Straight
Outta
SKOKIE

Straight
Outta
SKOKIE

The Krockey Chronicles

1968

Al Krockey

MAGICAL JOURNEY
MEDIA LLC

Straight Outta Skokie: The Krockey Chronicles: 1968

By Al Krockey

Magical Journey Media LLC
www.straightouttaskokie.com

Published October 2025

Editing by: David Aretha
Cover design by: Tanja Prokop
Publishing Consultant: Sharon Woodhouse, Conspire Creative
Interior design by: Andrea Reider
Author photos by : Charles Cherney

979-8-218-78282-5 Paperback
979-8-9930430-0-5 Ebook - Kindle

Please Note: This memoir reflects my personal memories and interpretations of events. While I have attempted to portray them truthfully, some names, identifying details, and characteristics have been changed to protect privacy. Conversations and scenes have been recreated from memory, and some may be composites. Any resemblance to persons not explicitly acknowledged is coincidental.

Printed in the United States of America.

Dedicated to my loving parents,
Arthur and Lorraine Krockey

Preface

One quiet morning in March 2020, as the world began to shutter itself in fear, I found myself sitting alone on the twenty-first floor of a high-rise on Chicago's lakefront, sipping coffee and staring out over Lake Michigan. The sunrise painted the water in soft pastels, and for a brief moment, I felt a calm I hadn't known in weeks. But then, reality returned.

The city was in lockdown. I was seventy now, recently retired, single again, and—thanks to a virus I barely understood—quarantined in a five-hundred-unit building that suddenly felt far too large and far too empty. As a "people person" by nature, I was learning, uncomfortably, how solitude felt.

Trips to the laundry room or to pick up mail became the highlight of my days. The small convenience store in our basement, once an afterthought, had transformed into a lifeline, not just for groceries but for human connection—masked hellos and muffled how-are-yous. I walked the lakefront when I dared, clinging to those strolls as a way to hold on to my sanity. Still, something was missing.

Then one day, in an elevator ride scented with corned beef sneaking through our masks, a neighbor mentioned Kaufman's deli in Skokie. They were doing curbside pickup now. Just hearing that name—Kaufman's—was like flipping a switch. In a year filled with uncertainties, the familiar pull of an old deli sandwich felt like something I could hold onto.

That's how I found myself driving up to Skokie, the town where I spent my childhood and came of age. As I waited in the Kaufman's parking lot, I wasn't just hungry for corned beef. I was starving for connection to people, to places, to memories that felt safe, simple, and mine.

I took the long way home, steering past my old apartment at 8239 Knox Avenue, where my parents raised my sister and me. I parked across the street and unwrapped a piece of hot corned beef right there in the car. The smell, the taste—it unlocked something.

And just like that, I was no longer a seventy-year-old man, isolated in a pandemic. I was a kid again in Skokie, where the world had clear, simple boundaries.

Back then, growing up felt ordinary. But looking back, it wasn't. Not at all.

Skokie was our universe. Summers belonged to mornings of paper routes and neighborhood baseball games, afternoons at Oakton Pool, and then stopping on the way home for a ten-cent bag of fries from The Hut. Winter meant shoveling snow off the basketball court to play a pick-up game of two-on-two, ice skating in Oakton Park, and warming up in the adjacent Oakton Community Center, where one of the moms handed you a hot cup of cocoa.

Our lives were centered around food, making sure we were home on time for supper or visiting our favorite hot dog place, be it Big Herms, Poochies, or The Hut, just to name a few. Or spending time in one of the many sit-down delis like Zweigs, Sam and Hy's, or Mr. Ricky's. Picking up lox and bagels at Kaufman's Bagel & Delicatessen or New York Bagel & Bialy. Taking your bike just over the border to the Sarkis Café in Evanston. Sarkis wasn't just a restaurant; it was a theater, and Sarkis himself was the star. We would go to a Friday night dance at Devonshire Center or the Legion Hall in Lincolnwood and end up at Alberti's or LaRosa's for a pizza, or maybe Jack's, the all-night diner.

We were free to hang out and play pinball at Twin Orchard or Oakton Bowl. Play pool at All Star Lanes, The Q Inn, or the Royal

Cue. Go to the Old Orchard Mall, where the guys wanted to meet girls and the girls wanted to meet guys. Take the Skokie Swift or 97 bus to Chicago and catch the Howard Street L train to go see the Cubs or White Sox, or a movie downtown at one of the many Chicago movie palaces.

We didn't know it then, but we were part of something rare and a place where kids belonged to a village, where neighbors were as much family as friends. Life wasn't perfect. It never is. But we were safe. We were free. And we were alive in a way that sticks to your bones.

In 1968, I was eighteen years old, coming of age in the most culturally explosive era in American history. But the story of how I got there? That story begins in Skokie, long before the world outside came crashing in, back when a simple block of co-op apartments, or split-level houses, was an entire universe.

Contents

CHAPTER 1
A Change Is Gonna Come   1

CHAPTER 2
The Hustler's Boogie   59

CHAPTER 3
Protest Installments   103

CHAPTER 4
The Pan Is Hot!   125

CHAPTER 5
College Deferment and Christmas Tree Weed   135

CHAPTER 6
Broken Stride   173

CHAPTER 7
Life Is a Highway of Roundabouts   187

CHAPTER 8
The Sunshine State   215

Chapter 1

A Change Is Gonna Come

This story begins on Thursday, April 4, 1968.

At 7 a.m., my mom entered my room and told me it was time to get up and go to work. "Let's go, Krockey; everything goes on in the morning," she yelled...nicely. You see, my full name is Alan Krockey, although most of my friends called me Krockey, and when my mom, Lorraine, wanted my or my dad, Art's, full attention, she would call us both Krockey. Although sometimes my family and my friends did call me Al or Alan, and occasionally people would refer to me as Krock or The Krock.

Work was not an option for this eighteen-year-old kid. My family was struggling as a result of my father's business partner leaving town with our family's life savings. I was determined to hustle a buck any way I could and maybe one day become a rich and successful entrepreneur.

It was spring vacation time, and my friend Norm was picking me up to go to our jobs as souvenir peddlers outside Wrigley Field. So, my mom made us each a bagel with cream cheese, and we headed for the Skokie Swift. As we walked toward the train platform, groups of Black women of all sizes, shapes, shades, and ages came walking off the Swift. Most of these women were housekeepers from the South and West Sides of Chicago who were going to clean the houses of these North Shore white suburbanites.

As we got closer, we ran into Maurice Smiley, who worked at Twin Orchard Bowl, maintaining the sixty-four pinspotters and lanes at the large, modernistic bowling establishment where we would hang out. Maurice—or Smiley, as we called him—was very active in his church on the west side, and, along with his wife, he was an active member of the Chicago Freedom Movement. Both had marched with Martin Luther King when Dr. King lived on Chicago's west side two summers before in 1966. Accompanying Smiley that morning was his beautiful wife, Samantha (Sam), who also worked at the BA (as we called the bowling alley). Sam was the head cook at the Twin Orchard Grill and could cook up a storm. As they approached, I greeted them both.

"Hey, Maurice. Hey, Sam."

"Where are you two Jewish gangsters off to so early?" Smiley asked.

"We're on our way to work at Cubs Park," I replied. "You know Eddie's got the souvenir stands down at Wrigley."

"Well, it's a beautiful day," Sam said as she smiled.

"You guys know my lovely Sam."

Sam then remarked, "Isn't it a shame all those beautiful Black ladies have to go clean for all these white folks?"

Shaking his head, Smiley replied, "Change is going to come, fellas. I just know it. Change has got to come."

"Right on," I replied.

Smiley smiled and said as Sam waved goodbye, "See you later, fellas."

After getting off the Swift at Howard Street, we hopped on the "L" headed for Wrigley Field. As soon as we entered the train, we ran into two girls we knew from Skokie, Barb and Cindy, whom we both greeted. Cindy responded, "Is that you, Krockey? I can't believe it. You grew so much. I saw you last year at one of the dances at the

Lincolnwood Legion Hall and you were shorter than me, and I'm only five-foot-two."

"Yeah, I grew seven inches in the last year and a half."

Then Barb said, "You guys both let your hair grow long. Wow, you both look cool, but so different: Norm with that strawberry blond hair and red mustache, and you, Krockey, with that thick black hair down to your shoulders. Wow!"

Then Norm said, "You girls both look great," with me smiling and nodding in agreement. Norm was always real smooth with the ladies. I was always a little shy. Norm asked, "Where are you girls headed?"

"My dad's law office downtown. His secretary is off this week, and he asked us to come down and help during spring vacation. Then we're going shopping in Old Town for bell-bottoms," said Cindy, the Jewish petite brunette whom I liked and thought was cute.

Barb, the tall Irish blonde with blue eyes, started to flirt a bit with the almost six-foot-tall Norman. We all made small talk, which led Norm to ask Barb, "What are you and Cindy doing tonight?" Barb looked at Cindy for approval and then told Norm they were free. "How about me and the Krock come by about 6:00 and we take you two out?" Barb wrote down her number and address right before we got to the Addison/Wrigley Field stop. We said goodbye to the girls and stepped off the train and went down the stairs to what one day would be called Wrigleyville.

We headed down Addison Street toward Sheffield, where Eddie Shay and his partner, Al Stein, had their two double garages behind two six-flat Greystone buildings, which they used as their warehouse. This was well before bleachers would sit on top of these Greystones. As we walked down Sheffield, you could smell the ham on the bone coming out of Ted's Grill and feel the ballpark and the neighborhood around it getting excited and ready for the preseason game on Sunday against the White Sox. There was a certain vibe when I was around Wrigley Field that gave me energy and a good feeling about being alive. This was pre-gentrification, when mostly working people, both white and Hispanic, lived in this unique and vibrant neighborhood around the ballpark

Our bosses, Eddie Shay and Al Stein, were well-connected guys. The two had gotten together because Stein's father was a partner of Eddie's uncle, and the two partners were known as the Lettuce Kings down at the South Water Market. The two Lettuce Kings introduced Eddie and Stein to Sergeant Donny Hayes, who ran the task force for the Chicago police in and around Wrigley Field. You see, back then, the Cubs were still owned by the Wrigley family, and both the Wrigleys and most of baseball had yet to see the full potential revenue in merchandising. So, with the sergeant controlling the outside of the ballpark, Eddie and Al were given the best spots on Cubs property for a small daily donation. The boys now had the five best spots right outside Wrigley Field.

As we walked up to the two double garages, Eddie yelled out over the sound of the L train above in his ball-busting voice, "C'mon, let's go. Move your ass; we got a lot of Chinese to do."[1]

"Go fuck yourself," Norm barked back. "I'm going for coffee—you want some?"

"No, I got some but get your ass back here. On second thought, get me a scratch sheet," Eddie said. "How about you, Krock, you want something?"

"Yeah, bring me a Kayo Chocolate Drink in a bottle, not a can." Right then, I started to hear and see some of the other peddlers coming down the alley toward the garages like a parade. Some were drinking coffee while a couple of the old-timers were drinking wine out of a paper bag. Some were part of Eddie and Al's crew; a couple were union guys who worked inside the ballpark for the Cubs, and

---

[1] "Chinese" was the process of getting the souvenir buttons, pennants, hats, and other various novelties ready to sell. It was called Chinese because most of the items came from China.

some were independents who bought wholesale from the two partners and who had their own spots.

One of the independents, Ballpark Benny, worked the come-in (before the game) with a badge board[2] and pennants over by the station entrance. His aim was to catch the folks coming off the train. Once all the people entered the ballpark, he would then move closer to Sheffield and Addison for the blow-off[3] after the game, catching people as they left the ballpark and headed back to the L.

Benny was a fifty-year-old, carefree soul who lived in a rooming house as a lot of his older ballpark cronies did. Benny loved to tell the story that during the Depression, Al Capone once gave him a fifty-dollar bill for a pennant. His best friend, Little Sol, was an ex-jockey who had won the Melbourne Cup in Australia but later got caught using a buzzer to fix a race and was then banned from racing for life. Little Sol would hobo in from Sacramento every spring, stopping in places like Reno and Denver, and would always share his stories of his road adventures with us. Little Sol worked both the come-in and the blow-off on the corner of Waveland and Clark on the opposite side of the park from Benny.

And then there were the specialists like New York Whitey, who was a dinger. Whitey would wear a veteran's hat with a patch over one eye and pin an American flag on a person's lapel, shirt, or dress as they walked down the street. Whitey would then just put out his hand and

---

[2] A "badge board" was a thick piece of felt attached to a three-foot-by-six-foot wood frame with a folding stick so the board would stand in place. We would pin various buttons on a badge board and have six drilled holes in the top to display the pennants we sold. We would also have a bunch of pennants sitting in a pocket sewn in the back of the badge board, so we could grab one quickly to hand to a customer and still have our display.

[3] The "come-in" was catching the folks coming to the ballpark and selling them a souvenir before they enter the park. The "blow-off" was catching the people on the way out who may have wanted a souvenir to take home from their day at the ballpark.

the good folks of America would proudly hand him over their money. That's how you dinged, and Whitey was the grand master of dinging. Whitey worked all over the country wherever there was a crowd and warm weather. Whitey would always talk out of the side of his mouth, always telling us about how he'd been making a C-note a day since World War II and how this Vietnam protesting shit was hurting his action. Of course, Whitey was always broke, because he loved the ponies, and whenever he wasn't working, he'd be at the track.

Another of the many specialists was a peddler called Shopping Bags, who sold rubber (balloons) and carried them around in, you guessed it, two shopping bags. Shopping Bags would take the bus and just come for the blow-off. As soon as he got off the bus, he would walk over to the gas station on Clark Street, across from the ballpark, and use their air hose to blow up what was called a worker. A worker was a balloon ten times bigger than the ones he would sell. On many occasions, people, after buying the balloons, would try and blow one up and realize the balloons they had bought were much smaller than the so-called worker that Shopping Bags displayed. If someone complained, he would start screaming back at them, oftentimes yelling racist remarks.

Because the balloons were only two for a quarter, most people would back off and go away. One time, after selling two African-American teenagers balloons and refusing to give them back their quarters when they tried to return them, they then proceeded to pop Shopping Bags's worker balloon with a cigarette, after which Shopping Bags started screaming, "There's going to be n***** blood around here. I'll kill these motherfuckers." One of the ballpark coppers came over and told Burl (Shopping Bags's real name) to "calm down before he got himself hurt." After smoking two Pall Malls, Shopping Bags calmed down and jumped on the bus like it was a normal day at work, then headed for the F&T Polish cafeteria on Milwaukee Avenue and Ashland to have his supper.

Norm headed down the alley with his coffee, my Kayo drink, and Eddie's scratch sheet. It was time to do Chinese and get the hat stands and badge boards ready for the preseason game Sunday against the Cubs' crosstown rivals, the White Sox. The Cubs and the Sox were scheduled to play two preseason games before the regular season opened on Monday. This was years before the American and National Leagues would have regular-season interleague games. The first preseason game for these two Chicago teams was scheduled to be held on Saturday at Milwaukee County Stadium. You see, the Milwaukee Braves had left for Atlanta in 1966, and the Milwaukee Brewers would not start playing there until 1970. Eddie and Stein had thought of going up to Milwaukee to just work the blow-off on Saturday but had decided to instead get ready for Sunday's Sox-Cubs game at Wrigley, and of course, the home opener the following week-end against the Cardinals. The Sox home opener would be Tuesday, but we rarely worked at Comiskey Park because the Sox didn't draw too well at that time.

I asked Eddie, "Why aren't we going to Milwaukee Saturday?"

"Too much heat working at County Stadium in Milwaukee. Last time we went up there, we all got pinched for working on county property."

As I was digging "Cowboys to Girls" by the Intruders on my little transistor, which I had placed on one of the shelves in the garage and set to the soul station WVON, I heard Eddie call out, "Krockey, bring those badge boards out and grab those boxes of buttons and start putting them together. As soon as you've got enough Cub buttons, start making up Sox buttons." Eddie then told Hymie, one of the younger neighborhood kids, "Go help Krockey with the buttons."

"Krock, make sure when you guys pin the buttons on the badge board, you put fifty percent Cubs, twenty-five percent Sox, and then add the Cardinals, Yankees, Detroit, and a couple of the other top teams. When you and Hymie are done with the buttons, grab those

Cubs and Sox pennants and start putting the sticks in and then make bunches of twenty with rubber bands."

All the badge boards had holes drilled on the top of the badge board frame where you would stick five or six pennants in for display, or what peddlers called a flash. You would do this on game day once you were set up in your spot.

Stein yelled out from the next garage, "Norm, you roll those hat joints (stands) out.[4] Don't scratch them up now. I just had Kenosha and Frankie Collins paint them yesterday. Tuffy, grab those boxes of hats and start sorting them by team and size, and put the adjustable ones separate and up front. Good job getting those hat joints lined up, Norm. Now, right behind you are all the plastic batting helmets. We sorted them yesterday."

Stein went on to say, "Norm, put one box of Cubs helmets, a box of White Sox, and one assorted teams' box on the bottom shelf."

Norm then asked Stein, "Should I grab these Pittsburgh and Oakland helmets? Don't we need to make up the Bleacher Bum helmets?"

"No, not yet. Stevie (Eddie's brother) is over at Sports Corner trying to persuade the Duchess to get off her barstool and come over and help us out."

The Bleacher Bums had emerged in '66 when the Cubs were still not drawing very well. There were always these ten or so guys

---

[4] A "hat stand" was about six feet wide with four shelves about four feet high, with another two feet high of board behind the top shelf. The bottom three shelves held the inventory in boxes till on game day, when you rolled out the stand to its location. You would then unpack the boxes and make a flash (display) using the top shelf to line up your all your Cubs hats along with those of the visiting team and the other top teams. You would line up all of your stock so you could grab the best sellers as quickly as possible, trying to serve as many people as possible, as the crowd would come rushing out of the ballpark.

who showed up in the left field stands with construction hats, and they called themselves the Bleacher Bums. Then this last season, as the team got better and the crowds grew a little more, other fans started showing up with yellow construction hard hats, and many had "Bleacher Bums" written across the front in black felt pen. So, toward the end of the '67 season, Stein started taking the Pittsburgh and Oakland yellow plastic batting helmets, which sort of resembled a yellow construction hard hat, and we would take the P or the O off and take a magic marker and write Bleacher Bums on them, and they would sell like hot cakes.

The problem was, Al Stein didn't have the best handwriting, but the Duchess in her former life was a calligrapher, writing out fancy wedding invitations. The Duchess, a fifty-year-old, skinny, redheaded widow, was Ted's sister and would help at Ted's grill during the busy hours. And when she wasn't working, she'd be next door at the Sports Corner Bar nursing a beer. Stevie and the Duchess walked over to the garage. The Duchess greeted everybody and asked Stein, "How many helmets do you need me to write on, Al?"

"About six dozen, D."

"Okay, give me a sawbuck and send one of the kids to the corner and get me a six-pack of Old Style."

"You got it, D. Stevie, here's some money. Please go get the Duchess a six-pack of Old Style, and when you get back, help Tuffy finish up so we can get a count of each stand's inventory."

The two partners had a nice operation that only got bigger over the years, eventually opening stores and warehouses. In 1968, they had the five best locations surrounding Wrigley Field for selling souvenirs. They had three stands that were set up for both the come-in and the blow-off. These stands would be set up on game day by 9 a.m. and not shut down until the last fan left the ballpark.

Back then (up until 1988), the Cubs only played day games. The first of these stands was on Waveland Avenue, right in front of the back gate, squarely on Wrigley Field property and across from the fire station. This was not only a place for fans to enter and exit but where the players entered and exited as well. Norm and I had been given this spot by Eddie. The two partners paid us twenty-five percent of the gross, which would go up to thirty percent in '69. Ours was a big stand that included a hat joint and a badge board. The next stand like this was on the southeast corner of Clark and Addison, which also served as a parking lot.

The partners leased this, and Eddie would one day buy and build a big souvenir store there. This parking lot spot was run by Eddie's sixteen-year-old younger brother, Stevie. Stevie would have two helpers, one to help with the souvenir stand and one to help park the cars. The third spot that worked both the come-in and the blow-off was just outside of Henry's Hamburgers on Clark Street between Addison and Waveland. They had a variety of guys who would work at this spot, like Mooch Sands, Shane, or the two old-timers, Comedy and Cancer. It would all depend on who showed up and who Eddie and Stein decided to give it to on a particular day.

The two big stands that only worked the blow-off were right at the front gate on Addison toward the Sheffield side on Wrigley Field property. These were referred to as the main joints and would be rolled out and flashed by the seventh inning. Eddie would handle the one that was busiest. As the people rushed out after a Cubs victory, Eddie had the ability to handle four or five customers at a time, working out of an apron and giving exact change faster than any of us could believe or do. No one counted money faster than Eddie. The last spot was a little way down from Eddie, but also busy. This stand was usually run by Chuck Marcus, one of Eddie's high school buddies who would be going away to college in the fall. Chuck was somewhat of a square guy and eventually became an accountant.

All the stands had helpers, mostly young Hispanic kids from the neighborhood. Eddie had a young helper named Manny. Manny's older brother was one of the leaders of one of Chicago's biggest Latino gangs. Eddie took Manny under his wing, and years later, he would sell him a small interest in one of his stores. Stevie had Hymie Gonzalez and a guy everyone called the Termite who would park the cars. Norm and I had Tuffy, this young neighborhood hillbilly kid from Kentucky whom everyone liked and who helped us out and had our backs.

Sometimes on game day, especially on the weekends, more guys would show up than there were stands. Eddie and Stein always tried to give a guy work when they showed up. When that happened, they would give these guys a bunch of pennants with sticks or a work box[5], which might have in it anything from souvenir buttons to hats to anything with "Chicago Cubs" printed on it that would sell. The only drawback was that these guys were not allowed to work up close to the gates or near one of the other stands, so they didn't do terrific business, but at the same time they made something for the day. Believe it or not, it would still be a couple years before pro sports and concert t-shirts became a popular souvenir item and would be sold around the country in work boxes just like these.

"Hey, Krock," Eddie called out from his makeshift office in the back of the garage. The office had a small desk, two chairs, and a payphone that Eddie was able to get installed through a friend at the phone company. As I walked to the back of the garage, Eddie was rolling a joint from a bag of grass sitting on his desk when the phone rang. "Hello, Jake." Eddie spoke into the phone and asked if his order was ready. When he hung up, he told me it was Jake Rubin, the wholesaler who owned Novelty Premium, where Eddie and Stein would buy some of their merchandise. "You want to take a ride to Jake's with me and pick up the order?"

---

[5] A "work box" is a cardboard box with a strap attached that you would hang around your neck to carry the box of items to be sold.

"Sure," I replied. "Is there enough room in the car or should we take the van?"

Eddie had a brand-new gold Pontiac LeMans convertible he had just bought that I really admired. "You can drive with me, and Norm and Mooch Sands can drive the van."

Just then, the phone rang. It was Jake again, asking Eddie if he would stop at Arnie Fisher's store at Maxwell and Halsted and pick up two gross of skimmers on his way to Jake's Novelty Premium, which was right next door to the International Amphitheatre at 42nd and Halsted. Jake was buying up all the skimmers he could, as it was an election year and both Democrats and Republicans loved to wear these straw hats called skimmers with their candidate's or party's names printed on a ribbon wrapped around these straw hats. In addition, later that year, the Democrats would be holding their convention at the Chicago Amphitheatre. Eddie finished rolling two joints and called out to Mooch and Norm, who were both now standing in the office doorway. Eddie then asked, "Did you guys finish your work?"

"Yeah, we just rolled the hat stands back in the garage and Stein inventoried everything," Norm replied.

Then Eddie said, "Here, Norm, you and Mooch take the keys to the van, and here's a joint of that ganja weed that Ronnie Casman just brought back from Jamaica."

"Where are we going?" Mooch asked.

Eddie replied, "You and Norm follow us in the van. First, we are going to stop at Breyers, Arnie Fisher's store in Jew Town[6] and pick up an order of skimmers for Jake Rubin. You can park right behind

---

[6] "Jew Town" in Chicago typically referred to the Maxwell Street Market area, a historical neighborhood on the Near West Side. It was once a predominantly Jewish immigrant neighborhood and the location of the Maxwell Street Market, a vibrant open-air market. The area is also known as the birthplace of Chicago blues music and the "Maxwell Street Polish" sausage sandwich.

Breyers, and we can grab lunch on Maxwell Street. After we eat, we can go by Jake's and drop off his skimmers and pick up my order."

As I was getting into Eddie's car, I asked if he was going to put the top down. "It's a little cold but what the fuck, why not?" Eddie said. "It's not too bad. It's like fifty or fifty-five degrees. It beats winter. I heard you started smoking a little weed this year, Krock."

"Yeah, I think I was the last cat of our group to try it." Once I started smoking, I loved it. I was a big music fan. I loved all music: soul, blues, jazz, rock and roll, country, and American standards. If it was good music, I was into it. So, smoking weed, listening to tunes, and seeing live music became some of my passions.

As we drove down to Maxwell Street, Eddie passed me the joint he had rolled. I took a couple hits and turned up the radio as Otis Redding's "(Sittin' On) The Dock of the Bay" was playing. It had just recently come out, and I couldn't get enough of that song. As the four of us entered Breyers through the rear entrance, we were greeted by Arnie Fisher, who always had a warm smile, and his store manager, James Jackson, better known as Lips, a Black kid who was about my age and had gotten that name playing trumpet in his high school band. He had no desire to become a musician as most of the musicians he knew were always broke, although I had heard he was one hell of a horn player. Instead, Lips wanted to be a lawyer and had just started night school at the University of Illinois Circle Campus right down the street from the store. After leaving the Marshall High School marching band and entering law school, he no longer wanted to be called Lips, but preferred being called Mr. Jackson or J. J. to his friends and coworkers as a sign of the respect he thought a future lawyer deserved.

Arnie Fisher owned two stores on Halsted near Maxwell Street—Breyers at 1304 S. Halsted and Leeds Men's Wear at 1318 S. Halsted. Both stores carried the widest variety of hats in the city, and the latest in fashion—that by 1968 was catering to mostly Black customers, although they still sold a variety of hats and fashionable clothing to many of Chicago's top musicians, politicians, and gangsters. Arnie told Lips to show us where the skimmers were in the basement. Then Eddie said, "Krockey, go down the street to the hot dog stand and get us lunch."

"Arnie, you and Lips and the girls want lunch?" Eddie asked. Arnie had two saleswomen on the floor: Maria, a young, petite Mexican gal, and Fran, an older, extremely well-dressed Black woman who was the store's go-to fashion coordinator.

"No, we just ate," Arnie said.

"Mooch, Norm, what do you guys want to eat?" Eddie asked.

"Get me a Polish sausage, with everything and lots of grilled onions," Norm said.

"Me too," yelled Mooch, and I shook my head in agreement.

"Okay, Krock, here's a sawbuck. Get us four Polishes with everything and fries, and get some drinks."

As I walked over, I could smell the hot dogs, Polishes, pork chop sandwiches, and those grilled onions that were always piled high. I could hear a blues harp calling me down Maxwell Street. So, I walked over and realized it was Jew Town Eddie Burks playing harp, and he was sitting in with John Guitar Embry's band.

As I was really getting off on the music, Norm tapped me on the shoulder. "I thought you were getting lunch; c'mon, we need to get back. That weed kicked in and I'm starving," Norm said.

I told Norm, "Check these cats out." So, we stayed till the end of the song and then picked up the Polish hot dogs and went back to Breyers to eat.

"Where the fuck were you?" Eddie screamed.

"Listening to this really cool blues band on Maxwell Street."

"C'mon, eat up," Eddie said.

"Boychik, you dig the blues? Who was playing?" Arnie asked.

"John Guitar Embry's band, and he had Jew Town Eddie sitting in on the harp," I said.

Arnie then told me, "You know, Krockey, the best blues harp player was Little Walter, who just died a few months back, and I bet you didn't know that the great Little Walter made his first recording right down the street in the back room of Bernie Abram's Maxwell Radio and Record, which housed and was released on the Ora Nelle recording label. I can remember sometime in the late '40s or early '50s when Little Walter and Muddy Waters first got together. They would come down to Maxwell Street and play. Of course, once their records became popular, they stopped playing on Maxwell Street, but they would still come into both stores and spend big money on the latest fashions. Muddy still stops in for clothes or a new hat on occasion."

Just as I took the last bite of my Polish, Arnie walked into his office and motioned me to follow him. Arnie's office had a big desk with a credenza behind it, and on that credenza sat the nicest, best-sounding stereo I had ever seen or heard. It was a McIntosh Amp and Tuner, and alongside was a Garrard turntable with KLH speakers hanging from the ceiling, just like the speakers out front in the store. On one wall was a couch, and on the opposite wall were shelves filled with record albums, mostly jazz and blues. "Arnie, I just love this stereo."

"Yeah, you know Stuart and Joel who help me out at Christmastime?"

"Sure," I said.

"Well, Stuart is now working at a stereo store in Morton Grove and he set this all up for me. It cost me a fortune. Here, boychik, listen to this *Hoodoo Man Blues* album by Junior Wells with Buddy Guy on guitar. Oy, I just love Junior's harp playing," Arnie said.

After a couple songs, I asked Arnie where I could find this record. "You go over to Grand and State to the Jazz Record Mart and ask for

Bob Koester. Bob's got the biggest selection of blues and jazz. Much bigger than Maxwell Radio and Record, and Bob happens to have a little record company called Delmark Records that put out this Junior record. Tell him I sent you."

Just then, the door opened and a gorgeous Asian woman walked in dressed to the nines. "Kim. I told you four o'clock, not noon," Arnie said. "Krockey, I've got to go. Tell Eddie and the boys goodbye, and you guys stop by anytime." As Arnie smiled and closed the office door behind him, I could see Kim giving him a little peck on the cheek.

"Arnie said to say goodbye," I said, and I asked Eddie who the woman was.

"It's his goomar, and keep it to yourself. He's married to a nice Jewish lady with a couple of kids."

After leaving Arnie's store, we drove over to Novelty Premium, and we all walked in carrying the boxes of skimmers we had just picked up at Breyers.

"Where should we put these, Jake?" Eddie asked.

Jake was sitting in his boxer shorts playing gin with his number one helper, Mike "The Schleper" Schiropsky. Jake looked up with a cigar in his mouth, pointing to a corner. "Mike, put them over there near the campaign buttons."

Mike walked over to show us where to put the skimmers. "Put them right here next to the Mayor Daley buttons," Mike said.

The warehouse was filled with cardboard boxes that all looked similar, but Jake and The Schleper knew where everything was. Jake sold every kind of souvenir for every kind of event. He was the peddler's peddler. They sold everything from flying birds to flags from all nations—Polish flags for the Polish parade, Irish flags for St. Paddy's Day, a Puerto Rican flag for Puerto Rican Day. Basically, Jake had a flag, a button, or a hat, for every country, nationality, sports team, political party, stock car race, concert, or any other event that drew people. He had a big sign in the warehouse from the importer of the binoculars he sold that said, "Put the Show in Your Lap."

Jake sold more of these binoculars than anyone in the country, especially when there was a big concert at the International Amphitheatre. I loved working at the different events at the Amphitheatre, be it a circus, a rodeo, or especially a concert. I even got to work and saw the Beatles in '66, where I was selling binoculars out of a work box while yelling, "Put the show in your lap." I loved to work the balconies; we would walk down the aisle where a young couple might be seated way up in these nosebleed seats and just hand the girl the binoculars while sticking our hand out toward her date. This worked ninety percent of the time because the guy didn't want to be embarrassed and not buy his date the binoculars after realizing how far away they were sitting from the stage.

Jake always had peddlers coming in for merchandise and would give credit to his regulars. "Are you guys still going to the schvitz[7]?" Jake asked.

Norm told him, "Why, sure, of course. Why don't you come meet us at Division Street? Tuesday after work?"

Jake replied, "You know I could really use a rub. Do you guys have a broom?"

"Brand new," Norm said.

Jake smiled and spoke. "All right, I'll meet you there. I'll give you both a platza[8]." Eddie and Mooch weren't schvitzers.

"What do I owe you for my order?" Eddie asked.

---

[7] Schvitz is a Yiddish word for sweat. In this instance, the Schvitz refers to a Russian-Turkish steam bath

[8] A "platza" treatment, also known as a rub, is a traditional Russian banya (steam bath) ritual involving a massage specialist lightly slapping or massaging the body with a bundled twig known as a broom, typically made of oak or birch leaves. This treatment is performed in a steam room to maximize the effects of the oak leaf broom and the heat. This can be done using a broom that has been soaked in just hot water or a bucket of hot soapy water for more of a soap scrub effect.

"Here, the bill is right on top of your order," said Jake as he lit his cigar. "You owe me $540."

Eddie looked at the invoice and asked, "Are you sure this is correct? Because Stein will be all over me if it's wrong."

"If you like, we can unpack the boxes and check," said Jake as he puffed on his cigar.

"No, I trust you, Jake," Eddie said.

"More importantly, I trust you. If it's short, you let me know and I'll square it. Don't forget to let me know if I gave you too much," Jake remarked, smiling. Everyone laughed.

"Here's your dough," Eddie said as he handed Jake the cash.

"Will see you guys," Jake said as he puffed on his cigar.

"Try and make it to the bathhouse Tuesday, Jake. My old man might come down," Norm said. Jake and Norm's father had grown up in the same Lawndale neighborhood on Chicago's West Side.

As we all carried the boxes of souvenirs and walked toward the van, Eddie told Norm and Mooch, "You guys, meet us at the garage. We need to drop off this order, and then I'll give you guys a ride back to Skokie." Eddie dropped me off first, and as I was getting out of the car, Norm told me he was going to pick me up at 5:45.

"Where are you guys going?" Mooch asked.

"We got a couple dates," Norm replied. "We're going to go down by the lake and maybe get something to eat and hear some music. Why? You and Ava want to come?"

"Yeah, man," Mooch replied in his Bronx accent. He and his family had moved in down the street from me a couple years ago from New York.

"Okay, here's what we're going to do. I'll pick Krock up at 5:15, 5:30, and Eric (Mooch Sands's real name) will go over to Ava's house, and I'll pick you and her up at her house. Then we can pick up the girls at Barb's, which is around the corner from Ava's. All right, see you later, Krock," Norm said.

Eddie then yelled out, "Krockey, here's some dough for today. See you Sunday."

Mooch and his girlfriend, Ava, were greasers. While Norm was a collegiate dresser, who recently started to dress like a hippie, I was all over the place. I went from athlete/collegiate type to greaser when I was ditching school a lot and hanging at Frank Perentie's Que Inn. Then, after getting thrown out of Niles East High School, I entered a private high school downtown in the Loop called Britannica to get my high school diploma. It was then that I started to dress like a full-blown hippie. Britannica was basically a school that taught you how to pass your GED and was filled with misfits from all over the city and suburbs of Chicago. I was able to graduate in February, while Norm and most of my friends my age would not graduate for a couple of months, sometime in June.

Eddie and Mooch had graduated the year before, as they both were a year older. Eddie had joined the Army Reserves to avoid getting drafted and going to Vietnam, as many guys who were draft-aged did. The reserves had required Eddie to go away for basic training the previous summer for three months, followed by another three months of duty; now, he would only have to go away for two weeks of training every year for another five years. Norm and I were planning on getting a college deferment by entering junior college in the fall. Vietnam was on everyone's mind as all of us knew someone who went over there and never returned. We also knew a few guys we had grown up with who had just returned and were having a hard time adjusting. I was very outspoken against the war in Vietnam and had attended a few protest rallies.

By the time I got home, it was three o'clock. I plopped down onto my bed and nodded out for an hour or so. I awoke to my old man coming up the back-porch stairs of our two-story, four-unit co-op with his work boots clomping, wearing his backward Cubs hat and work clothes soiled from a day of picking up scrap metal and driving his truck. My dad had bought our tiny two-bedroom co-op apartment in Skokie with a VA loan a few years after getting out of the Army, where he served six years as a medic during World War II, winning a Bronze Star and being nominated for a Silver Star. My dad had told me about the Battle of the Bulge and how he had treated so many men for frostbite. He would always remind me of this in the wintertime when he would make me wear two pairs of socks. What he didn't tell me until years later on his deathbed was how, at the end of the war, he had been assigned to Buchenwald and Dachau concentration camps, mainly because he was one of the few medics who spoke Yiddish, where he would stay on to help treat many of the Holocaust survivors.

For as long as I could remember, my dad took a bath every day after work and would lie down for a half hour before supper.

While I was growing up, my mother would always tell me not to bother my father when he first walked through the door, but tonight, I needed to ask him if he wouldn't mind if I took a quick shower before his bath.

"Dad, do you mind if I take a shower before your bath?"

"No, go ahead," my dad said. "Where are you going that you need a shower?"

"I got a date."

"No kidding—you need some money?" This was a nice gesture as I knew he was struggling with money after recently being robbed by a partner he had taken in to open a small scrapyard in Des Plaines. Now, my dad was responsible for the lease and was trying to find someone to invest in his dream. I had grown to dislike the scrap business after working for him when I was younger. It just seemed to me that there were easier ways to make money than pushing around fifty-gallon drums of scrap and coming home filthy every day.

"No, Pops. I worked at the ballpark today to get ready for the Sox and Cubs game on Sunday, and Eddie paid us."

"Okay, go take your shower and don't use all the hot water. I'm going to walk Schnaps and water the flowers and grass."

After showering and getting dressed, my fourteen-year-old sister, Sherry, came into my room with a freshly ironed shirt. "Here, Mom said to give this to you. Where are you going on your date? Who are you having a date with?"

"Cindy Miller. She goes to Niles North." At the time, Skokie had three high schools: Niles West, Niles North, and Niles East, where I had been thrown out of and where my sister attended.

"I don't know her. Is she cute?" my sister asked.

Before I could answer, my mom asked, "You sure you don't want supper? I'm making salmon patties with Jewish spaghetti and farmer's chop suey." This is what Jews call a *milchig* (dairy) meal. No meat. Farmer's chop suey, the way my mom made, it was basically a salad with cucumbers, tomatoes, and scallions topped with sour cream. The Jewish spaghetti was made by taking noodles, Campbell's Tomato Soup, and lots of seasoning and then baking it in glass bakeware, where it would form a nice crust, and nobody made salmon patties like my mom. The best.

"No, Ma, I'm going to eat later."

"Okay, have a nice time."

Just then, Norm pulled up and honked his horn. I ran down the front stairs, and my dad was out front with the dog, talking to a neighbor. "See you later, Pops."

"You look nice, but you still need a haircut. You look like a beatnik." And then, as always, when I left the house, since the age of five, he would say, "Safety," and I would have to answer first.

I jumped into Norm's mom's blue Ford Falcon. "Hey, Krock, you're not going to believe this: Barb called my house right after I walked in and asked if we could pick them up on Michigan Ave in front of the old water tower. It seems these two chicks went shopping in Old Town and now they are on the way to Oak Street to look at shoes."

I tried turning on the car radio, but Norm's mom still hadn't had it repaired. "What's with the radio, Norm? How come your mom hasn't had it fixed?" I asked.

"Too busy with work, and now my sister Judy is pregnant again," Norm said, shaking his head. As we pulled up to Ava's parents' house, we spotted Mooch with a Winston in his mouth and with his arm around Ava. Ava was a greaser with a blond bouffant hairdo, tight slacks, and a tight poor boy sweater underneath her leather jacket. She looked much older than her age and was very attractive with a super body. Eric was wearing black pants with a black shirt under his black Cabretta jacket, his usual greaser attire. He kind of looked like Al Pacino in *Carlito's Way*, but not exactly. Maybe it was that Bronx thing.

Norm, almost six feet, with long brownish-red hair and a mustache, had on blue jean bell-bottoms with a knit shirt and a Levi's jacket, while I was like five-foot-seven, skinny, with long black hair, and the beginnings of a weak beard. I had on a green Army jacket with a peace sign sewn above the left breast pocket over a tie-dye t-shirt and blue jeans.

As far as shoes, Ava was wearing flats while the three of us were wearing some variation of what they called shit-kickers, a popular style of boot back in the late '60s. I suggested to Norm that we take Lake Shore Drive, and Ava and Eric both yelled their approval. Ava always called Mooch "Eric" and would get angry when we referred to him as Mooch. Norm asked, "Does anyone have papers? I've got some ganja from Casman."

"How much did Casman bring back from Jamaica?" Eric asked.

"What am I, his bookkeeper? I don't know, a few pounds," Norm said.

Then I said, "I think he was able to maybe bring back two or three pounds. On the first trip, he brought back maybe a pound that was sewn in the lining of a big straw basket they would sell to tourists. Then, Ronny Casman came up with this idea to bring a golf bag with those plastic tubes for the clubs. He told me the bag would have a few golf clubs and a bunch of those plastic tubes stuffed with ganja. He said the customs guys never even took the cover off the golf bag. He sold Cookie Gordon a pound and Norm and I split a pound."

Then Norm said, "I'm going to stop at Four Heads on Sheridan. Krock, you run in and get two packs of Blanco de Negro," Norm directed with a smile. Four Heads was a head shop on Sheridan Road, next to the 400 Theater. I walked in as the smell of incense and the sound of "Third Stone from the Sun" by Jimi Hendrix filled the air, surrounded by the store's psychedelic posters, black lights, and smoking pipes of all kinds. This was one of our go-to head shops on the North Side, a year or two before the iconic Adam's Apple would open near California and Granville. I went right to the counter and had my usual greeting exchange with Matt, the proprietor of this fine establishment.

"How you doing?" I asked.

"Okay, how you doing?" Matt replied and went on to tell me, "Last night I checked out the opening of this very groovy new music venue up on Clark and Lawrence, the Electric Theater. Really cool place with this outta-sight light show. They had a band from Canada called the Paupers, and they were pretty good. But listen to this, man. I was talking to the owner, Aaron Russo, and he said they are going to bring in all the heavy bands that play the Fillmore East and West."

"Wow," I said. "Maybe I'll check it out tonight. Give me two packs of Blancos."

"Here you go."

"See you later, Matt."

"All right, man, stay righteous."

When I got back in the car, Norm handed Mooch the bag of weed and told me to give him the papers, as Mooch could roll a much better joint than I could. "Here, roll like three sticks, Eric."

As we headed down Lake Shore Drive with its view of the lakefront, and after taking a couple hits of weed and feeling the lake breeze, I had a nice buzz going, although I was a little anxious about seeing Cindy. Norm got off at Michigan Avenue and drove right past the Water Tower Pumping Station, where we could see the girls standing. Norm went around the block a few times when Ava shouted out, "There's a parking space." Sure enough, we had managed to find a metered spot right on Chicago Avenue in front of Seneca Park.

Norm and I walked over to meet the girls, who were each carrying two bags. "You ladies look really cool. I like those paisley bell-bottoms, Barb," Norm said as he grabbed Barb's bag.

"Wow," I said. "Cindy, those blue and white striped bell-bottoms are boss, and that suede floppy hat is really cool."

I grabbed Cindy's bags. "Here, Krock, let's put the bags in the trunk, and Eric, you grab those two blankets, and we can sit in this mellow park and smoke this ganja, man," Norm ordered nicely. Ava told Norm she didn't smoke and that she liked beer. "No problem," Norm said. "My old man works for Country Club Malt Liquor, and I happen to have two six-packs here in the trunk underneath the spare."

"Here, Ava." Norm handed Ava one of the six-packs. We headed toward a grassy area away from the playground, where a few kids were playing while their parents looked on. Eric then spread out both blankets. We all sat down as Ava offered us all a beer.

"Not for me," I said. Barb and Cindy shook their heads, both saying "no, thank you" in unison, but Eric and Norm each took a can. "Eric, light up a couple of those spliffs, man," I said, as Eric then handed me one of the joints, which I gave to Cindy after taking a hit.

We all sat around in this little park surrounded by tall buildings, white clouds, and blue sky while smoking and sharing this excellent Jamaican herb with each other. The weed had just started to hit me as I lay my head back on the blanket, and a minute later Cindy took her hat off and lay her head back next to mine. As we looked toward the few white clouds in front of the blue sky with all the tall buildings surrounding us, I noticed one building that had a purple-blueish top that was trippy. I told Cindy to check it out as it seemed to change shades of purple and blue as the sun was setting. When I looked over at Eric and Ava, they were making out, and behind them on the swings were Norm and Barb, with Barb sitting on Norm's lap, kissing. This made me a little anxious as I wasn't quite sure if I should try and kiss Cindy. Just then, Cindy rolled over and gave me a surprise kiss, and I relaxed, and we started necking for a while when Norm yelled out, "You guys want to eat?"

Mooch responded, "Yeah, I'm starving. How about pizza?"

"Should we eat down here, or should we go to Leona's on Sheffield near Belmont? They have the best thin pizza," Norm said.

"We love that place. My dad takes us there," Cindy remarked.

"Okay, Leona's it is," Mooch said as we gathered the blankets.

Ava asked, "Does anybody want this last beer?" When everyone shook their heads no, Ava chugged it down, and we all jumped into the car. Mooch and I went in the back seat, with Ava sitting on Eric's lap and Cindy on mine. Norm got behind the wheel, with Barb sitting right beside him, her hand on his leg. Mooch lit up another joint and we passed it around. Even Ava took a hit as she was a little tipsy after that third beer.

Nighttime was upon us as we headed down Division Street, going west past Wells. We were now approaching the Cabrini Green housing project when I noticed a large crowd out front of the fire station at Division and Larrabee. As we drove past groups of Black residents, some were shaking their fists at us. Some were yelling profanities and things like, "Get out of here, whitey!" My eyes focused on two Black women crying as they embraced each other. *What is going on?* I wondered.

The car radio wasn't working; we had no idea that Dr. Martin Luther King Jr. had just been assassinated in the last hour or two.

When we reached the three-way stop at Division and Crosby, someone threw a stone at the passenger door, and now, with the car stopped, a man jumped on the hood of the car, beating his umbrella on the windshield. After he hit the windshield a second time, nobody even noticed that the radio came on as a small crack appeared on the windshield. Norm screamed, "What should we do?"

"Get the fuck out of here," Mooch screamed.

Norm hit the gas as the man slid off the side of the car and then threw the umbrella at the car as we pulled away. When we got to Halsted Street, I told Norm, "Get the hell off Division Street. Take Halsted."

In the meantime, Cindy was crying and holding on to me tightly. Norm asked Eric for one of his Winston's, though Norm had quit smoking a year earlier. We now had the windows open to let the smoke out, and we could hear sirens coming from all over. "Hey, the radio is working now. Must have been from when the guy hit the windshield with the umbrella," Barb said as she reached for the dial. The radio was on WVON, as I had set it there before. But before Barb could move the dial, a DJ came on and announced that Dr. Martin Luther King Jr. had been shot at the Lorraine Hotel in Memphis and that the station had just received a call from the Reverend Jesse Jackson, who had sadly been with Dr. King at the time of the assassination.

As we listened intently, Herb Kent, the WVON DJ, came on and spoke about King's accomplishments and his nonviolent protests, after which, Kent, known as the "Cool Gent," urged the city to stay calm during this sad time. Then the Cool Gent played Curtis Mayfield's "People Get Ready" by the Impressions.

When Norm reached North Avenue, I told him to take North Ave west toward the Kennedy Expressway. Norm then said, "Let's go to Town & Country instead of Leona's." Town & Country Restaurant was a Greek diner just west of the Kennedy on North Avenue. As we pulled into Town & Country, we could see it was crowded, and we would have to wait. There were also a bunch of cops huddling around in the parking lot with sirens sounding in all directions.

I spoke up, feeling a little shaken and not ready to sit in a restaurant. "Let's get the hell out of here. There's a new music place called the Electric Theater up north on Lawrence and Clark that Matt from Four Heads told me about. Why don't we call in a pizza to go from Leona's, and then we can go hear some music up at this new place?" Then Norm said, "There's a pay phone inside Town & Country. Does everybody like cheese and sausage?"

"No, Barb and I only like cheese," said Cindy.

"Mooch, go inside and order an extra large, half-sausage, half-cheese."

Ava interrupted, "His name is Eric."

Norm replied, "Okay, Eric, please order an extra large, half-sausage, half-cheese, and get some drinks. Unless you guys want some beer? There's still a six-pack in the trunk." We all agreed on beer.

After picking up the pizza, Norm asked, "Where should we go to eat the pie?"

I answered, "Let's go by Eddie's garage. It's only a few blocks away from Leona's. We can park across the alley under the L tracks and eat."

"Good idea, Krock," Norm said. So that's what we did. Ever since the man threw his umbrella at the car, we were listening to the reports from WVON and the plea from the radio jocks for the city to stay calm. We had no idea that the next day, April 5, on the West Side, protests would turn into violent riots with stores on Madison Street and Roosevelt Road being burned and looted. On the South Side, the Woodlawn area would see much of the same. We would discover a week later that the rest of the South Side had escaped major chaos, mainly because the two large street gangs, the Blackstone Rangers and the East Side Disciples, cooperated to control their neighborhoods. Many gang members didn't participate in the rioting, due in part to Dr. King's direct involvement with these groups. In 1966, Dr.

King had moved with his family into an apartment building on the West Side, trying to bring better wages and living conditions to Blacks living on both the West and South Sides.

After finishing our pizza and beers, we headed to the Electric Theater, soon to be renamed the Kinetic Playground. As we got closer to the front door, I recognized the doorman, Herbie, a short Black man dressed in his black karate garb. I knew Herbie from him doing security at different concerts around Chicago. Herbie was rumored to be a black belt and as tough as nails. "What's happening?" Herbie asked. It was obvious Herbie hadn't heard about the assassination and what was going on in the different parts of town. So, all of us told Herbie what we had just witnessed and heard on the radio. After that Herbie told us, "You guys, get your asses inside, no charge."

"Wow, thanks, Herbie," I said, shaking his hand with a soul grip. Then Mooch gave Herbie a soul handshake and said to Herbie, "Righteous, man, right on."

"Stay cool, guys," Herbie replied.

As we walked into the Electric Theater's main room, we were taken in by this incredible light show, especially because we were all so stoned. In a somewhat circular room, a huge gondola hung off the ceiling, filled with projectors and strobe lights for this psychedelic light show. None of us had ever seen anything like this before. There was a band on stage named the Paupers, which none of us had heard of before that night.

"Where should we sit?" asked Cindy.

"I guess there is only seating on the floor," I replied. So, we found a place where we could all sit on the floor.

"This is fuckin trippy," Norm said.

After we all sat down, we became mesmerized by the strobes and images being projected on the walls and ceiling. Soon, Cindy and I were lying on our backs when she turned to me and spoke. "This is one of the craziest nights I have ever had."

I remembered just then what Smiley had said to me that morning, that change was going to come. Things were surely changing, I thought to myself, but I just wasn't sure how it would all turn out. Just then, Cindy reached over and kissed me. We started to make out as the band played a song called "Magic People," and as Norm said earlier, it was trippy.

As we were necking, I could hear Norm say to Barb, "Let's take a walk."

Then Ava said, "We'll go with you. C'mon, Eric."

As they left, we kept necking, and I realized Cindy had no bra on as I placed my hand on her breast. After a while, the band stopped playing and people were leaving, and a couple of people almost tripped over us. We had not realized that we had been listening to the band, watching this amazing light show, and necking for almost two hours. We got up to look for everyone, and as we walked around, we saw Eric and Ava coming out of this little room, which the Electric Theater called meditation booths. Then Norm and Barb popped out of another booth. I thanked Herbie as we walked out, not knowing that I would be coming back almost every weekend as the Electric Theater/Kinetic Playground would be booking the best bands in the world.

After we dropped the girls off, Norm suggested we go to Jack's, a twenty-four-hour neighborhood diner in Skokie where we would often end up at two or three in the morning. But tonight, I told Norm, "Maybe we should go home. This has been one crazy night."

Mooch said, "Fuckin A, man. We could have gotten our asses kicked in front of Cabrini or maybe even shot and killed."

"All right, let's go home," Norm said. "My old man is going to shit when he sees the windshield, and my mom's probably worried, as she always watches the ten o'clock news with Fahey Flynn after she walks the dog."

As I got out of Norm's car, I could see my father looking out the window from our second-floor apartment, but when I walked in, he had already gone back to his bedroom. I walked to the back of the apartment to my bedroom, which was really an enclosed sunporch about six feet by eight feet. While walking past my parents' room, I could hear my dad telling my mom that I was all right and to go back to sleep. To get to my bedroom, I had to walk down a hall past my parents' bedroom and through my sister's bedroom. As soon as I walked through my sister's bedroom door, my sister, Sherry, sat up in her bed and told me. "Someone killed Martin Luther King, and now the Blacks are really upset and starting to freak out."

"Yeah, I know all about it."

"Mom and Dad were really worried, especially Daddy," Sherry said.

"I'm exhausted, Sher. Let's talk in the morning," I said, and Sherry answered back, "Good night, I'm glad you're home."

In the morning, my mom woke me to tell me that Eddie had just called and said to take the day off, and he would see me tomorrow bright and early. "If you get up, I will make you fried matzah. Which reminds me, next Friday night is Passover and we're going to Aunt Ray's."

"Thanks, Ma, but I'm really tired and want to sleep."

"Okay, you can sleep today because there's no work, but don't make it a habit."

I didn't get up till noon. I walked into the kitchen and, to my surprise, Art, my dad, was sitting at the kitchen table in his work clothes, enjoying fried matzah and onions, which smelled delicious. I looked at my mom. "All right, I'll make you some too." As my mom smiled, I walked over to lift the percolator, and to my surprise, it was full. "I just made coffee for your father. Grab two cups and there's cream in the fridge."

"What are you doing at home, Pops? I don't think I have ever seen you home on a weekday unless it's the High Holidays or a relative's funeral."

"I don't know, it's meshuga. I went to drop off a load of scrap by Lissner Iron and Metal, over on Goose Island, and the off-duty cop that works there doing security told me there could be trouble in certain neighborhoods. I was about to leave Lissner and go to my next stop, a screw machine outfit on West Lake Street by Pulaski, and the policeman said not to go to the West Side. He was telling us that Cabrini Green, which is only a few blocks from Lissner's scrapyard on Goose Island, had some trouble there last night. Hopefully, things will calm down. Martin Luther King was a great man. I understand how the Shvartzes feel. I hope things calm down."

"I hope so too, Dad. But I've got to tell you something. Last night we were in Norm's mom's car with our dates, and we didn't know about the trouble brewing from the assassination, and we drove by Cabrini Green. It was crazy. I saw a bunch of ladies crying and hugging each other, and then somebody threw a rock at the car and then, suddenly, this guy about my age beat his umbrella on the car's windshield. Luckily, we were able to get out of there."

Then my father said, "Thank God. I better call Charlie Walker and see how he's doing." Charlie Walker was my dad's one Black friend. They had met in the Army at the Battle of the Bulge. As my dad told it, Charlie was a medic in the 761st Tank Division, an all-Black unit that became a big part of defeating the Germans in the Battle of the Bulge. This was one of the few times where Black and white troops fought side by side in an army that was primarily segregated. The 761st Tank Division became known as the Black Panthers, whose name would later be adopted by the radical group of the '60s. The Black Panthers and their tanks played a big part in winning the Battle of the Bulge.

My dad, who was also a medic, had met Charlie as they both ended up in the same hospital tent, treating the wounded and frostbitten. While treating these patients, working side by side, they discovered they were both from Chicago and became fast friends, exchanging addresses and promising to get together for a beer when the war was over. Not sure they would ever see each other again, Charlie took off with his unit the next day. A few comments were made to my dad about being friendly with a Negro. But my dad, who had been a victim of prejudice against Jews his whole life, related to these Black soldiers.

As fate would have it, they would meet again at the end of the war at the Buchenwald concentration camp. Charlie's 761st Tank Division, along with another Black unit, the 183rd Combat Engineers, had just liberated Buchenwald. A week later, my dad had been assigned there because he spoke fluent Yiddish and was a medic. Charlie would tell my dad that when his unit first saw these poor skeleton-looking souls moaning from pain and hunger, he cried like a baby, as these prisoners about to be freed would look upon these Black soldiers like they were from Mars. Most of these people had never seen a Black soldier, but they would become so grateful for the help they received from these kind men.

I know that many of the 761st and 183rd had been highly decorated, as Charlie received the Bronze Star. My dad had also received the Bronze Star, but he did not talk about that experience and the horrific things that he and Charlie had seen until right before his death. I'm sure sharing this experience is what made their bond as friends so very strong. Following Buchenwald, my dad was also sent to Dachau to treat the survivors. My dad did end up sharing some of these horrors with me during the last couple weeks before his death in 1984.

After they both got out of the Army, Charlie got married to Marva and had twin girls, Denise and Felice. The girls were a couple years younger than my sister, Sherry. When Charlie first came out of the Army, he became a house painter, picking up jobs here and there. He would also help my dad on the truck a couple days a week. Then, when I was about ten, my dad got a hernia. For about a year, he would go to work with this big leather contraption called a hernia belt that would hold his guts in while he loaded and unloaded his truck.

After suffering with the pain for about a year, he went in for hernia surgery and asked Charlie to help him out and take over his route while he recovered. Charlie agreed, taking over the route for a little over a month, and went on to expand the business, picking up a few more stops through people he knew. When my dad finally recovered, he asked Charlie if he wanted to be partners. But Charlie hated the scrap business and told my dad, "No, thank you," and that he liked being a painter. Wanting to help his friend and repay Charlie for helping his family, my father went to see his old friend, Big Joe Arnold, who was a connected guy and a union organizer. Soon after, Charlie had a good union job painting offices in the Loop.

A few years after Charlie became a union painter, he was able to save enough money for a down payment on a beautiful jumbo three-flat building on South Chappel Avenue in Chicago's South Shore Neighborhood. Charlie, Marva, and the girls lived on the second floor, his parents on the first floor, and his brother and his family on the third floor.

When our family went to visit Charlie one Sunday, my mom could not get over how big and nice their apartment was with its formal dining room, three bedrooms, a large kitchen, and two bathrooms, and she complimented Marva on how beautiful the apartment was. On the way home, my parents had one of their big arguments about how much bigger and nicer Charlie's apartment was compared to ours and why couldn't we have a bigger place.

When my dad hung up the phone, he said, "I just spoke to Marva, and she told me that Charlie had just called her to tell her he was coming home early as his bosses had told everyone to go home early, and then Charlie told her to make sure the girls don't go out after school as there were rumors flying around that there could be trouble."

"Stay in the neighborhood today, Alan. No going into the city," my mother said. "I want you home for dinner. It's Shabbos and I'm making chicken."

"Okay, Ma, I'm just going to go play some basketball and I'll be back for supper."

"When you're done playing, please go over to Oakton Bakery and pick up a challah and have them slice it. Be home by five and we will eat about six." I went over to the playground we called Future Park because for years they had a sign up in this empty field that said, "This Will Be a Future Park." So, we always called it Future Park, even though when it finally opened, they put up a sign naming it Winnebago Park. As I walked over to the courts, I could see a couple of the neighborhood guys playing a game of HORSE. "Hey, Joey. Hey, Jim. How's it going?"

"All right, Krockey, how's it hanging?" asked Joey.

Just then, Pete Wingerski walked up. "Let's play two-on-two," Jim said.

These three guys had all gone to St. Peter's grammar school in downtown Skokie. Joey was about to graduate from Loyola University this June, as we were the same age. Joey Julius had always lived across the street from us on Knox Avenue with his three brothers, sister, and mom in a three-flat that Mrs. Julius owned. Mr. Julius had died some years back, as I don't remember ever seeing him. Jim Gorman, who was also our age and went to St. George High School in Evanston, lived on the next block on Kilpatrick Avenue, a few doors down from the Wingerskis. Pete Wingerski was a year older and had graduated the year before from Niles East.

When we first moved to Skokie a few months after I was born, my neighborhood was primarily Catholic with both St. Peter's a few blocks away in downtown Skokie and St. Lambert's about a mile east of where we lived. But while growing up in the '50s and '60s, a major migration of Jews from Chicago's West, South, and Northwest Sides had moved to Skokie.

After a bunch of games, Joey's brothers, Jim and Jerry, came by the courts to tell Joey it was time for supper. Soon after the game broke up, my friends headed home, while I headed to Oakton Bakery on my bike to pick up the challah my mom had asked me to get. When I walked into the bakery, the owner, Abe, told me, "You're lucky your mom called me. You got the last challah, and she added four brownies. She also told me that if you eat a brownie or take a piece of the challah, she will cut your hands off. Here, take a couple of these small brownie cookies with the nuts."

"Thanks, Abe. See you tomorrow." As I approached our building, my dad was out front watering the grass.

"Alan, go turn the water off and roll up the hose. C'mon, we can wash our hands in the basement and go up the backstairs." When we got up the stairs and after taking our shoes off, Sherry came out of her room and we all walked into the living room to watch the local news with Floyd Kalber and Len O'Connor while my mom stayed in the kitchen preparing the Shabbat dinner. I noticed the table was set, and as I went to grab a piece of challah bread, my mother slapped my hand. "We're going to eat in less than an hour; you will spoil your appetite."

"Please, Mom, just one piece."

"Okay, just one piece." My father winked at me as he spread a little chopped liver on pieces of the egg bread for the three of us, using the small plates my mom had placed on the table. As we sat down in the living room after my dad turned the TV on, images of burning buildings appeared on the screen as we heard Floyd Kalber describe the riots that had just started to escalate on the West Side.

Over the next several days, looters broke into stores and set buildings on fire, mostly on Chicago's West Side. A two-mile stretch of Madison Street running through east and west Garfield Park was devastated, with more than one hundred buildings destroyed by fires. Looting and fires also broke out in Lawndale along Roosevelt Road and around 63rd Street on the South Side. Fires also raged across a few other neighborhoods on the South Side and the Near North Side.

Acting Illinois Governor Samuel Shapiro activated nearly seven thousand Illinois National Guard troops the day after King's assassination to support police officers and firefighters in Chicago.

Churches and schools that didn't shut down held memorial services for King on April 5, remembering his nonviolent protests and calling for unity in the city. On April 6, Mayor Richard Daley called President Lyndon Johnson, seeking federal troops. "Mr. President, we're in trouble. We need some help; it's starting to break down in different places. We need help as soon as we can get it," Daley told Johnson.

Late in the evening of April 6, five thousand additional federal troops were ordered into Chicago to support the National Guard and local police. Daley placed Chicago under a citywide curfew for anyone under twenty-one. The city's downtown neighborhood and Rush Street area were totally deserted that Saturday night. According to newspaper reports, hundreds were left homeless on the West Side, and thousands in the city were without electricity.

Daley told reporters after the riots that he had ordered police "to shoot to kill any arsonist or anyone with a Molotov cocktail in his hand." To "maim or cripple anyone looting any stores in our city."

Police were originally ordered to use tear gas on looters and rioters instead of shooting, but by Saturday night, Chicago police commanders called for aggressive action against rioters. Photos of the riots show buildings ablaze and the National Guard patrolling Chicago's streets with rifles.

By the end of the Chicago riots, at least nine people were killed and 1,200 injured. Over 200 buildings were destroyed. The destruction had cost nearly nine million in property damage across the city, according to the *Chicago Tribune*.

The next day, Saturday, I woke up to find only my sister home playing her Supremes records. "Hey, Sher, where's Mom? Did Dad go to work?"

"Mom took the day off, and went shopping, and Dad went to work. They both said not to go to the city. Stay in the suburbs," Sherry replied.

After I read the *Sun-Times* report on the riots, I turned to the Sports section and saw that the Cubs were still going to play the Sox in Milwaukee today but had cancelled their game scheduled for Wrigley Field on Sunday.

I called Norm and he said, "Meet me at the BA for breakfast."

When I got to the bowling alley, Norm was the only one at the grill counter, and he was talking to José, who worked alongside Samantha, preparing the food at the Twin Orchard grill.

As I walked toward the counter, Norm called out, "Krock, Sam and Smiley aren't coming in today. I guess Smiley's at Mount Sinai hospital after getting knocked in the head by some copper after trying to help some lady escape from her burning building. José said he just has a minor concussion."

"What about Sam?" I asked.

"She's over at the church cooking and serving meals for all the people who have lost their homes to the fires."

"Motherfucker," I shouted, "How can this be?"

For the rest of the day, I kind of walked around in a fog as we went from the BA (Twin Orchard Bowl) to other Skokie hangouts, finally ending up at the Q-Inn. Throughout the day, I noticed that most of the people I saw running around Skokie and doing their Saturday errands did not seem very affected, and that Chicago's West and South Sides might as well have been on the other side of the world. This was the first time I realized that most of the people in Skokie and the other North Shore suburbs were living in a bubble, including myself. Sure, there were some white suburbanites who had been affected, having stores or apartment buildings on the West and South Sides that had been destroyed and would never be rebuilt or reopened. But for the most part, there was little concern for the underlying inequality issues that Dr. King had so often preached about.

As we walked into the Q-Inn, through all the cigarette smoke, and with "Reach Out (I'll Be There)" by the Four Tops coming from the jukebox, I could hear a mix of racist and empathetic comments coming from the pool hall crowd. In the corner, there appeared to be a big game of straight pool going on between Jeff Williams and the Big Tuna. Jeff was being backed by Babe Caruso, who, along with his brother Nick, were the sons of a local mafioso named Rocko "the Parrot" Caruso. The Big Tuna, a three-hundred-pound mass whose relatives owned Sally's Ribs in West Rogers Park, had just choked, missing his last shot and giving Jeff a chance to run out four balls to win the game, which he did easily, taking twenty bucks off the Big Tuna and splitting it with Babe.

Jeff was a year younger than me; we had known each other since Hebrew school. A true anti-establishment left-wing hippie and already a big pothead, he had been the one to first talk me into smoking pot. He came over to talk with us. "How's it going, Krock, Norm?"

"It's crazy with these riots and all the fires and looting," Norm said.

Then, Frank Perentie, the owner of the Q-Inn, shouted out, "Fuck these shines."

Jeff yelled back to Frank, "Go fuck yourself, Frank. These people have been persecuted and abused their whole lives by people like you."

"Get the fuck out of here, Williams, you fucking hippie, and don't come back till you can show me some respect."

Then Jeff knocked over the gumball machine as we all ran out laughing while gumballs were rolling down the aisle of the Q-Inn.

When I got home that afternoon, Gary Garfield called to tell me that his father was having a poker game on Sunday afternoon and wanted to know if I wanted to help with getting the food set up and serving the drinks.

"What time is the game?" I asked.

"Around four."

"I thought they usually play on Thursday night."

"Yeah, they decided to not play Thursday after the King assassination. We should be able to make some good tips."

"Sounds great. The Cubs and Sox canceled their preseason Sunday game, so I will definitely be there," I replied.

Then Gary asked, "Hey, are you going to that party in Devonshire tonight?"

"Yes, sir," I answered. That night there was a party in the upscale Skokie neighborhood of Devonshire at the house of Jeff Williams's girlfriend, Michelle, whose parents were out of town. "What time are you going over there?" I asked.

"Probably later after it gets started, but I can pick you up at eight and we can go by the BA, or we can go shoot some pool at the Q-Inn. I've got my mom's Cutlass."

"Cool, love that car. I'll be out front at eight."

When I got home, I decided to take a nap. I was sleeping soundly till I was awakened by my parents yelling at each other, having another one of their fights, my father screaming and swearing. I waited till it got quiet and walked into the kitchen to find my father begging for forgiveness. He suggested to my mom that he would go pick up some deli at Kaufman's and after they would go see a movie. "Alan, take a ride to Kaufman's with me."

"Okay, Pops." One of the things that would make my dad feel good was going to the deli. He was struggling financially at the time and was suffering from undiagnosed PTSD. But when he was able to go to the deli and buy what he wanted, he would always enjoy himself and walk out feeling on top of the world.

Kaufman's was takeout only, with a deli on one side and a bakery on the other. Each side had its own distinct, wonderful smells. As we walked into the deli side, my dad took a number. "Hey, go over to the bakery and order a rye bread, a dozen bagels, and a half-dozen of those French onion rolls you like. I'm getting corned beef and potato salad for dinner and some lox and a couple chubs for breakfast. Here's some money."

"Sherry said she wanted an éclair."

"Okay, get two eclairs and a dozen assorted rugelach."

When we got home, my sister Sherry had set the table.

"Where's Mom?"

"She's in the bathroom getting ready. Here, give me the food and I'll put it on the serving dishes." My dad had turned on the news in the living room, his good mood fading as he watched the rioting going on in Chicago and across the country. My mom walked into the living room and turned the TV off.

"Enough with the bad news. Let's eat, Art, and then you need to get ready for the movies. We're going to see a comedy called *The Producers*. It's playing at the Skokie Theatre and starts at eight."

"I like the Old Orchard theater better," my dad said.

"We're not going to the Old Orchard, Art. They have some *farka-kte* movie about apes on the planet."

"Okay, Babe," my dad answered while taking a bite of one of the pickles he bought, his good mood seeming to come back with each bite of his corned beef sandwich.

After my folks took off, I got ready and went outside to wait for my friend Gary Garfield. "Hey, G, how's it going?"

"I'm starving. Did you eat?"

"Yeah, we had corned beef from Kaufman's. You want to go back to my house? I think there's some left over."

"Nah, I feel like a hot dog. Let's go to Big Herm's."

As we walked into the small hot dog stand, Howie Brown was working along with Herbie, the grill man. Howie was as big as a house and a year older than us, and when Howie wasn't working at Herm's or with his girlfriend you could find him at one of the many Chicago-area racetracks that ran flats in the day and the trotters at night. The grill man, Herbie, with his do-rag and processed hair underneath, kind of resembled James Brown. "What will it be, fellas?" Howie asked.

"Just a hot dog with everything, fries, and a large orange Nedlog."

"How about you, Krockey?"

"Nothing for me—I just ate."

Howie laid down his racing form and made Gary his hot dog while making a fresh batch of fries. Howie handed Gary his order in one of their red baskets lined with wax paper.

Two Skokie cops walked in. Bill Hicks, a detective, and Bert Podolak, the juvenile officer. We all knew both officers too well from previous encounters and constant harassment of our teenage crowd. Last summer, I had been arrested at the Burger King down the street from Herm's for a fight I'd gotten into after some guy called me a dirty kike. After that, I had to report to Podolak every month as part of my probation/supervision, which had just ended last month.

"What will it be, officers?" Howie asked.

"Let us have two of those steak sandwiches to go," Officer Hicks replied.

As Herbie started to make his famous skirt steak sandwiches, he asked, "You fellas want grilled onions?"

"Pile them on," Podolak replied.

Hicks said, "Not for me—my ulcer is acting up. Too much aggravation with these hippies and now with the Blacks, and all this rioting. They better not start that shit in Skokie."

"Right, Herbie?" Herbie just smiled at him with his big gold tooth shining brightly in Hicks's eyes. Officer Hicks liked to bully Skokie's teenagers and the Blacks who would come across McCormick Boulevard into Skokie from Evanston to buy liquor. (Evanston was a dry town in those days.)

"Here's your sandwiches."

"How much do we owe you?" Officer Podolak asked.

"On the house," Howie said.

"Thanks," Podolak said.

"Stay out of trouble, fellas," Hicks said, giving us all that condescending look of his. After they walked out, Herbie shouted, "Why the fuck didn't you charge those motherfuckers?"

"Yeah, I know, but Herm told me not to charge Hicks and Podolak. It seems Big Herm cut a deal with them after he got caught speeding leaving The Cork Restaurant last week. Krockey, you guys want to go to the trotters with me tonight? Brett Hanover is running."

"No, Howie, we're going to a party right around the corner from your parents' house. You want to come?" Gary asked.

"Nope, I'm going to the track. Maybe I'll stop by later with my girlfriend."

"See you, Howie. Take care, Herbie," I shouted as we walked out.

I asked Gary where he wanted to go. "C'mon, let's go shoot a couple games at the Q-Inn and then go to the party."

"I don't know. Frank was really pissed when Williams knocked over the gumball machine this afternoon."

"Don't worry about it. Just because you were with him, he can't blame you."

As soon as we walked into the pool hall Frank hollered at me, "Where's that fucking Williams? He owes me a half a hundred for the broken gumball machine. When you see him, you tell him to bring me that half a yard or he will never play here again."

"Give us table eight in the back," Gary said.

As we were playing our third game of eight-ball, Kenny David walked over. "Are you guys going to the party at Michelle's? You guys want to buy some hash?"

"No thanks, Kenny, but we're going over there after we finish this game."

"Can you give me a ride?"

"Sure, Kenny, but first tell me how much acid and other stuff you are carrying," Gary said.

"Just a couple tabs of acid and a little hash." Gary and I had not tried acid yet, but it seemed that more and more of our friends were experimenting with LSD and other psychedelics like mescaline and mushrooms. We gave Kenny a ride over to the party.

I told Kenny, "If we get stopped by the cops, you better be ready to eat both the acid and the hash."

Kenny gave me that goofy smile of his and replied, "No problem. I love acid, and with the hash kicker, it might be mellow. Hell, I'm going to take one tab now. But I promised my girlfriend that I'd save the other one for her, so please don't get stopped or Patty will kill me. She's a giant acid freak."

When we arrived at Michelle's parents' house, a few people were hanging outside in the backyard. I spotted Jeff Williams sitting on a lounge chair with Michelle next to him. "Hey, Jeff, how are you doing?" I asked.

"Cool, Krock, very cool."

"Jeff, we just came from The Q-Inn and Frank is pissed. He said that if you don't bring him fifty bucks for the gumball machine, he is never going to let you back in."

Jeff looked at me with a crazy stare and then said, "Wow, man, check those fireflies."

"What are you going to do about Frank?" I asked.

"Wow, man, you're really bringing me down. Can't you see I'm tripping?" Jeff said in an angry voice. Jeff's girlfriend, Michelle, who never took any drugs, not even pot, motioned for me to move on while rubbing Jeff's back and whispering to him to look at the beautiful fireflies. As I walked through the house, I could hear music coming from the basement. It was Archie Bell and the Drells singing "Tighten Up."

As I entered the basement, I could see it was filled with smoke, and mostly the greaser crowd, where the rest of the house was younger kids, mainly collegiate types and a few hippies. But this greaser crowd had some fabulous dancers. And now there were eight of them doing a line dance to "Tighten Up"—four girls and four boys moving in sync. I was truly impressed, as I was a pretty good dancer myself.

Out on the floor was Mooch Sands dancing along with Ava, and a short little five-foot-four tough guy named Jimmy Grimes who hung around the All-Star Bowl. Jimmy danced in the line with Marge, his six-foot-tall fiancée with her beehive hairdo. There were two other couples in line next to them, but I only recognized one of the guys. A guy named Gene Marines, who had crazy hair that stood straight up. They were in the groove that night, dancing in Mr. and Mrs. Lake's basement.

If Mrs. Lake could see what was going on in her house, she would freak out. The Lakes had gone down to Miami for ten days to see Mrs. Lakes's mother over the Passover holiday. Before they left, they pleaded for Michelle and her sister, Yvonne, to come with them. Michelle was finishing her junior year at Niles North and had convinced them, with Jeff's encouragement, that she needed to study and that she promised to watch over her younger sister, now a freshman, and that they would both take care of the house. As I walked up the stairs, I could see Yvonne necking with this short little guy who looked like Woody Allen, Freddy Schwartz, who was Stereo Stu's little cousin. As I walked through the house, I ran into Norm and Barb, who were parked in a beanbag chair in one of the bedrooms.

Norm looked up at me with a bizarre expression I had never seen before, "Krock, we can't move—we're stuck in this quicksand." They were obviously tripping, so I helped them both up. After that, Norm gave me a bear hug. "Krockey, you saved our lives." Then Barb hugged me and gave me a big kiss on the lips.

"Wow," I said and then asked, "Hey, have you seen Cindy?"

"She's around here somewhere. Check out the other rooms," Barb replied.

I walked down the hall and heard Cream's "Crossroads" coming out of one of the bedrooms. I walked in and saw two naked bodies on the bed in what appeared to be Michelle's room.

"Don't you knock, man?" as this guy who appeared to be a few years older than me turned his head. I recognized the guy right away as being one of the members of the Flock, a local band that I had just seen a few weeks before at The Cellar in Arlington Heights. Then the girl sat up, covering herself with a blanket. I couldn't believe my eyes; it was Cindy.

My heart fell into my stomach as I turned around and left the room, only to hear Cindy scream, "We're on acid! Come back and trip with us." I ran outside and could barely catch my breath.

As I started to walk toward Skokie Boulevard to try and hitch a ride home, I heard Gary G call my name, "Hold up, man." When he caught up to me, he asked, "What happened? Why did you run out?"

"Fuck, man, I went upstairs and ran into Norm and Barb who were tripping their asses off. But, if that isn't crazy enough, I walked into Michelle's room and found Cindy there with one of the guys from the Flock, both stark naked in bed and tripping on acid. Man, I couldn't take it, so I ran out. It's not like she was my girlfriend or anything, but we made out the other night, and I was hoping she might be."

"Don't sweat it, Krock, there's plenty of fish in the sea."

"Hey, Gary, it looked like you were having a good time with that girl you were talking to. If you want to go back, it's cool. I was going to hitch home anyway."

"To tell you the truth, her braces kind of turned me off, and I didn't know that many people at this party."

I replied, "Yeah, where was everybody? I didn't see too many people we knew. Just the greasers and a bunch of the younger crowd."

Then Gary said, "I forgot that Hayman had mentioned to me that a lot of people were going to see Simon and Garfunkel at Northwestern in Evanston. By the time I tried to get tickets, they were sold out. Come on, let's go to Jack's. You want a Marlboro?"

"You know I don't smoke cigarettes."

"Well, I'm out of pot, and I thought it might relax you."

"No, thanks." When we walked into Jack's, it was even more crowded than the usual Saturday night. There was a big line with people waiting to get a table or a booth. "Hey, Gary, let's grab those two stools at the counter; otherwise, it will take forever." After we sat down, I heard someone call my name from the booth behind us. It was Steve Yonover with his date, Helene Brakman; Bruce Hayman and Bonny Gaigerman; and Donnie Siegel and his girlfriend, Francie.

As we turned on our stools, Gary asked, "How was the show?"

Almost in unison, all three girls said, "It was wonderful."

"I tried to get tickets," Gary said.

"There were a lot of empty seats," Hayman replied.

"I was told it was sold out," Gary said.

Then Siegle told us, "It was, but because the City of Chicago had a 7 p.m. curfew due to the riots, a lot of kids who lived in Chicago never made it."

"Wow, bummer," I replied.

"Did you guys go to that party in Devonshire? How was it?" Bonny asked.

"Not so great. A lot of people were taking LSD. The greaser crowd from the All Star Bowl were there, and mostly a lot of younger kids."

"I will never do acid," Helene said.

Then Hayman asked, "How about you guys?

"No, not me," I answered.

"No acid for me either," Gary said.

"Well, I'd like to try it someday," Bruce said, as Yonover gave him that cuckoo motion with his hands.

We turned back around on our stools when Pearl the waitress asked, "What will it be, fellas?"

"I'll have the patty melt, fries, and a chocolate phosphate," I said.

"Same for me, Pearl, but give me a Cherry Coke instead of the phosphate."

As we headed home, I asked Gary, "Is it cool if I sleep in your basement tonight? I don't feel like going home and waking my parents, who would start asking me a million questions."

"Sure."

When we got to Gary's house, he gave me a blanket and pillow. He went back upstairs to his room, and I went downstairs to the Garfield's finished basement. They had a first-rate jukebox and since everyone was sleeping on the second floor, I figured I wouldn't wake anyone and picked out the record *That's Life* by Frank Sinatra to lullaby me to sleep. As soon as my head hit the pillow on that couch, I fell into a deep sleep. Around 8 a.m., somebody started shaking me, telling me to wake up. "Krockey, get up."

As I opened my eyes, standing there with his hands on his hips was Charlie Garfield, Gary's older brother, and his Chinese girlfriend, Ling. Charlie had met Ling when delivering food for the Pekin House on Devon Avenue. Ling's father, Mr. Wong, who managed the Pekin House, worked alongside his wife, Mae, and his daughter, Ling, who both waitressed. Ling knew her father would never approve of this romance so Ling and Charlie snuck around. Charlie would wait up all Saturday night and pick up Ling on Sunday mornings. She would tell her parents she was going to early mass at the Catholic church in Rogers Park. Charlie barked, "Krockey, hurry up and put your pants on. Ling, please turn around."

I put my clothes on before walking up the stairs. When I reached the top of the stairs, Charlie called out to me, "Take it easy, Krockey, and don't tell anyone about Ling or you will catch a beating."

"Ling who? See you later, Charlie."

Gary always slept late, so I went on my way and didn't bother to wake him.

I was walking back to my family's apartment, which was only three blocks from the Garfields' townhouse on Main and Kilpatrick across from Kenton School, when Norm pulled up with the window down and shouted for me to get in.

"What are you doing here?" I asked.

"I was on my way to your house to pick you up to go to Sunset Baths. When I called my house this morning to let my parents know I had slept at Buggy Faustine's, my father answered. He told me he ran into Jake Rubin and his wife last night at the Cork Steakhouse on Dempster and that Jake had mentioned to him that he had seen us and that we had talked about going to Division Street Baths on Tuesday. Then my old man told Jake that Division Baths was temporarily closed because of the rioting and suggested we all go to Sunset this morning. Oh, man, what a night. That fucking acid kicked my ass."

"How was the party after I left?"

"Fucking crazy. I'm not sure how long after you left because I was so spaced out. But, Barb and I were lying on the grass in the backyard when the cops showed up. As soon as I saw Hicks, Barb and I took off through the neighbors' yards and kept running till we were like five blocks away. What we didn't realize was Gene Marines and his girlfriend, Tootsie, were right behind us, and right behind them was Shane and his new girlfriend, Bonny Kanter, the one from North, not the one from Niles East."

"When did Gary Shane get there?"

"Right before the cops got there. Anyhow, Shane said that he and Bonny had walked to the party and suggested that we go pick up his car by his parents' house, which was right down the street from where we were all standing. So, we all hopped into Shane's Malibu and drove to the Lakefront in Evanston. As soon as we got into the car, Gene offered Shane and Bonny the same acid we were on and now all of us were tripping. We ended up somewhere in Evanston by the lake, where they had these big rocks along the shore. We sat there all night smoking pot, talking, and waiting for the sun to come up. I never really talked to Gene Marines before. Did you know he was like twenty-one or something? He told us all about when he lived in San Francisco and how cool it was, and that we should all go out there sometime."

He continued, "Then the sun started to come up, and the colors of the sky over the lake were incredible. Really trippy. You have got to try acid, Krock. Then Shane dropped everybody off and took me back to my car in front of Michelle's house. I could see Michelle, Yvonne, and little Freddy cleaning up the house through the picture window. After I knocked on the door, Michelle opened it and was crying, telling me that Jeff and Kenny had been arrested and that Officer Podolak had made her call her parents so that he could talk with them, and that her parents were cutting their trip short and coming home tonight. Then, little Freddy came to the door and said that Ira and Bobby Sussman, who were at the party, called their dad, Harvey, the lawyer, and that Harvey and Jeff and Kenny's fathers were down at the police station, hoping to bail them out. What a night."

"Take me by my house so I can pick up some clean clothes, and I have a brand-new broom. You want to borrow some clean stuff?" I asked Norm.

"No, my old man is bringing me clothes. You can tell your parents you slept at Buggy's if you want. His parents are down in Florida."

"No need, I can tell them the truth that I slept at Garfield's. I'll be right back." When I walked in the door, I saw it was 8 a.m. and my mom was washing dishes.

"Did you sleep by the Garfields?"

"Yeah, Ma. Where's Dad?"

"Your father is painting the back stairs." When I opened the back door, there was my dad on his knees painting the porch like he did every spring.

"Hey, Pops, I'm going to the schvitz with Norm, his dad, and Jake Rubin. Why don't you come with us?"

"Wish I could, but once you start a job, you must finish. Haven't I always taught you that?"

"Yes, Dad, but you paint these stairs every year, and you could use a schvitz. My treat."

"Thank you. But you know, I always paint the stairs after the winter with all the snow, ice, and salt."

"See you later, Dad. Don't work too hard." He just looked up and smiled. You see, my dad loved working on his building and was very proud that he was able to buy each of the co-ops' four units separately over time and eventually own the whole building. Unfortunately, he was currently going through a rough patch financially. Which is why all I had on my mind, besides girls, was my burning desire to make money.

I got into Norm's car and we headed to the schvitz. There were three schvitz or Russian/Turkish bathhouses in Chicago. The one we were going to that day was Sunset Bowl and Health Club, the most modern, built in the early '50s and located in West Rogers Park, not far from Skokie. The other two were Luxor Turkish Bathhouse, built in 1923, and Division Street Bathhouse, built at the turn of the century, around 1900. Both Luxor and Division were close to downtown Chicago.

The three places each had their own personality with different features and different clientele, but all three had one popular feature: a steam room. These rooms were built of concrete, brick, and tiles with glass doors. In a corner of each room is a brick oven in which granite boulders, approximately the size of watermelons, are heated to extreme temperatures by gas jets; hot water is then thrown on the rocks by the customers or attendant as desired. When this happens, the water instantly evaporates, creating steam inside the oven and heating the brick enclosure, thereby raising the air temperature in the room.

The bathers will sit or lie on one of the three levels of tiered wooden benches, which allow for dramatically different temperatures at the various heights. Cold water is provided by taps located under the benches. When overwhelmed by the heat, a bather will dump a bucket of frigid water over their head while still in the hot room or may step outside to use the cold pools.

Sunset and Luxor, also called North Avenue, both had Olympic-size swimming pools, while Division Street just had a small cold pool for cooling off. Of the three, Division Street had the best heat. One other common element was the *platza* or rub. The traditional Russian platza is when you are just beaten lightly with a flat oak leaf broom. But here in these Chicago schvitz houses, the popular soap rub, also called a platza, is given with a round oak leaf broom while you lie down, and a professional platza specialist or a friend will scrub you with this oak leaf broom after soaking the broom with hot soapy water. The oak leaves contain a natural astringent, which will open your pores, remove toxins, and take off layers of dead skin.

After one of these rubs while you are still covered with soap, you or the rubber will throw a cold bucket of water over your head and body. There is nothing as refreshing and invigorating as a good rub. Some described the platza as "Jewish acupuncture." Since I was a young boy, I have been addicted to this tradition, having been taken first to Division Street Baths when I was only five by my Zadie, who at the time lived in that neighborhood with my Bubbe.

Sunset had a different crowd than Division or Luxor, which were closer to downtown Chicago. Both Luxor and Division in general had more politicians, judges, lawyers, and entertainers, along with Chicago's top gangsters. Sunset, which sat in the basement of a bowling alley, was more working class with car salesmen who worked down the street at the many dealerships on Western Avenue; home improvement guys, commonly called tin men; insurance salesmen; installment dealers; store owners; and a variety of other businessmen from scrap dealers to plumbers to professionals.

Sunset was also a major gambling spot and had a big card room with a few resident bookies if you were so inclined to bet on a horse or ballgame. All kinds of games were played there. Guys sat around in sheets playing gin rummy, the most popular game. They also played panguingue, clobyosh, pinochle, and of course all types of poker. The big poker game was run by Sunset Health Club's manager, Jerry. The big game was only spread on Wednesday and Friday.

As we headed down the stairs from the bowling alley, we bumped into Stewie Cohen and his dad, Arnie, who was the bartender at the Black Angus, a popular steakhouse down the street from Sunset Baths. Right behind them was Lenny Patrick and Irv Singer. Irv was the frontman owner of the Angus, but it was rumored that Lenny Patrick and his mob associates owned a piece of this popular restaurant and would frequently be seen at the Black Angus enjoying a meal or hanging at the bar. In fact, Stewie's dad, Arnie, was brought in by Lenny to run the bar and keep an eye on things.

"Hey, Stewie, why are you leaving so early?"

"I got here at five o'clock to meet my dad after he got off work."

"I thought they opened at 7 a.m."

"Normally they do, but they opened early for us."

"Oh, I get it."

"Okay, catch you later, Stu."

Then Lenny Patrick said, looking at Norm, "What are you smiling at?"

Norm replied, "Nothing, sir. Just going for a bath."

Norm and I looked at each other, started laughing, and ran down the stairs as we had just smoked a joint on the way over. When we got to the locker room, Norm's dad, Hawk (Henry) Friedman, was talking to Jerry, the manager, and Irv Kahn, a bookie who was a bathhouse regular. Irv and Jerry were complaining about that prick Lenny Patrick, who they said kept raising the amount they had to pay every week for protection from the outfit.

"Krockey, you bring a broom?" Jake Rubin shouted as he walked out of the steam room.

"Just picked up a new one from José on Division Street. It's been soaking in my parents' basement for two days, so it should be nice and soft."

"Good because the brooms they have here are shit compared to José's. That kid José is the best broom maker I've ever come across, a real artist. C'mon, Hawk, let's get some heat and I'll give you a rub," Jake told Hawk Friedman as he grabbed the broom and the bucket of soap from me. The hot room was crowded but cleared out after about twenty minutes. I sat on the top bench, feeling the heat hug me, still a little high on the weed, and waiting till I was super hot before throwing a cold bucket over my head.

"Wow, what a rush!" I shouted, my mind clearing as the cold water hit. I felt invigorated and relaxed at the same time.

After I threw the cold bucket over my head, one of Sunset's professional masseuses walked in. Joe Lubin, a former boxer who worked there as a rubber and masseuse, was friends with my dad's friend Eddie Lander, also a boxer. My father was a big boxing fan and would tell me stories about how after getting out of the Army, he would go see Joe Lubin and Eddie Lander fight at Marigold Gardens. And how his friend Eddie Lander was cousins with the one-time champion boxer Barney Ross. "Why is it so crowded, Joe?"

"Well, with the riots and everything, I guess Division and Luxor closed for a few days. So, some of their Sunday guys came here."

After we gave each other platzas, with me getting the last rub, Norm's dad said, "Let's eat."

We dried off in the locker room, wrapping big white bed sheets around us before walking over to the dining room. Billy Joe, the Black masseuse who worked there with Joe Lubin, called me over. "Krockey, you got another one of those reefers you gave me last time you was here?"

"Not with me, but there's half a joint in Norm's car I can give you when we leave."

"Cool. You're the best, Krock."

In those days, all the bathhouse dining room tables had a bowl of sour pickles and sour tomatoes, along with a basket of rye and black bread sitting out. As soon as we sat down, Hawk Friedman barked out the orders. "Give us a bottle of red and a bottle of white. Jake, do you want maatjes herring?"

"Of course," Jake replied.

"Okay, then bring us an order of maatjes herring, a couple lox plates, and some scrambled eggs with onions. And toast four bagels to start. What kind of bagel do you like, Krockey?"

"I like an onion bagel," I said.

Norm said, "Give me that, too."

"Okay, give us a couple onion bagels, a pumpernickel for Jake, and I'd like a poppy seed."

"No poppy seed, but we do have sesame seed," the waiter replied.

"Okay, sesame seed."

Norm started to pour the bottle of Montreal club soda, referred to as white, into everyone's glass with ice, and then proceeded to top it off with the red strawberry pop, also made by Montreal.

They brought out the maatjes herring first, which I had never tasted before, because all my mom ever bought was pickled herring in wine sauce, which I loved, and schmaltz herring when my Zadie was alive. Then, Jake, after taking that first bite of the maatjes herring, looked up with a smile on his face and spoke. "Come on, boys, try some. It tastes just like a woman."

As he was putting the herring on three small plates, I said to Jake, "You sound just like Dylan."

We all laughed. It turned out that I really liked this maatjes herring. We were just finishing eating when Gary Garfield and his dad walked by the restaurant, towels and sheets in hand, on the way to the locker room. I called out to Gary, "Garfield, what are you doing here?"

"I called your house, Krock, to tell you the game was canceled for tonight, and your mom told me you went to the schvitz, and when I mentioned it to my dad, he said, 'Great idea,' and here we are."

Then Gary's father, Art, chimed in, "Yeah, we couldn't get enough of the Thursday night poker regulars to come, as a few of them live downtown and are staying home until things quiet down around the city. How are you, Hawk? Long time," asked Art.

"I'm good."

Hawk replied, "And you and the family?"

"Can't complain—we're moving along. How about some top-shelf brandy, fellas?" Art Garfield offered, as he removed a bottle of Martell Cognac from his gym bag.

"Of course—why not? You want some food?" Jake replied.

"No thanks, we're going to eat after we take some heat."

"But let's all have a shot first," Mr. Garfield replied. So, we all took a shot as Mr. Garfield and Norm's father talked about their mutual friend, Seymour Taradash, and the junkets to Vegas he was running to the Stardust out in Sin City. It appeared that both Hawk Friedman and Art Garfield and their wives were booked on the same junket, the July 4th weekend at the Stardust Hotel in Las Vegas. After the drinks, we went back into the heat, washed the herring smell off us, and went home. Gary and his dad stayed, and as I found out later, Art cleaned up in a gin game.

When I got home that afternoon, after having two shots of brandy, an hour and a half of heat, a rub, plus the weed, I passed out around 2 or 3 p.m. and did not wake up till about ten that night. After that point, I tiptoed through my sister's room so as not to wake her and then continued down the hall past my parents' room. My parents' room door was closed and it appeared that they were also sleeping.

I walked through the kitchen into the living room and turned on the TV just in time for the start of the ten o'clock news. The news reported that the rioting had started to quiet down. All this after eleven people had died, forty-eight had been wounded, and over 2,000 were arrested, as well as ninety policemen being injured. Daley had set a curfew, with 10,000 policemen, over 6,000 National Guardsmen, and an additional 5,000 Army troops sent in by President Johnson after a request for help from the mayor.

The news showed all the buildings and businesses that had been destroyed by fire, showing that hundreds would be left homeless and that thousands were without power. A commercial came on, and I went into the kitchen and made myself a peanut butter and jelly sandwich with a glass of milk. While sitting there finishing my sandwich, watching the news, I thought about how crazy and scary this all was and that none of it made any sense.

Then my dad came into the living room after waking up to use the washroom. "What are you doing, Totty?"

"I guess I fell asleep after the schvitz around 2:30 and just woke up."

"I was tired myself after painting the whole porch. I took a bath, ate supper, and then fell asleep on the couch until your mother made me get up and go to bed. I just got up to pee and heard the TV. Your mother is reading her book."

My father then switched the channel from Fahey Flynn and Joel Daly over to Floyd Kalber and Len O'Connor, who he liked better. He could also do a pretty good impression of Len O'Connor. It seemed Floyd and Len were reporting pretty much what I had just heard on the other channel as my pops listened intently. "You know, Alan, that most of the Black folks living on the West and South Side are good hardworking people who have been discriminated against for years just because of the color of their skin. Many of these folks are churchgoing people. I think their faith is what helps many of them to keep going." As my dad explained, you could see sadness in his face.

I asked, "Then why do some of them riot and destroy their own neighborhood?"

"Well, that's a complicated question. As I see it, it only takes a few to wind up what appears to be mostly younger people, teenagers. Many of these kids are broke and with maybe just one parent. Discrimination and many of the other circumstances Blacks find themselves in today make it easier to lose hope, especially when one of your leaders, like Dr. King, who preached hope, is assassinated."

Then news from the Vietnam War came across the screen. My dad went on to say, "It's so unfair and ironic that many of the boys being killed over there are Black. In fact, most are minorities—Mexicans, Native Americans, and such. You know, Juan Martinez, the mechanic at the Enco gas station on Oakton and Kostner? Well, in addition to being a superb mechanic, he won the Silver Star over in the Pacific during World War II. Did you know that his son, Juan Jr., enlisted?"

"Yeah, I heard. He was a year ahead of me in school and a hell of an athlete. I hope he will be okay."

"I pray so too, Alan. You know, son, when you were in trouble at school, I told your mom that maybe you should go into the Army. I'm so glad you didn't join the service."

Chapter 2

The Hustler's Boogie

As the summer of 1968 slowly rolled on, my days became somewhat routine when the Cubs were in town and very different when they were not. When the Cubs were at home, I would go to work at the ballpark, but when the Cubs were on the road, I would look for any way I could to make a buck. I had all kinds of jobs and hustles on the Cubs' traveling days. I tried selling door to door as an installment dealer, working as a stock boy at various stores, selling flowers on street corners, and then eventually just selling small bags of pot, which we called lids.

In late June of that year, my dad asked me to help him one day in his fledgling scrapyard as he could no longer afford to pay the workers, letting go of his only helper just a week before. My job that day was to take scrap copper tubing that had iron fittings on the end and cut off the iron fittings so my dad could sell it as clean #1 copper, which would make him a nice profit. I hated the work, but my dad needed help. It was about lunchtime and my dad had walked down the block to pick up lunch for us. While washing my hands for lunch, I heard a car pull up and honk its horn. As I walked outside to see who it was, I saw my dad getting out of a really cool, cream-colored 1960 Buick LeSabre convertible. "Pop, whose car is that?"

"It's yours," he said.

"Pop, you can't afford to buy me a car."

"I didn't buy it. Do you remember that thieving partner of mine, Harry Orloff, who ran off with the secretary and all the company's money?"

"Yes, I do. He was a real asshole for leaving you holding the bag and now you owe all this money to the banks and big Joe. What about him?"

"Well, I ran into him last night, and with the help of Big Joe we convinced him to sign over the car along with some of the money he owed me. At least Joe got all his money, and I no longer have to pay him juice every week. Now I can work on paying the bank off, so we don't lose the building. Remember when you first left school and I promised you that if you went back to high school and graduated, I would buy you a car? Well, a promise is a promise. Anyway, because the car is eight years old, I could probably only get a couple hundred for it. It's yours, Totty. Enjoy your new car and please take care of it."

"I promise, Dad."

As we enjoyed our Italian beef sandwiches with sweet and hot peppers, I could see a proud tear rolling down my dad's cheek along with a big smile on his face, which I hadn't seen since Harry ran off and left my dad broke. My dad was still in debt and would go on struggling for a couple more years, but on that day he felt proud and happy. He was as excited about the car as I was, and we shared one of the very few father-and-son special moments we would ever experience.

Now that I had my own car, I started to come up with all kinds of ideas to make money. Around this time, bell-bottoms were coming into fashion. The problem was that you had to go to Old Town to find this new style of pants. None of the department or men's stores around Skokie or on Devon in Chicago were carrying this new style. So, one day, I decided to take a ride and go see Arnie Fisher down by Maxwell Street to see if maybe he was selling these hard-to-find pants for men and women. Sure enough, my hunch was right. Arnie, whose stores always carried the latest in fashion, had just got in a big order of three styles of bell-bottoms. These included blue jean bell-bottoms, engineer stripe bell-bottoms, and paisley bell-bottoms, which the girls really liked. I asked Arnie what he thought about me selling bell-bottoms out of the trunk of my car at the various places where my friends and other teenagers hung out.

"It sounds a little crazy to me, but if anybody can do it, Krockey, it's you. I know your father is struggling and you're working at the ballpark. So, I'll tell you what I'm going to do. I will give you two dozen pairs of these trousers in various sizes on consignment to start. Go see if you can sell them. If you don't sell them, you can bring them back, as long as they are in the same condition as when I gave them to you. And if you need more, I'll sell you more. Listen, I pay five dollars a pair. I'll charge you eight dollars, and you can sell them for whatever. But try to get fifteen or twenty as that's what they charge in Old Town."

On weekday nights, I would hang out with my friends at Skokie's various teen hangouts. These included the Burger King on Dempster, which we called BK on D, the Q-Inn, down the street from BK on D, as well as the Twin Orchard Bowl and various other spots in Skokie, Evanston, Lincolnwood, and Chicago's Rogers and Hollywood Park neighborhoods. Well, for about a month, it went very well with kids trying on these bell-bottoms in the washrooms of these hangouts. I even sold a pair to Frank Parente at the Q-Inn. If the pants needed to be shortened, I would send them over to Sam the tailor, a Holocaust survivor, who only charged a dollar to shorten pants. But within a month, the stores in downtown Skokie, like Raymonds and Mister Juniors, started selling the same bell-bottoms at a good price. I had a nice run selling a little over four dozen pairs and banking a little over three hundred dollars.

After selling my last pair of bell-bottoms, I wanted to give Arnie the balance of the money I owed him, so I headed down to Maxwell

Street. As I walked into Breyers that Sunday, the store was crowded and you could hear "Stay in My Corner" by the Dells coming out of the speakers. "Hey, Lips, how's it hanging?"

"Not as good as yours. I heard you made some good coin selling bell-bottoms out of the back of that fine Buick of yours. I got to give it to you, man; you're a hell of a hustler for a white kid." We both laughed. "He's over at the other store today."

As I walked over to Arnie's other store, Leeds Menswear, I could smell those grilled onions from the hot dog and Polish stand next door. As I was about to walk into Leeds, Arnie came out. "What's up, Mr. Krockey?"

"Nothing, Arnie, just came by to square up."

"Come on, Krockey, I'm walking over to Manny's to have lunch. We can square up there."

"Sounds good—I'm starving."

Manny's was, and still is, a cafeteria-style Jewish deli and has become a Chicago institution. As we stood in line looking at the hot food specials, Arnie yelled out, "I will have the stuffed veal breast with a side of spaghetti."

As Arnie waited for his plate of food, I moved down the line to where they served their famous corned beef sandwich. "Hey, Gino."

"Hey, Krockey, what will it be?"

"Give me the corned beef on rye and a potato pancake."

"You got it," Gino said. Gino, who was about my age, ran Manny's sandwich station always with a smile as he sliced your choice of meats—and he still works there today.

As we grabbed a table and sat down, I looked around the room and noticed a very diverse crowd enjoying their lunch. "What are you looking at, boychik?" Arnie asked.

"All these different kinds of people eating together."

Arnie then went on to explain, "Yes, sir. Manny's is a real melting pot all right. But they all have one thing in common: They all love eating and meeting at Manny's. Here, look over there. That's my lawyer, Leonard Fisher, eating with Congressman Dan Rostenkowski and the politician George Dunn. And at the table next to them, you can see from their uniforms are two city garbagemen, the three-hundred-pound Italian and the skinny Black guy."

"How do you know he's Italian?"

"He's got 'Rocky' written on his uniform and a tattoo on his left arm with the Italian flag. What, do you think he's Jewish? The skinny Black guy he's eating with has 'Tyrell' written on his shirt. You need to be more observant, Alan. And as usual, in the corner is my bookie, Leo Weiss, and today it looks like he is eating with his mob friend, Fat Herbie Blitzstein. In the front by the register, you will notice a table of Black politicians from around the city who meet here every week after church. All kinds. How's your sandwich?"

"Delicious. How's your veal?"

"Like butter, but way too much food."

As we were having coffee, I handed Arnie an envelope, which he stuffed into his inside coat pocket. "Thank you. You know, Krockey, I wasn't sure you were going to sell all those pants. But I'm sure glad you proved me wrong. You should maybe think about opening your own store one day. Right now, you're a hungry kid trying to make a buck, and that's a good thing. But you should keep your eyes open for a business that will not only do good and make you money, but something that you enjoy working at. Something you can build. I need to get back to the store."

I grabbed Arnie's check out of his hand, and we headed toward the door where you paid. Manny and Mrs. Raskin were behind the register. "Well, this is a first: Arnie Fisher not picking up a check. Who's the little pisher?" Manny asked.

"Krockey, this is Mr. and Mrs. Raskin. Meet Krockey."

"That's your name?" Mrs. Raskin asked.

"No, my name is Alan Krockey, but everyone likes to call me Krockey. I know your son Kenny; he's friends with my cousin Michael."

Mrs. Raskin replied, "Well, good to meet you, Alan. See you tomorrow, Arnie."

As we walked out, Arnie waved his hand and shouted, "Goodbye—see you tomorrow."

We then crossed the street, walking right past the window of Chernin's Shoes, when I spotted a pair of Frye boots in the window, thinking these would look real boss with my new bell-bottoms. I thanked Arnie for all his help, said goodbye, and walked into Chernin's to buy the Frye boots.

After going to the Electric Theatre the weekend they opened, it would soon become the place I would go to almost every weekend, as well as some weekdays, when they would have a band I wanted to see. I returned a few weeks after my first visit to see the Siegel Schwall Blues Band along with my friend Jeff Williams, who, like me, was also a fan of the blues. Sometimes, Jeff and I would hang out with this older guy, Gene Marines, who would fill us in on Chicago's music scene. While hanging out or shooting pool at The Q-Inn or at Gene Marines's favorite spot, East of Edens restaurant, located in the All Star Bowl, Gene would hold court and tell us about all the bands he had seen at Big John's and Mother Blues down in Old Town. Siegle Schwall was one of the bands he mentioned but that I had never seen.

When I would ask Gene to take us to these bars, he would always tell us we were too young to get in. Around this same time, I had also started hanging out at the original Jazz Record Mart on Grand and State. It was at the Jazz Record Mart where I first learned about the Chicago Blues scene. Bob Koester, the owner of this top-notch record store, would point out these white blues bands that played around Chicago, like the Paul Butterfield Blues Band, Charlie Musselwhite's Southside Band, and Siegel Schwall Blues Band, all with albums of their own. He said they were only imitating, but they were also learning from these extraordinary Black bluesmen. And, at the same time, they were subconsciously helping to create a genre that would come to be known as blues rock.

I told Bob Koester that I loved the first two albums by the Paul Butterfield Blues Band as well as Charlie Musselwhite's *Stand Back*. I really liked these blues rock bands and found that I could easily relate to Corky Siegel, Mike Bloomfield, Harvey Mandel, and Barry Goldberg, who were all Jewish kids like me from the Chicago area. Although they were a few years older than me, seeing guys much like me playing this unbelievable music must have subconsciously encouraged me to identify with these musicians and the blues rock these guys were now playing.

Bob Koester loved to share his knowledge of blues and jazz. The first day I met Bob, he would begin to introduce me to what he called "the real blues masters": the original bluesmen like Robert Johnson, Big Bill Broonzy, and Lightning Hopkins, along with the great Chicago blues masters like Muddy Waters, Howlin' Wolf, Otis Rush, Little Walter, and Willie Dixon, just to name a few. He would also tell me about all the bands he was recording on his Delmark label, like Magic Sam, J. B. Hutto and the Hawks, and the Junior Wells record *Hoodoo Man Blues* featuring Buddy Guy, the same recording that originally brought me into his store after Arnie Fisher had played it for me and recommended I visit the Jazz Record Mart and meet Bob.

This introduction started me on my path to collecting records and a further love of record stores. My first purchase that day, in addition to *Hoodoo Man Blues*, was BB *King's Live at the Regal, The Original Folk Blues* of John Lee Hooker, and *Super Blues*, a collection of songs by Muddy Waters, Bo Diddley, and Little Walter.

When Jeff and I arrived at the Electric Theatre that first Friday of May, I said hello to Herbie with the usual soul handshake, thanking him for letting us in for free that first night. "Tonight it's four dollars, my man," Herbie said, smiling and directing us to the ticket window.

"Krock, can you lend me a deuce?" Jeff asked.

"I guess, but you already owe me a fin from that last card game."

"Check this out: Tim Buckley is also playing. Michelle has his record, *Goodbye and Hello*, and it's fuckin groovy, man."

"Cool! Let's go in."

As I started to walk in, Jeff grabbed me and whispered, "C'mon, let's take one more hit of this Afghani hash. We can go between those buildings down the street."

"Nah, I'm already stoned from all the hash and pot we smoked in the car on the way here. Which, by the way, was not cool. I got three lids down my pants that I brought here to sell. You go ahead and take your hit of hash. I'll just wait here."

While waiting for Jeff, I ran into this guy everybody called Crazy Steve, whom I would run into at almost every concert I went to for years. Jeff came back and we went in, as a band we had never heard of, Michael and the Messengers, was leaving the stage. Just then, we spotted Ronnie Singer and his soon-to-be wife, Candi Fassio. They were a few years older than us. Ronnie was from my neighborhood, a former greaser who used to race cars, and had fallen in love with Candi after meeting her at one of the hippie coffee houses on Wells Street in Old Town. Candi, an Italian girl whose father owned Fassio's Restaurant, a popular Italian restaurant, was this Mama Cass-looking flower child with a heart of gold, while Ronnie and his greaser crowd were rumored to be messing with hard drugs, mainly heroin.

"What's up, guys?" Candi asked.

"Nothing too much. I've got some fine Afghani hash. You guys want a hit?" Jeff replied.

Ronnie pointed to one of the meditation booths as the three of them headed to the booth. I told them I was going to take a walk around. Candi waved back as they entered the booth. As I was roaming around, going past the sound booth, I could see a tape recorder, which caught my interest. "Are you guys recording tonight?"

"Yeah, man, we're recording Tim Buckley tonight," answered one of the sound men.

"Wow, cool. Do you mind if I stand here and watch for a while?"

"Sure. Hey, man, you smell like pot. Do you happen to have a joint you could spare?"

"No, but I do have some weed. If you have some papers, we could roll one."

"Yeah, I've got some backstage. Follow me, but I need to hurry. Buckley goes on in fifteen minutes."

I followed the sound guy backstage, and as soon as I pulled out the three bags of weed, the sound guy asked me, "Do you want to sell any?"

"Sure, but they're twenty dollars a lid as this is for real Jamaican Ganja."

"Cool. I'll take two."

No sooner had the sound guy rolled a joint and taken that first hit, and then passed it to his buddy Mark Dylan, whom I recognized as one of the clerks who worked up at Laurie's Records in Evanston but was now working here as a stagehand. Mark ended up buying the third bag. After that we all walked back to the sound booth where I watched Tim Buckley accompanied by a bass player and a conga player. I enjoyed Tim's performance, which seemed kind of ad-libbed but with some interesting guitar.

A few weeks later, when I listened to Buckley's *Goodbye and Hello*, it sounded completely different from the concert I heard. The album was more straight-ahead. Maybe Tim took a hit off that Ganja before he went on. Siegel Schwall was finishing up their set, which I really enjoyed, but nothing compared to when I had heard the Butterfield Blues Band at the Cheetah[9] the year before. Butterfield and Bloomfield

---

[9] The Aragon Ballroom had changed its name to the Cheetah for a short time and then eventually went back to using the Aragon Ballroom as its name.

had blown me away that night at the Cheetah. While Siegle Schwall put on a really good show, it lacked the intensity that Butterfield and Bloomfield brought. I found Jeff and we headed home, with Jeff crashing in the back seat of my Buick. While driving home I thought about how I could probably sell a shitload of weed at these concerts coming up at the Electric Theatre. But how could I get more than three lids in there? Hm, something to think about.

That following weekend, the Mets were at Wrigley and drew a nice crowd all three days. Norm and I did pretty well on Friday, picking up sixty bucks each, even after the Mets' Jerry Koosman, pitching a two-hitter, beat the Cubs and Fergie Jenkins 5-1. After the game that Friday, Norm and I had put our stands back in the garage and were getting ready to leave when Ruby Bluestein walked up to the garage and asked, "Eddie, do you have those binoculars I asked you to pick up for me from Jake Rubin?"

"I got them right here, Ruby. What's the matter, Ruby? You don't look so good."

Eddie said, "Well, I'm kind of in a spot. Comedy and Cancer were supposed to work the concert with me tonight, over at the Coliseum, and they're off on a bender somewhere. We were going to use Comedy's car."

Ruby looked over at Norm and me. "Hey, fellas, I'm in a spot. My cousin Morry has got the X at the Coliseum and I told him I would take care of him if he let me and my crew work googs (binoculars) for tonight's concert. How about we jump in that Buick of yours, Krockey, and I buy you and Norm dinner tonight, and you guys work this show with me? We should be able to clean up."

"Who's playing?" I asked.

"The Doors, and they're supposed to be the biggest thing since the pope."

"You're right, Ruby, they are a big band. Not my cup of tea, but the girls love them, and they have a big following."

"Where's the Coliseum again?" Norm asked.

"You know, Norm, they're calling it the Syndrome now. I saw Cream with the Mothers there last month with Barry Paddor and Cookie Gordon. It's a new place for big concerts over on South Wabash."

I replied, "There is nothing new about it; they just changed the name."

"But there are a lot of seats way up high so we should be able to sell the hell out of these googs," Ruby replied.

"What do you think, Norm?" I asked.

"Sounds like we could make some scratch, Krock, and maybe have some laughs."

"You guys should go. You might meet some hippie girls."

Eddie piped in, "Yeah, but I'm sweaty from working all day."

Ruby then told us, "That's okay, fellas, my cousin sent over these clean vendor uniforms. I got them right here in this shopping bag."

"Are you crazy? Are you out of your fucking mind? I'm not wearing those fucking goofy uniforms," Norm barked while we all started laughing.

"What is so funny?" Ruby asked.

"C'mon, Ruby, we will look like Good Humor men," I answered.

"Fellas, we either wear the uniforms or my cousin Morry won't let us work. It's a union venue. My cousin said if we wear the uniforms, he will make sure we get past the union with no trouble."

Norm replied, "Okay, Ruby, here's what we're going to do. What time are we supposed to be there?"

"I'd say by 6:30 or 7:00 the latest. The show starts at 8:30."

"Anybody else working with our crew?"

"Yeah, Little Sol; he said he'd meet me at the bar next to the Coliseum around 6:30."

Then Norm asked, "You still live on North Avenue above the Luxor Baths?"

"Sure do."

"Good, we can take a quick steam, clean up, and have that tasty bathhouse salad and scrumptious brisket that they make. Did you ever smoke reefer, Ruby?"

"I was smoking reefer before you guys were born."

"We had a feeling you were some kind of beatnik back when. Do you mind if, after we get dressed, we run up to your apartment and roll a few joints?"

"No problem, fellas."

"Thanks, Ruby. Krock and I will pay for your entry to the schvitz, and you buy us dinner."

Ruby was about fifty at the time, about my dad's age. But he was very different from my dad or Norm's dad. On the one hand, he was one hell of a small-time hustler, a real specialist. But, on the other hand, he seemed a lot more educated and hipper than the other peddlers who hung around the ballpark. Right after the war, Ruby had found himself broke, having lost all his accumulated Navy pay in a craps game on the boat while sailing back from the war in the Pacific. When he landed in California, he somehow met New York Whitey, who would school him in different ways to hustle a buck.

Being broke, Ruby wound up traveling around the country with Whitey for a couple of months, learning various hustles. Whitey's main hustle was dinging. As I mentioned earlier, Whitey would wear a veterans hat with a patch over one eye and pin an American flag on a person's lapel, shirt, or dress and just put out his hand, and the good folks of America would proudly hand him over their money. But, after a couple of weeks on the road with Whitey, Ruby came up with his own style of dinging. Ruby would have these business cards made up that read "World War Two Veteran Deaf Mute." He would put his veterans hat on and walk down any busy street like Broadway in New York, State Street in Chicago, or Collins Avenue in Miami and hand people these cards and pin an American flag on their lapel. And, with this wave of patriotism sweeping across America after the war, most folks would hand Ruby various amounts of money, and on most days he would out-earn New York Whitey.

But after a few months and now having a few bucks in his pocket, Ruby decided this wasn't for him as he became tired of people looking down on him as some sort of beggar. Also, he had his fill of Whitey and his schemes. Shortly after that, he came upon what Ruby called a legitimate hustle, which was working factory blow-offs. Ruby and his sometimes-partner, Mikey Halprin, would go to large factories like Ford or GE on payday and sell anything like kids' windup toys, telling these tired workers as they left work to bring home a nice toy for their kid or the newest fad item for their wife, like a lava lamp or a game of Twister in a box.

On occasion, these factories would call in the cops and try to have the peddlers arrested for working on company property. But when they tried to pinch Ruby, he would go into his dummy act, handing the officer his WWII Deaf Mute card, making a sad face that only Ruby could, and the cops would send him on his way. He was very proud of the fact that he had never been pinched working a factory blow-off.

After sitting in the steam room and cleaning up, we wrapped our sheets around us and walked into the Luxor Baths dining room with its crowd of characters eating or playing cards. We all said hello to Bernice, the small Black woman who worked for Dave Schaffel and his wife, Pearl, who together owned the restaurant and had gone home early that day. Bernice was often the only woman there, except when Pearl came in to help or on ladies' day. Bernice was not shy about putting someone in their place if they were rude or got out of line. Yet she was always with a smile and had a carefree sense of humor. Bernice walked up to our table, "What's it going to be tonight, fellas?"

"Krockey, please pull that sheet up. I've seen enough Kosher salami to last me a lifetime." We all laughed, including Bernice.

Norm ordered, "Give us a big bottle of red and a bottle of white, a bathhouse salad, and three brisket plates."

Bernice shouted nicely to her helper, Mike Singer, who drove a Montreal pop truck during the day and helped out at the bathhouse restaurant a few nights a week, "Mike, please bring my hungry friends here some bread and pickles, and a big bottle of Montreal strawberry pop and a bottle of seltzer water." Bernice's bathhouse salad with fresh tomatoes, onions, lettuce, cubed mozzarella cheese, and Kosher salami and her special vinegar dressing, along with the most tender brisket and roasted potatoes, always hit the spot after taking a steam.

At the long table next to ours, eating the same meal, were the Friday regulars who came every Friday afternoon, giving each other platza rubs and then enjoying dinner and talking or playing cards into the night. This group included Roy Walker, a fire adjuster; Jack Rogen, a home improvements contractor; Joe Sheade, who had a furniture factory; Benny Testa, Chicago's biggest produce wholesaler (Benny had fresh produce delivered to the bathhouse every day); Augie Gonzalez, a truck driver who gave the best rubs; and Gussie Alex, a highly ranked city hall fixer for the outfit. Also at the table was Moe Gelfond, who was at the baths every day selling clothes out of his locker. Moe sold everything from socks and underwear to pants and shirts, some of which he would keep in one of the bathhouse lockers.

Ruby then pointed out Joe Colucci playing gin with Little Caesar Di Varco at a table in the corner. Joe Colucci, at one time, owned with his partner, the politician, Parky Cullerton, gambling joints all over Chicagoland. Starting out with newsstands, he became one of Chicago's biggest bookmakers. But in the early '50s, Joe gave it all up, telling me years later that the mob had pressured him for a bigger cut and even kidnapped him once. Joe right then and there said he handed his whole operation over to the outfit and, without skipping a beat, opened a Kaizer Fraizer car dealership on Madison Street, as well as owning other properties along Madison Street. He said, "I would rather be friends with those outfit guys than partners."

Colucci would eventually buy Division Street Baths a few years later in 1978. Joe "Little Cesar" Di Varco owned a haberdashery with Big Joe Arnold and ran Rush Street for the outfit. I was familiar with both men, having grown up with Caesar's son Vince, whom I was friends with, and having first met Joe Colucci when my dad had bought a used truck from him. Both Joe Colucci and Caesar were not over five feet tall, but as Ruby pointed out, these were powerful men.

After finishing dinner, Norm and I bought some fresh underwear and socks from Moe. After, we walked back to our lockers and got dressed, putting on the vendor uniforms Ruby had given us. We walked over to pay Moe for the socks and underwear. Upon seeing us, Moe said, "What's with the uniforms, fellas? I got some beautiful blue jeans, Krockey."

I answered, "Not today, Moe; we are on our way to the Coliseum to sell binoculars with Ruby and we are required to wear these goofy-looking uniforms."

"Good luck, boys. See you later."

We went up to Ruby's one-bedroom apartment. The very small apartment was loaded with books: mostly history books and biographies. Then I noticed on the wall a diploma from the University of Illinois: Rubin Bluestein, class of '39. "You went to college, Ruby? What did you major in?"

"American history and political science. I became a teacher. I taught history at Marshall High School for two years before going into the Navy in '42."

"Wow!"

"C'mon, Krock, start rolling joints," Norm yelled, and Norm and I rolled.

Ruby asked, "How many of those marijuana cigarettes are you making?"

I replied, "As many as we can before we have to leave."

Ruby pointed out, "Well, we better get going in the next fifteen minutes." We ended up rolling fifty-three joints.

When we arrived at the Coliseum, Ruby got out to get Little Sol from the bar next door and told us to meet him behind the building where there would be a sign that said "Deliveries." We drove to the delivery area and waited in the car for Ruby and Little Sol. Norm and I took out our big work aprons that we would normally use at the ballpark. These peddlers' aprons were used to store the cash we took in and make change for the customers quickly. We each proceeded to put twenty singles, four fives, four tens, and one twenty in the three front pockets, while using the back zipper pocket of the apron to hold the twenty-five joints each that we had rolled earlier, while we each stuffed one lid down our crotch. When Ruby walked up with Little Sol, Norm and I stepped out of the car and put our aprons on. Ruby seemed to know the security guy, who told us we could park the car near the wall after we unloaded our merchandise. Once inside, Ruby took us behind the stage, where he had four workboxes waiting. We then divided up the gross of binoculars, putting thirty-six binoculars in each work box.

Ruby said, "You and Norm take the East Side, and me and Sol will work the West Side, and be careful with that tea. If you get pinched, I don't know you and won't be able to help."

As Norm and I were about to walk into the arena from the backstage area and climb the stairs to the balcony, we ran into Dizzy Lavin, one of the many madcap characters we grew up with in Skokie. "Hey, Krockey. Hey, Norm."

"What's up, Mike? (Dizzy's real name.)"

"Ah, it's crazy. I'm here with these two groupies I met when I was here a few weeks ago to see the Mothers and Cream. They know all the rock stars. Ah, it's crazy, unbelievable. We partied with some of the Mothers of Invention after the show a couple weeks ago. Ah, it's crazy;

I ate some mushrooms tonight and forgot my weed at home. Cynthia, the one groupie, asked me to bring some pot for this party with the Doors after the show. Do you guys have any grass?"

I replied, "Just so happens we do. We have two lids and fifty-three joints."

Dizzy excitedly replied, "Unbelievable. Ah, that's crazy unbelievable, ah that's crazy unbelievable. I'll take it all. How much?"

Norm replied, "Give us a hundred bucks and we will give you the two lids and fifty joints; we want to keep three joints for ourselves. Twenty-five each for the lids and fifty for the joints."

"Cool, that's unbelievable," Dizzy said, pulling out forty dollars and a check for $110.53 from the Skokie Montgomery Wards in Old Orchard shopping center in Skokie, where he worked in the restaurant on the top floor. "Can I give you the check, and you can keep the difference?"

I replied, looking over at Norm, who was smiling, "Here, Michael, you don't have to do that. Just sign the check on the back. Michael Lavin and I will give you back your ten dollars change. Here's a pen and ten dollars." Dizzy signed the check and handed it back, thanking both Norm and me as he started to walk away.

"Dizzy, didn't you forget something?" Norm yelled out.

"Oh, yeah."

"Here, Mike, you had better have one of the girls put this in her purse and hold it for you," suggested Norm.

Dizzy replied, "Good idea. Ah, it's crazy, you guys. Thanks, I really appreciate it." One of the groupies told Mike to hurry it up.

As they walked toward one of the dressing rooms, Norm looked at me with a smile and said, "That was way too easy. Let's get rid of these googs and go home." While we were upstairs on the balcony after the show had started, Norm called out to me, "Check out the guy dancing on the mountain of speakers to the left of the stage." Sure enough, it was Dizzy Lavin dancing with his shirt off, doing his thing.

I must say, although I had not been a big Doors fan, that Jim Morrison and the Doors put on a very cool show playing the songs off their new hit album, with the crowd all on their feet and loving it. We sold out all the binoculars in less than an hour and went backstage to wait for Ruby and Sol, who showed up ten minutes later after they sold out as well.

Ruby said, "Let's go next door to the bar and straighten up; it's too fucking noisy in here." After cutting up the dough, we asked Ruby and Sol if they wanted a ride.

"No, we're going to stick around and have a couple of beers and wait for my cousin, who is going to meet us here after the show. He'll give us a ride. Hey, by the way, what happened with all that Mary Jane?"

I replied, "Sold it all to one guy in like five minutes. Drinks are on us."

As we walked out, I put a five on the bar and we headed home. We would find out later that right after we left there was a small riot. The audience rushed the stage and Dizzy sprained his ankle after falling off the speakers. With the sixty dollars each we made at the ballpark and the thirty dollars apiece on the pot, plus Ruby paying us a dollar-fifty for each binocular pair we sold to total another fifty-four dollars each, we picked up $144.00 each for the day. The Cubs would go on to beat the Mets on Saturday and then split a doubleheader on Sunday, adding another $130 each to our bankroll, for a weekend total of $274 each: more than most grown people made in a week after taxes back in 1968.

The Cubs headed to Los Angeles that Monday to begin an eight-day road trip. Wednesday rolled around and I was getting low on pot, having just three lids left, and thought this would be a good time to invest in a couple more pounds. I called all my connections and every-body seemed to be out of any kind of weed. I asked Cookie Gordon, whose real name was Randy, if he had any ganja left, and he said he had a few ounces but had promised two of them to someone and was keeping the rest for himself. Even Manny, who worked for Eddie, with his Latin Kings connections, was out of their Mexican pot.

On Friday, Canned Heat was playing at the Electric Theatre. I became a big Canned Heat fan after buying their album *Boogie with Canned Heat*. In those days, there was a thing called the Columbia Record Club. A few months earlier, I had stumbled on an ad for the Columbia Record Club, which basically gave you ten albums for a dollar if you bought an album a month for a year at the regular price. Not having a checkbook at the time, I stuck a dollar bill in an envelope that was attached to an ad in the *TV Guide*, made my selections, and mailed it in. Lo and behold, a couple weeks later, I received these ten exceptional LPs, including *Boogie with Canned Heat*, Procol Harum's first album, the Beatles' *Magical Mystery Tour*, Hendrix Axis's *Bold as Love*, the Rotary Connection's first album, Spirit's first album, and Cream's *Disraeli Gears*, as well as fresh copies of *Mary Wells Greatest Hits* and the *Drifters Golden Hits*, which my sister and I had worn out by playing these two favorite albums of ours over and over.

I also ordered *Frank Sinatra Live at the Sands*, giving this celebrated album to my mom, who loved it and played it often while she cooked or did housework. I never bought any more albums at full price from the Columbia Record Club, and for years, they sent collection letters to my parents' house where my mother would always rip them up before my father could see them.

That Friday afternoon, Mark Dylan, who was now working as a stagehand at the Electric Theatre after quitting his job at Laurie's Records, called me at my parents' house. "Krockey, we just finished the sound check for Canned Heat, and Fito, the drummer, asked me if I could get him some reefer. Nobody around here seems to have any. Can you bring some? I'll get you in for free."

"Well, I've only got three lids left, but I can sell two."

"Okay, come by the backstage entrance at seven or seven-thirty. The opening act probably will go on about seven, and Canned Heat about nine."

"Cool, I'll be there, but I'm with two of my buddies."

"That's okay. Give me their names and I'll put them on the guest list, but they will need to go to the box office and come in through the front. I can only let you come backstage."

I went by Jeff Williams's house to pick him up for the Canned Heat show that night. I arrived at Jeff's house, and he was there alone. Both his parents were still at work while his older brother was off at college, and his younger brother was off playing somewhere. I followed Jeff into his room as he handed me his hash pipe, and I took a hit.

"Listen to this," he said as he picked up his acoustic guitar and played along with John Lee Hooker's "Boogie Chillen" on his turntable. "Sounds pretty good, Jeff."

"Yeah, I've been practicing. I can't wait to hear Alan Wilson and Canned Heat play the boogie."

Then I said, "I love that album. Let's go—we need to pick Paddor up at his house in Lincolnwood." We drove over to Barry Paddor's big fancy house in Lincolnwood, where he was waiting outside.

Barry jumped in my Buick and the first thing he said was, "Let's boogie."

All three of us were big fans of the *Boogie with Canned Heat* album, and we were very excited to see the show as none of us had ever seen them play live before. When I told Jeff and Barry we were going to boogie for free that night, they couldn't believe it. I explained to them that I was bringing one of the in-house roadies a couple of lids for Canned Heat, which is how we got the freebies. We parked a few blocks away, and I told Jeff and Barry to go to the box office, where they would have tickets waiting under their names, while I needed to go to the backstage door to drop the weed off, and that I would catch them later.

I knocked on the door, and sure enough, Mark opened the door and told me to get my ass inside to follow him, and to be cool, as there were some plain-clothes cops walking around. Following Mark into the big dressing room where Canned Heat was, I was a little nervous, having never been in a famous band's dressing room before. Walking in, it appeared Bob the Bear Hite was sleeping on the couch, while Alan the Blind Owl Wilson was off in a corner strumming his gold Les Paul, while Fito was talking to a girl in the opposite corner. Henry Vestine and Larry Taylor had not yet arrived.

Mark called out to Fito, and Fito replied, "Hey, man, you got the stuff?" Almost sounding like Cheech from Cheech and Chong, as he was also a Mexican American with the same accent as Cheech Marin. As Fito walked over with this girl, I immediately recognized her as Cynthia, one of the groupies who was with Dizzy at last week's Doors concert.

Mark introduced me to Fito as Krockey, and Cynthia said, "I know you; we met last week. You're the guy that sold Michael that good pot at the Doors concert."

I smiled at Cynthia while nodding my head, and then Fito spoke. "Well, hey, man, let's light one up. You got papers?"

"Sure do, but here I've got a few already rolled," I said, handing Fito a nice big spliff and Mark a few regular joints since he was nice enough to get us into the show for nix.

Mark said, "We should go outside because there are a lot of cops around here tonight."

Fito replied, "Hey, man, we always smoke in the dressing room."

Mark repeated, "Normally it would be cool, but for some reason there are a lot of cops here tonight."

Fito called out to Bob the Bear Hite, who had just lifted his three-hundred-pound body off the couch while downing a whole bottle of Pepsi. "Hey, Bob, we are going outside to smoke a joint."

"Why can't we smoke it right here?" Bob replied.

Fito answered, "Cops, man."

The Bear screamed "motherfucker" and then said, "Fuck it, I can use some fresh air, but let me take a whiz first." As we were walking out, the Blind Owl asked where we were going.

The Bear replied, "To smoke a joint and get some fresh air. C'mon with."

When we all got outside, Cynthia suggested we walk across the street to the St. Boniface Catholic Cemetery, noting her neighbor was buried there. So that's what we did. As I handed the Bear another joint, the Blind Owl started walking off by himself around the grave-yard, stopping at different graves and reading the headstones.

After taking a couple hits, Fito asked, "What kind of weed is this, man? It tastes good, man." The Bear nodded in agreement while taking a puff.

"It's Jamaican ganja," I replied.

"Man, I never smoked any Jamaican ganja. Have you, Bob?"

"No, man, this shit is good. Can you get any more?"

"No, I sold you guys my last two lids."

"Hey, what's your name, Corky?" Fito asked.

"No, it's Krockey," I replied.

"Well, hey, Krockey, see if you can find some more and come by tomorrow. I will put you plus one on the guest list."

"Cool, thanks. I'll try," I replied.

Right then, the Bear said, "Hey, we better get back," calling out to the Blind Owl.

"C'mon, let's boogie. We've got a show to do."

I went out front before Canned Heat came on and found Jeff and Barry, who were sitting on the floor, as most of the crowd were. Jeff offered me a hit of hash.

"Put that shit away," I quickly told him, "there's plain-clothes cops dressed as hippies."

"You're just being paranoid," Jeff replied.

"Paranoid my ass. Mark the stagehand said that one of the off-duty cops that works security told him that some shit might go down tonight."

"Okay, cool," Jeff replied and put away his pipe right as Canned Heat hit the stage. Within a few minutes of this high-energy mix of blues and rock, the whole crowd was standing while at the same time a bunch of hippies were dancing in front of the stage. They opened the show with "Rollin' and Tumblin'" with the Blind Owl switching back and forth from blues harp to incredible bottleneck slide guitar while the Bear sang and got the crowd on its feet. The whole set was mind-blowing. I thought Henry the Sunflower's solo on "Amphetamine Annie" was incredible until he topped it in the finale, "Fried Hockey Boogie," which displayed each member's incredible talent, each member taking a solo while the Bear was doing introductions to each solo while also singing and dancing.

This rocking boogie started out with Alan "Blind Owl" Wilson doing a tasty fingerpicking solo, followed by Larry "The Mole" Taylor with his in-the-groove moving basslines, keeping the crowd swaying and cheering. Next was Henry "The Sunflower" Vestine playing an electric guitar solo that ripped with sustain and had the crowd cheering for more. But Adolfo "Fito" de la Parra just blew the crowd away with this incredible drum solo, mesmerizing everyone there. Bob "The Bear" Hite ended the set with a line that my friends and I would be repeating for months: "And don't forget to boogie."

On the way home that night, I remember thinking that was probably one of the best shows I would ever see. Boy, was I wrong. That summer and into the fall and winter and well into 1969, I would go to the Electric Theatre, soon to be called the Kinetic Playground, almost every week, discovering amazing music. I also had started reading Rolling Stone and The Chicago Seed, both of which gave me the heads-up on all these far-out bands coming out of San Francisco, London, and elsewhere.

A couple of days after the Canned Heat Show on May 21, we were working at Wrigley. The crowd was small that day as school would not be out for a few more weeks, and we barely made lunch money. I was planning on going to see Steppenwolf at the Electric Theatre that night with Norm and wanted to get there early to sell a couple of lids before the show. Unfortunately, Norm and I were on our way home from Wrigley, and we got stuck on the Skokie Swift for two hours because the train in front of our train had broken down. Now, we would be arriving late at the concert, missing the opening act, but hopefully in time for Steppenwolf.

When Norm and I pulled up to the theater later that night, there were a ton of cops. A crowd had gathered as we all watched people leaving the theater in handcuffs. This old man next to me kept yelling to leave the kids alone as he drank his bottle of Old Style beer out of a brown paper bag. I asked him what had happened.

"The coppers raided the joint like it was a speakeasy."

I could see Mark sitting in a paddy wagon along with the rest of the backstage crew. I told the old man that that was my friend in the back of the paddy wagon.

"Don't worry, kid, they won't hold him. Probably just looking to shake the owner down. This is Chicago, kid, where everything's a shakedown and a payoff." The old man was right. Two days later, the Electric Theatre was open with Steppenwolf headlining, and all charges against the owner, the employees, and the patrons were dropped. It was rumored that not only was there a big payoff, but from then on, the cops would leave everyone alone, including the patrons.

The summer rolled in with me working at the ballpark, going to concerts, and hanging out with friends while trying to meet girls. On days when I wasn't working, especially on hot, humid days, we would go to Morse Beach in Chicago or Tower Beach in Wilmette. On other days, you could find us at a variety of places: Twin Orchard Bowl, All Star Bowl, The Q-Inn, The Royal Que, Howard Paulina Pool Hall,

Burger King on Dempster (BK on D), Sarkis's Grill, Jack's restaurant, Old Orchard Mall, and Fun Fair amusement park.

We would also gather at Devonshire Park and would often go into Chicago to Hollywood Park, where Chicago kids our age hung out, as well as The Gold Coin restaurant on Howard and California in Chicago. Sometimes, on a Friday or Saturday night, when we weren't parked on the floor of the Electric Theatre/Kinetic Playground, we would venture down to Wells Street in Old Town. This was the "happening" place where Chicago's hippies would gather. Record stores, head shops, the coolest clothes stores, groovy music, and comedy venues. Always a fun adventure.

*****

It was close to ninety degrees by noon on August 9 as I walked out my front door wearing my orange bathing suit, towel in hand. I jumped into my Buick, turned on WVON, and heard Hugh Masekela's "Grazing in the Grass," which was the perfect groove as half my friends and I were headed for Morse Beach on this steamy Chicago day.

After I picked up Norm, he told me to head over to Cuzzi (Bobby) Kahn's as Cuzzi's father had taken his car keys away from him and told him he wasn't allowed to drive his brand-new GTO except for work for at least a week because he had gotten three tickets for drag racing on Edens Highway. Bobby's parents had bought him this beautiful automobile last June after he had graduated high school. This was quite an accomplishment, considering Bobby was not the brightest star in the sky. Bobby Cuzzi Kahn had a job delivering prescriptions for Endler's Drugs on Church Street. This allowed him the opportunity to steal various barbiturates and speed, which were both starting to become popular, especially the barbiturates. This was a year or two before Quaaludes.

When we got to the beach that day, it was packed with mostly younger teenagers, as the families were further down toward Touhy Beach. I could see lots of people I knew, both from Skokie and Chicago, sitting on towels and blankets, or swimming in Lake Michigan. My visits to the beach over the last couple of years had slowed down. When we were thirteen or fourteen, we came almost every day in the summer, along with hundreds of kids our age, all taking the Skokie Swift or the 97 bus to the Howard L train, then transferring to another L for a short trip to the Morse stop. After arriving at the beach, we would often get into a potluck game, a game much like blackjack, where the dealer has the advantage, and then we would proceed to lose all our dough to the older guys who were dealing as well as cheating. But now, we were the older guys. It looked like there were a few card games going on as well as a craps game. The transistor radio from the snack stand was blasting, "Hello I Love You" by the Doors, as most of the transistor radios on the beach were tuned to WLS or WCFL. "You want a hot dog, Krock?" Norm asked.

"Absolutely. Plenty of that brown mustard."

"How about you, Cuzzi?"

"Sure, just a little mustard."

Norm then ordered three beach hot dogs and three Pepsis. Beach hot dogs were different from the well-known Chicago hot dog with all the trimmings. These were more like a Wisconsin brat served only with brown mustard.

After downing the dogs, Norm said, "Hey, there's Barb and Cindy on that blanket near the lifeguard tower. Let's go sit by them."

"Nah," I said. "I've had enough of Cindy. You and Cuzzi go. I'm going to check out the card game."

"All right, Krock, let me know how the action is." As I wandered over to this potluck game, I noticed a craps game being played on a blanket. The same older guys who had taken my money when I was thirteen were now doing the same to these kids. The thing is, you never play dice on a blanket because with one slight pull of the blanket, it can affect the roll of the dice. The two older guys were artists on the blanket, knowing exactly how to move the blanket without it being noticed. When I was thirteen, Babe Caruso, who was a few years my senior, had confided in me after seeing me lose all my money. He had told me that they do it with their toes, keeping their feet behind them. As I watched these kids lose their money, I was always amazed by the skillfulness of these guys' toes. As I looked over at the potluck game, there were a few guys my age passing the deck around and mostly to each other and not allowing the younger guys to deal. Of course, the dealer always has the advantage, just like in blackjack.

As this was the only potluck game going and my friends were not interested in the game, I started to walk back to where Norm, Cuzzi, and the girls were sitting. As I turned around, one of the guys from the game, whom I knew, tapped me on the shoulder. It was Barry Pearle, who had gone to Sullivan High School. I was always bumping into him either at his main hangout, The Gold Coin Restaurant on Howard and California, or Hollywood Park, and at various pool halls, as he was a pretty good pool player. But where we got to know one another was when we ran into each other the night Cream played at this teen club called The Cellar in Arlington Heights back in April.

I had gone there that night with Cookie Gordon, but as soon as we got there, Cookie ran into a friend of his and told me he would be right back. I didn't see him the rest of the night. I would find out later that he was using heroin. When he left, I saw two girls from Skokie who were younger than me, Andy Cohen and Donna Lachman, who came there with Barry Pearle. I guess Pearle was hot for Andy, and Donna had come to see Cream. When the show was over, I asked Barry if he could give me a ride home. Then Barry Pearle suggested we all go to Jack's Restaurant. We all agreed and ended up sitting in Jack's for a couple of hours talking about how electrifying the Cream show was with Clapton, Bruce, and Baker.

"What's up, Krockey?" Barry asked as he walked away from the potluck game and tapped me on the shoulder. "Are you going to the Hendrix show tomorrow?"

"Oh, man, I completely forgot to get tickets. I guess I'll have to go down there tomorrow and see if I can find a scalper."

"No need, bro, I'm getting six tickets tonight from my friend and I can sell you two. I'm meeting my friend Daryl Schwartz at the Gold Coin on Howard and California tonight around ten."

"You're blowing my mind, Pearle. Wow! Thank you, man!"

"I know you dig the electric guitar, Krockey, and this guy is the best. This might be better than when we saw Cream with Clapton."

"All right, see you tonight," I said as I walked away.

Later that night, after Cuzzi got off work, he picked me up in his GTO and we headed for The Gold Coin. Originally, Norm was going to go to the Hendrix show, but he decided to go up to the Chain O'Lakes to join his family on their boat. As soon as I got into Cuzzi's GTO, I lit up a joint and asked, "How did you get the car?"

"My dad said, since I worked all day, he would make an exception. Make sure you don't burn the seats," Cuzzi said as I passed him the joint.

When we rolled up to The Gold Coin, I said to Cuzzi, "It's really crowded tonight. Hey, there's a spot; pull in."

There were a bunch of people standing outside, and a line going inside waiting for a table. As we walked past the restaurant's big window, I heard someone knock on the glass. It was Barry Pearle motioning for us to come in. He was sitting in a booth with his new girlfriend, Jody, and had saved a seat for Cuzzi and me. After we sat down, I asked Barry how he had gotten the tickets.

"You're not going to believe this. I told you I was getting the tickets from my friend Daryl. You know him. Well, it turns out that Elaine Chess, who is Darryl Schwartz's girlfriend, whose brother is Marshall Chess and whose father is Leonard who owns Chess Records with his brother Phil. Well, because of Marshall's involvement in the record business working for his father, he became friends with Hendrix's manager, Michael Jeffery, who also manages the Monkees. Well, about a week ago, Daryl was at Chess's house picking up Elaine in his new yellow Corvette when Marshall pulled up.

"Hey, man, nice car," Marshall said to Daryl.

"Thanks," Daryl replied.

"Is this your new boyfriend?" he asked his sister.

"Yes, this is Daryl."

"Good to meet you, Daryl. I'm Marshall. Hey, man, would you be interested in a two- or three-day gig?"

"What, robbing banks? Only kidding. What kind of gig?" Daryl asked.

"I just received a call from a friend of mine, Michael Jeffery, who is Jimi Hendrix's manager, asking if I knew someone cool who could pick up Jimi at the airport and be his driver while he's in town, as well as show him around Chicago."

"Are you shitting me? Sure, I'd love to," Daryl replied.

"Okay, but you must be sure you're willing to take Jimi wherever he wants to go, as well as be at his beck and call and get him whatever he needs within reason. I'll make sure you are reimbursed for any out-of-pocket expenses."

Daryl replied, "Are you kidding? It would be an honor."

"Okay then, I will get you his itinerary and some tickets for the show. How many tickets do you need?"

"Do you think I could get ten or twelve for me and my friends?"

"No problem, I should be able to do that."

"What about me?" Elaine asked Marshall.

"You can go to the show with your sister Suzie and me, and we can all meet Daryl at the show."

As we were sitting there waiting for Daryl, munching on French fries with ketchup, Angie, the waitress, came over and told Barry that Daryl was on the restaurant phone and wanted to speak with Barry. Barry came back to the table, telling us that Daryl would be here in an hour, around 11:30, and was bringing a guest.

Then I said, "Is he bringing Jimi?"

Barry gave us all a big smile, telling us, "Yep, Daryl said he wanted to come right before closing at midnight so the place would not be as crowded. He said Jimi was starving, having spent the better part of the day with Cynthia [Plaster Caster[10]] and her friend."

Then I said, "Wow, I think they are the same girls I met at the Doors show with Dizzy Lavin and then another time at the Electric Theatre when Canned Heat played."

Then Barry went on to say, "The two girls had come to Jimi's room to show him the cast they made of his dick last February when Jimi played two shows at The Opera House."

When Daryl pulled up to the Gold Coin that night, a half dozen people were standing outside, and a dozen or so people inside could not believe their eyes. As I observed through the window, one of the guys, Marcus David, standing outside, handed Jimi a joint. Jimi was wearing a paisley silk shirt, silk scarf, velvet pants, and a gangster-type hat tilted on his head. It turned out, after Daryl had picked Jimi up at the airport, and before going to the hotel, Jimi had asked Daryl if he knew where Smokey Joe's clothes store was. Jimi had heard from other musicians that Joe's was the place for boss threads in Chi-Town.

"Sure, Jimi, it's down by Maxwell Street, or as some people call it 'Jew-town' because of all the Jewish store owners." Daryl told us later that after they walked out of Smokey Joe's with three big bags of

---

[10] As described in Wikipedia: Cynthia Dorothy Albritton was born in Chicago. Shy as a young girl, Albritton sought out a way to contact the opposite sex. In the late 1960s, she became caught up in free love and rock music. Albritton studied at the University of Illinois, Chicago. In college, when her art teacher gave the class an assignment to "plaster cast something solid that could retain its shape," she hit upon the idea of casting erect male genitalia, which would then go flaccid and exit the mold. Finding a dental mold-making substance called alginate to be sufficient, she found her first celebrity client in Jimi Hendrix, the first of many to submit to the idea.

clothes, all these people were following them. Jimi spotted a hat in a window across the street at Bryers, Arnie Fisher's store, the very hat he wore that night at The Gold Coin.

Daryl and Jimi had taken a couple more hits from Marcus's joint before walking into The Gold Coin.

Jimi turned to Daryl and said, "Hey, motherfucker, does this place have pancakes? I'm starving."

"Me too," Daryl replied as they walked in and took the booth right next to ours. Daryl introduced us as his friends who were big fans. As Jimi ate, a few of the young crowd came over for autographs, while two older couples sitting in a booth stared at Jimi like he was from outer space.

Jimi's show on August 10 at the Auditorium was mind-blowing, including the opening act, Soft Machine. We had tenth-row seats. I knew I was watching something special, observing how Jimi, being left-handed, was playing an upside-down right-handed guitar, and would use an old blues technique using the thumb of his fretting finger to play the bass notes while using the other four fingers to create a sound with voicings: a guitar master, the likes I had never heard or seen before.

After the show, the last thing I remember is getting into Cuzzi's GTO, heading to the afterparty at Jimi's hotel, and Cuzzi offering me a Seconal. I had not eaten since lunch, and that Seconal came on like a Mack truck. I had never taken any downers or really any kind of pills before. The next thing I remember is Cuzzi helping me up the stairs to my parents' apartment. Thank God my parents had gone to Nippersink Manor in Wisconsin for the weekend with my sister and our downstairs neighbors, Gerti and Al, along with their two daughters, Cindy and Bonny. Nippersink Manor was an affordable resort in Wisconsin that featured live entertainment, dining, dancing, swimming, and other activities. This was maybe the second time in my life that my parents had left me alone in the apartment.

Skokie

Alan Krockey, 1957

Al Krockey and his sister, Sherry

The Krockey Family, with friend at the Auto Show

Mom, in front of 8239 Knox Avenue, Skokie

Skokie, leading suburb of new home construction, 1954
(*Courtesy of Skokie Heritage Museum*)

Downtown Skokie, 1950s (*Courtesy of Skokie Heritage Museum*)

Lincoln Avenue & Oakton Street (*Courtesy of Skokie Heritage Museum*)

Lincoln Avenue (*Courtesy of Skokie Heritage Museum*)

Oakton Pool (*Courtesy of Skokie Heritage Museum*)

Skokie Theatre (*Courtesy of Skokie Heritage Museum*)

Old Orchard Theatre, by Mike (*From Creative Commons*)

Old Orchard Theatre poster (*From the author's collection*)

Twin Orchard Bowl (*From the author's collection*)

Old Orchard Mall (*Courtesy of Skokie Heritage Museum*)

Fun Fair Amusement Park (*Courtesy of Skokie Heritage Museum*)

Henry's Drive-In (*Courtesy of Skokie Heritage Museum*)

Jake's Snack Shop, which became Jack's Restaurant, Skokie
(*From the author's collection*)

Big Herm's, Skokie (*From the author's collection*)

The Corner Hut (*Courtesy of Skokie Heritage Museum*)

Skokie Swift platform, by Roger Puta (*From Wikimedia Commons*)

Sam & Hy's advertisement (*From the author's collection*)

The Cork Restaurant, matchbook cover (*From the author's collection*)

Alberti's Italian Pizzeria advertisement (*From the author's collection*)

McDonald's, Skokie, advertisement (*From the author's collection*)

Chapter 3

Protest Installments

When I woke up on Sunday morning, I found myself in my parents' bed, as it must have been easier for Cuzzi to plop me down there, as my room was all the way in the back of the apartment. I still had all my clothes on, including my leather vest, paisley shirt, and blue jean bell-bottoms. In my haze, I started to remember Cuzzi pulling off my Frye boots after plopping me down and me struggling to help. I got up that morning, put some coffee on, and showered. Every Sunday, we had the *Sun-Times* and the *Chicago Tribune* delivered, as my mom and dad liked to sit around and read the paper while enjoying their traditional Sunday breakfast of lox and bagels, with some scrambled eggs on the side.

I read the front pages of both papers. The coverage was all about the Vietnam War and the upcoming presidential election. There was an article about how a US fighter bomber accidentally killed eight Americans and wounded fifty with rocket and cannon fire. "Fuck, no way I'm going to Vietnam," I said to myself out loud. Norm and I had recently enrolled at Central Y Junior College to get a college deferment and would be starting school in September. The newspaper also talked about the Republican presidential candidate, Richard Nixon, and his running mate, Spiro Agnew. It went on to talk about how Nixon had gone to President Johnson's home in Texas to receive a briefing on the war and the recent Paris negotiations.

Finally, the papers went on to talk about the upcoming Democratic Convention and the possible presidential candidates, which included Hubert Humphrey, Eugene McCarthy, and, just today, George McGovern jumping in, which I felt could hurt McCarthy, who took up the mantle of Bobby Kennedy when Kennedy was shot earlier in the year. I liked McCarthy because he was against the war in Vietnam, and now McGovern was running with some similar ideas. We would find out soon enough as the Democratic Convention was being held in Chicago at the International Amphitheatre and was only a couple weeks away. One thing was for certain: Jake Ruben was going to sell a lot of skimmers and campaign buttons.

As I was reading the sports section, I was reminded that tomorrow, August 12, the Cubs would open a four-day homestand against the first-place St. Louis Cardinals, followed by a four-game series with the Cincinnati Reds, and then four games with the Atlanta Braves. The Cubs were now in second place, but still fourteen games behind St. Louis. We always cleaned up when the Cardinals came to town, as busloads of people would make the trip from St. Louis to Chicago's Wrigley Field and especially now that the Cardinals looked like a shoo-in for the pennant. Sometimes we would sell as much Cardinals merchandise as Cubs. The Reds also drew well, as Cincinnati was like St. Louis, in which you could drive to Chicago in four or five hours. Chicago was and still is a popular vacation destination for people from St. Louis and Cincinnati, and, of course, Wrigley Field remains one of the many star attractions for visitors to the city.

After talking with Eddie on Sunday night, we decided we should get to the ballpark by seven to get everything ready for the week's homestand. On Monday morning, I picked up Norm around six and drove to the Skokie Swift, as parking and traffic would be impossible around the ballpark with all the buses coming in from St. Louis. One highlight of the week for me happened on Tuesday, about fifteen or twenty minutes before game time. I was standing with Norm and Tuffy by our stand next to the back gate, and, as I mentioned earlier, this was also where the players entered and next to the team's parking area. Suddenly, this new Cadillac pulled right onto the sidewalk in front of the back gate, almost hitting us and knocking over our stand. Then, Cubs manager Leo Durocher jumped out looking like he had a long night.

The usher inside the gate came out and yelled, "What the fuck, Leo?"

"Sorry, Jerry, I'm fucking late and got to get on the field before game time." He tossed me the keys and told me, "Hey, kid, I'm late and don't have time to park the car with all this traffic. Here's ten bucks to park my Caddie in the lot. The space has my name written on the ballpark wall. Give the keys to Jerry, the usher, after you've parked it. And be careful, the car is only a couple days old. Thanks, kid, see you around."

After that day, whenever Leo arrived, he would always say, "Hiya, kid" or "How ya doing, fellas?"

The following season, we would really get to know Mr. Leo Durocher.

The Cubs won the first two games. In the third game, the Cardinals started Bob Gibson, who would post a historic 1.12 ERA that season and win the NL MVP Award.Being friends with most of the Andy Frain ushers, on occasion they would allow me to enter the ballpark for a few innings whenever I liked. I would sometimes go inside Wrigley for a few innings to not only watch my beloved Cubs with Banks, Santo, and Williams, but to see certain visiting players I admired. I loved watching Bob Gibson. Watching Gibson paint the corners of the plate was like watching Picasso paint a masterpiece.

Other visiting players I enjoyed watching were Roberto Clemente, Willie Mays, Juan Marichal, Pete Rose, and Hank Aaron. Gibson pitched a one-hitter that day, beating the Cubs 3-1.

On Thursday, after the Cubs lost the last game, splitting the series, Eddie, Norm, and I decided to go to Francis's cafeteria on Clark before going to the newly named Electric Theatre, now called the Kinetic Playground. I had gotten a call from Fito of Canned Heat the night before, telling me they were replacing Julie Driscoll and Brian Auger and would be opening for the Mothers of Invention, and asking if I could get him a couple lids of weed, which I did. As Eddie was driving us over to eat at Francis's, he told us we were meeting his cousin Art Brown and asked if he could come along to the show tonight. I told him it was no problem. Fito left me four tickets. We got to Francis's, which had consummate homemade food and served its hot meals from steam tables much like Manny's did. Standing in front of the steam tables, I decided on chicken Kiev with kasha, Norm got the liver and onions, and Eddie and his cousin Art both had the matzah ball soup and a Reuben sandwich. Eddie's cousin Art, from Springfield, Illinois, looked like he was really enjoying his sandwich.

"I bet you don't get food like this down in Springfield," I said.

"No good deli in Springfield, but I've been spending a lot of time in New York, which has so many good delis."

Eddie, having not seen his cousin in a couple of years, then asked, "What's going on in New York?"

"Well, school for one thing. I'm taking classes at NYU and have gotten really involved in the protest of the war in Vietnam, in addition to hustling a little weed and acid on the side."

"Yeah, I knew you were going to school in New York, but I wasn't sure which school. How involved are you in this protest shit?"

"I'm not super involved, but I have been to my share of rallies and protests. It all started last summer while I was hanging out with this unbelievably beautiful hippie chick, Jenny, in the East Village and going to Tompkins Square Park with her. I was also selling a lot of grass at the time when I met this guy, Dana Beal, whom I would sell and buy weed from. Beal and his friends were always talking about legalizing marijuana. Anyway, one day the Grateful Dead showed up with this local band, the Fugs, to play a concert at Tompkins Square Park. This would be the first time the Dead played the East Coast. And then, Dana shows up with hundreds of rolled joints, and proceeds to get on stage while the Dead is playing, and then Dana proceeds to start throwing joints at the audience with all these cops around.

Suddenly, the park smelled like weed with 3,000 people pulling out their own stash or lighting up one of the joints Dana threw to the crowd. Normally the cops would step in, but with so many people at the concert they left us alone. That day I met these guys, Abbie Hoffman, who's a Yippie, and his friend, Stanley, who is really into acid. When I met Abbie at the concert, he told me, 'Hey, man, look, the cops aren't doing anything. We got a real smoke-in going, a real fucking smoke-in. This is so groovy.' Then Abbie went on to tell me, 'I heard the Dead made a deal with the city that they would play a free show in Central Park later this summer if they allowed this show, but the cops would have to be cool. Who knows, 3,000 people are a bunch of people to arrest.'

"Anyways, that's one of the reasons I'm in Chicago. Tomorrow, I'm going down to Springfield to see my family, and then I'm coming back to Chicago next week for the Democratic Convention and for the protest my Yippie friends are organizing. Hey, what time is the show tonight?"

"Not sure; the doors open at seven, but the bands usually don't hit the stage till at least eight-thirty or nine, sometimes even way later, like ten. I want to get there before eight so I can take care of business before Canned Heat goes on," I replied.

"You guys want some of this out-of-sight acid I got from my friend Stanley?" Art asked.

"Not me," I answered. But then Norm looked at Eddie and nodded.

"Is it really that good?" Eddie asked.

"Stanley Owsley's acid is the grooviest, out-of-sight shit I've ever had." Eddie and Norm both took the acid and we all went to the show.

"Norm, don't tell Joyce."

Norm replied, "No problem, Eddie. I thought you guys broke up?"

"No, we're back together for the moment."

After I went backstage to drop the weed off, I came out front and we all sat down to hear these two amazing bands. Within a half hour or so, you could see that my friends were tripping their asses off, as I had never seen Eddie dance, but all three of these guys were dancing with some hippie chicks who also looked like they were tripping, dancing in their bare feet and wearing long flowing dresses. One was sweating so much that her nipples showed right through her dress. My friends all had crazy looks on their faces like they were seeing or discovering something for the first time.

As I was sitting on the floor, listening to the music and watching my friends, all looking like they were having a ball, I started to think that maybe I should ask Art for some acid. But I didn't. I was always kind of afraid of acid, especially after the time I had seen a neighborhood guy, Mark Pitman, running down Dempster Street naked and then him walking into the New China Restaurant while my parents, sister, and I were waiting for a table last Christmas. He had very nonchalantly walked right by us, right up to this little Chinese hostess, and asked if he could order two egg rolls to go, while the whole restaurant watched. Of course the cops showed up and arrested him, dragging him out as he kept yelling, "I didn't get my egg roll!"

As we were finishing our traditional Christmas Chinese dinner that night, my father turned to me, looking very concerned, and told me, "You better not be taking that crap."

After the Cubs split the series with the Cardinals, they went on to lose all four to the Reds and then closed out the Atlanta Braves with a sweep by winning a doubleheader on the final day before going on a road trip out west. Norm and I did pretty well, splitting up close to $500 for the ten-day, twelve-game homestand, including two doubleheaders.

After that final doubleheader with the Braves, we were all tired. It was 7 p.m. before we finished putting the stands away. Eddie offered to give Norm and me a ride to my car at the Skokie Swift, so we wouldn't have to take the train home. On the way to my car, Eddie offered to buy Norm and me dinner at East of Edens Restaurant, which was located inside All Star Bowl. After we ordered our food, we ran into Buggy Falstein, who had a band called the Domineers, and was having a sandwich with one of the other guys from the band. The Domineers played in all the local teen dance clubs, including Devonshire Center in Skokie, The Legion Hall in Lincolnwood, The Green Gorilla in Des Plaines, and The Cellar in Arlington Heights, just to mention a few. Buggy, whose real name was Bobby, had been good friends with Norm in junior high and was a hell of a musician, playing both keyboards and guitar, and was also a pretty good singer.

"What's up, Buggy?" Norm asked.

"Not too much. Just came from rehearsal. We're playing Friday at the Legion in Lincolnwood. You should come by."

"Maybe," Norm replied.

"Yeah, the band has been busy. How about you guys?"

"We've been working," Eddie answered. "How about you, Krockey? Have you seen any good music lately?"

"I just saw Hendrix and we all went to see the Mothers of Invention and Canned Heat the other day," I replied.

"I wanted to see Hendrix but we had a gig in Wisconsin that night. By the way, this band, MC 5, is doing a free show Sunday in Lincoln Park at some peace rally before the Democratic Convention starts on Monday. They're pretty good. I saw them in Michigan when we were up there last month as their opening act."

"I might check it out," I replied.

Buggy and Norm exchanged hugs, and then Buggy and his band-mate took off. After Norm sat back down, Eddie told us that even though he did his one weekend this month, he was notified he would have to report to his National Guard unit this weekend and may have to stay on for a week in case there was trouble at the convention.

On Saturday, Norm and I went shopping at Raymond's and Mr. Juniors in downtown Skokie to buy some clothes for our first semester at Central YMCA Community College, which would be starting on September 9. After picking up a pair of jeans and a pair of khaki pants from Raymond's, I decided to get a couple button-down shirts from Mr. Juniors, as that's what I thought you were supposed to wear in college. For some time, I had mostly been dressing in tie-dye t-shirts, paisley shirts with big collars, and different colored bell-bottoms, along with my Frye boots or my Converse All-Stars. Norm was looking for a sweater and suggested we go to Marshall Field's in Old Orchard. As we were driving past the Old Orchard Theatre, I saw that *Hang 'Em High* was playing with Clint Eastwood. I had been a big fan of Eastwood's ever since *A Fistful of Dollars*, *For a Few Dollars More*, and *The Good, the Bad, and the Ugly*.

I suggested, "Norm, let's blow off the shopping and go see my man, Clint."

"I can't, Krock, I've got a date with Barb tonight."

"That's cool. I'm going out with that hippie girl I met last week at the Kinetic Playground, Helene. She's two years older than me and gave me a hand job in one of the meditation booths, which was out of sight. I'm not sure Helene or Barb will dig Clint. Let's go to the matinee; the two o'clock starts in ten minutes."

"No, let's get tickets for tonight's show, and Barb and I can meet you there with your date."

"Okay," I said.

So we all met at the show, and to my surprise, the girls dug the movie and were gaga over Clint.

After we came out of the show, Norm asked, "How about pizza?"

We all agreed on pizza.

"You want to go to Alberti's, La Rosa on Dempster, or Gulliver's?" Norm asked.

My date, Helene, said she loved Alberti's pizza.

Then Norm said, "Okay, cool. We will meet you there."

After we ate, I drove Helene home, and she invited me in. It seemed her parents' bedroom was on the second floor of this big house in a rich part of Skokie called Timber Ridge. Helene led me downstairs to the family room. After making out for a while, she took me by the hand to the spare bedroom in the basement and we started to get undressed. Ten minutes later, I was no longer a virgin. Helene was much more experienced than me, and over the next two weeks before returning to her third year of college at UCLA, Berkeley, she would introduce me to the pleasures of sex after telling me not to fall in love with her.

When I woke up on Sunday morning, my parents reminded me that we had our annual cousins' club picnic in Harms Woods, which was about twenty minutes from our apartment. My mom had been up early, making her fried chicken and potato salad as well as a dozen hamburger patties.

My sister Sherry asked me, "Are you going with us to the picnic?"

I told her, "Of course, but I'm leaving around one-thirty or so to meet my friends."

"You're not going to that protest downtown, are you?"

"No, I think there's some kind of peace rally in Lincoln Park, but don't tell Mommy or Daddy."

After seeing my cousins and eating my ass off at the picnic, I jumped into my car and headed over to Norm's house, which was only a few minutes away.

"What's up?" Norm asked.

"I brought you a piece of my mom's fried chicken and some coleslaw."

"Thanks. You want a beer, Krock?"

"Sure. Where are your parents, Norm?" I asked.

"They took a ride to Ray Radigan's in Wisconsin with my sister, Judy, and her husband, Les, for a Sunday afternoon dinner. Who needs Ray Radigan's when I have Mrs. Krockey's fried chicken? Cuzzi is picking up Buggy Falstein and then coming by here. He should be here soon. You have weed on you?" Norm asked.

"Yeah, I got like two lids."

"You had better leave most of it here. Only take a couple joints because I heard that the cops were busting people yesterday in Lincoln Park, especially after curfew."

When Cuzzi and Buggy arrived, Norm suggested we all go in his backyard and smoke a joint. "Yeah, let's smoke here. I don't think we should carry more than a couple joints in case the cops are busting people. Cookie told me they busted a bunch of people yesterday in the park because of curfew. We can park on Clark Street and walk to the park and smoke the joints."

Buggy responded, "Don't be so paranoid, Norm. It's supposed to be a peace rally and I told you guys, this band, the MC5, is playing. It should be fun and there should be plenty of chicks." After smoking a joint, we jumped into Cuzzi's GTO and headed to Lincoln Park.

After getting off the drive, Lake Shore Drive, at Fullerton going west, we saw groups of people heading for the park. As we inched west, Cuzzi said he wanted to park along Clark Street away from the crowds. When we got to Clark Street, we turned left, driving toward Armitage, but found no parking spaces. We were almost at North Avenue before we found a place to park. We started walking toward the music in the park. When we finally got close to where the MC5 was playing, I noticed that there was no PA and that the band had plugged their amps into a hot dog vendor's stand.

Norm tapped me on the shoulder. "Look at that mule in the Army fatigues. He just punched the shit out of that long-haired hippie." Right then, as the show was ending, more and more cops showed up, and now some were beating on people with their nightsticks.

"Let's get the fuck out of here," I told my friends.

As we started to run, I saw Ronnie Singer and his girlfriend, Candi, being thrown into the back of a paddy wagon along with Jeff Williams and Kenny David. When we finally got back to the car, there was this big fat cop leaning on Cuzzi's GTO, talking to an older woman.

"Excuse me, Officer," Cuzzi said.

"What the fuck do you want?"

"This is my car."

"Nice car, kid. I can see from your vehicle sticker you're from Skokie. I suggest you and your friends get in your car and get your asses back to Skokie before you get hurt."

"Yes, sir," Cuzzi replied.

So that's what we did. But instead of taking Lake Shore Drive, we drove west down North Avenue to the Kennedy Expressway.

"Let's go to Jack's," I suggested.

Then Norm said, "You know, I really have a taste for a hot dog at Superdawg."

"Yeah, me too," replied Buggy.

So off we went. Superdawg was a drive-in where you ordered through a speaker at your parking spot, and a waitress, or carhop, as they were called, brought you your food by hanging a tray on the car window. We all had Superdawgs with everything, which included mustard, onions, relish, a pickle slice, and a sport pepper, which came with French fries and a sour tomato on the side. All this came inside a little cardboard box. In addition, we all had root beer floats.

When the waitress finally came, Cuzzi said, "C'mon guys, I don't want you eating in the car."

So instead of hanging the serving trays on the windows, we had the waitress set them down on the picnic tables they had next to the parking lot.

"Man, could you believe the shit going down?" Norm said as we ate.

I replied, "I know, man, and the convention hasn't even started. And how about what they said on the radio on our way here about the same shit going down with the protesters at the Hilton and in Grant Park? I thought it was going to be a peaceful and groovy party. I'm staying away."

"No shit," said Norm while Buggy and Cuzzi nodded in agreement.

So that's what we did. We decided not to go to any more rallies or protests that week. On Monday morning, Jeff Williams called me. Sounded like he had been up all night after he, Kenny, Ronnie, and Candi had been arrested and then released. Jeff told me that when the paddy wagon with Ronnie, Candi, Kenny, and him arrived at the station, the cops let them all go, and they went back to Ronnie and Candi's to get high. I didn't ask what they got high on.

"Krockey, you want to go down by the Hilton with Kenny and me?"

"No, I'm against the war and everything, but I also don't need my head bashed in or to get arrested."

"C'mon, it will be fun. We're thinking of doing some mushrooms before we go."

"No, thanks, I'm starting a new job tomorrow with Norm until school starts."

"What about the ballpark?" Jeff asked.

I explained, "The Cubs are on the road till Friday, and we are only working a couple games in September, because that's when the crowds start to fall off. We're hoping this new job as installment salesmen, selling door to door, is something we could do while going to school." We would soon come to learn that this door-to-door installment business was on its way out.

As soon as I hung up with Jeff, Norm called. "You talk to Williams?"

"Yeah, just hung up. He sounded out of it," Norm replied.

"I hope he's not fooling around with that junk."

"Yeah, me too."

Then Norm said, "I'll come by and get you at nine."

"Where is their office?" I asked.

"Lincoln and California."

As we pulled up to the address, the building had a sign on it: Happy Shoppers.

Norm and I walked in and were greeted by Sol and Bernie Kogen. "Hello, Norm."

"Hello, Mr. Kogen. This is my friend, Alan Krockey."

"Call me Sol. This is my brother, Bernie."

"Good to meet you, fellas," Bernie replied.

Then Sol spoke. "Boys, we're going to teach you how to sell door-to-door as installment salesmen."

I then asked, "What do you guys sell?"

"We sell everything," Sol replied.

"What do you mean you sell everything?" Norm asked Sol.

"Well, back in the early '20s when my father came over from Poland, there were no credit cards or stores giving credit, and most of the immigrants barely spoke English. So, these peddlers from Europe would buy merchandise with the idea of, for example, buying a fan wholesale for three dollars and selling it for six. The problem was that most of these

European immigrants were poor, especially when the depression hit in 1929. So, they started selling with the installment plan. The idea is, take the fan as an example. When Mrs. Jones asks you how much, you tell her six dollars. She says, 'I don't have six dollars.' You tell her, 'I'll tell you what I'll do. Give me three dollars, and I'll come to your house every week, and you can pay me fifty cents each week.'

"After she says yes, you have accomplished two things. One, you sold her the fan, and you now have covered your cost, and in six weeks, you will have all your profit. And two, now you have a new customer that you can visit every week, building a relationship and of course selling her more merchandise. The idea is to keep getting more and more customers and building a route. At first, it's hard: cold calling, knocking on as many doors as possible."

"How do you know what to sell?" Norm asked.

Sol answered, "That takes some learning. You guys will come with me today, and I will explain more in the car, and you can watch me work with the customers. There are certain items you always carry along with these catalogs. You always carry a vacuum cleaner, a coffee percolator, fans in the summer, space heaters and blankets in the winter, and some toys for the kids. And of course, these catalogs, which have every item a housewife would want, from clothes to tools to jewelry, dishes, and of course, religious items. Sort of like your own Sears catalog. As you develop relationships with these folks, they will tell you what their wishes are, and it's your job to fulfill these wishes. And of course, in making friends with these people, they will then recommend you to their friends and relatives." So off we went in Sol's brand-new, turquoise blue Cadillac DeVille with its leather seats.

Then I asked, "Sol, why do you have a police spotlight with a handle attached next to your outside rearview mirror?"

"Oh, that's for when I'm calling on my night customers. You see, more and more women are working these days; in addition, some of their bigger purchases will need their husband's approval."

As we drove farther south down Kedzie Avenue, I asked where we were going.

"We are going to the West Side," Sol answered.

"Isn't that mostly Black?" Norm asked.

"Of course; most of my customers are black. Good, hardworking folk who still have a hard time getting credit. I also work in the Puerto Rican and Mexican neighborhoods. But I still do have a few white customers I see once a week. Mostly Polish."

As we pulled up to a nice two-flat greystone on Douglas Boulevard located across the street from a Baptist church, I noticed Hebrew inscriptions at the top of the church above the cross and stained glass.

"Hey, guys, look at the Hebrew carved into the church above the cross."

"Yeah, Krockey, a lot of the West Side churches were once synagogues," Sol responded as he went into his trunk, pulling out a GE toaster oven like my mom had, along with an electric heating pad.

After we knocked on the door, an old lady, about eighty with a housecoat and curlers in her hair, answered the door. "Hello, Miss Irene. How are we doing today?"

"I'm okay, Mr. K, you know how it is. Oh, Mr. K, you brought my heating pad. I asked my daughter, Martha, to get me a new one. Thank God she remembered. Oh, bless you." Miss Irene called out. "Martha, Mr. K is here with a couple of young gents."

"I'm getting dressed, Mama. I will be out in a minute."

"Are these your sons, Mr. K?" Ms. Irene asked.

"No, these are two new salesmen I'm breaking in."

"You boys are lucky. Mr. K is one of the good Jews."

"Why, thank you, Ms. Irene."

"My pleasure. Mr. K. How long have we known each other?"

Sol responded, "Got to be twenty years or so. Let's see, I got out of the Navy in '45, and you became one of my first customers. So, it's over twenty years."

Just then, Martha walked in wearing her CTA uniform. Sol greeted her. "Hello, Martha, are you still working at the L station on Lake Street and California?"

"I sure am. Two more years and I'll be sixty-five and getting my pension. I saw you brought Mama's heating pad. Praise the Lord."

"Amen to that," Irene responded as she laughed.

"Here's that GE toaster oven you ordered."

"I forgot what you told me the price was last time you were here."

"It's still eighteen dollars like I told you before and six dollars for the heating pad."

Right then, Sol pulled out his account book. "Okay, let's see, you have a balance of thirty-five dollars. I need nine dollars down for the toaster oven and three dollars down for the heating pad, and why don't you give me three toward the balance? Fifteen all altogether."

Sol drove us all around the West Side. Many of the stops were just collections where Sol didn't sell anything, but when he did make a sale you saw how these old-school guys worked, especially because most of Sol's remaining customers had been buying from him for years, and would look forward to a visit from Sol as if he were an old friend or relative.

After selling one lady a vacuum, the lady said, "Mr. Sol, I saw this same Hoover in the *Sun-Times* advertisement for Polk Brothers for ten dollars cheaper, up on Central Avenue."

Sol responded, "You know very well, Lucy, you are not going to take two buses over to Central Avenue and have them tell you cash-and-carry."

"I know, Mr. K, I was just trying to see if I could Jew you down," as all two hundred pounds of Miss Lucy shook with laughter. Sol sold these people anything he could. He even told us on a couple of occasions when his customers were looking to buy a new car and wanted his help getting a good price, he would drive them over to one of the car dealers he knew. They would give Sol a little commission and at the same time sell Sol's customers a car at a fair price. Sol was a master of selling religious items. From clocks with a picture of Jesus to crosses to pictures of the pope. On one of his stops that day, Sol brought a lady named Ruthie a new Jesus clock, which had a picture of a white Jesus along with the words "Time for Jesus." Once we were inside her large house with white painted walls that had white ceilings painted with glitter, Sol introduced us to Miss Ruthie.

Norm commented, "I like your ceilings, Miss Ruthie."

"Thank you. It's what they call stars in the sky paint, which I love and have in all the rooms of my house."

Sol said, "It does look good, Ruthie."

"Mr. Sol, here's the final five dollars for that new linoleum floor you got me for my kitchen some months back."

"Thank you, Miss Ruthie."

"What you got in that box?" Ruthie asked.

"Well, Ruthie, now that you've paid off that pretty linoleum floor, I thought I'd show you something that would look really good in your kitchen with your new floor."

As we were all standing in the kitchen, Sol took the clock out and placed it on the counter. Ruthie looked at me and Norm and asked, "What do you think, boys?"

Norm replied, "Ooh, that looks really nice." Sol knew that Ruthie was a churchgoing woman, having sold her many crosses that hung throughout the house and having recently sold her two pictures, one of Jesus and one of Martin Luther King, that hung in her bedroom.

Sol said, "The boys and I are going to step into the dining room while you spend a few minutes with the Lord to decide."

As we walked out to the dining room, we could hear Ruthie praying behind us. A few minutes later, Ruthie came out and gave Sol five dollars for the ten-dollar clock. She then asked Sol if he could come by next week and bring her one of those fancy mops like they sell on TV.

"Sure, Ruthie, see you next week. Before I forget, Ruthie, I stopped by your church last week and gave Reverend White a donation for you both for helping me to sell all those Martin Luther King pictures for the church."

On the way back to the office, Sol told us that after MLK was assassinated, every Black churchgoing person on the West and South Side wanted a picture of MLK. So, Sol and Bernie printed up a few hundred pictures. Sol went on to tell us, "Yeah, when the demand first started, we bought all these picture frames and Bernie and I, along with our wives and kids, framed almost three hundred pictures of MLK on our own. Then we went to see all the pastors of the Black churches with the idea of it being a good source of fundraising for them. The church would sell them to their congregants for ten dollars each. It cost us three dollars for the photos and frames. We would give the churches pictures on consignment. The church would sell them for ten dollars and keep three-dollars and fifty-cents, giving Sol and I six dollars and fifty cents, which amounted to a three-dollar and fifty-cent gross profit for Happy Shoppers Inc. Of course, we also sold dozens and dozens along our route and still do. One of our bestsellers."

After getting back to the office, Sol told us to meet him there tomorrow morning at eight-thirty.

Once we were back in Norm's car, I said, "Norm, I don't know about this job."

Norm replied, "I know. It does not look too promising."

I went on to say, "Did you notice that most of Sol's customers have been buying from him for ten or twenty years? That he had hardly any new customers? Sol must realize that this is a dying business. I'm sure he must know that stores like Sears and Wards are starting to give credit to the minorities. And even Polk Brothers and Harlem Furniture are now giving credit to Blacks and other minorities, even though Sol had told that lady that Polk Brothers didn't sell on installment." Giving Norm a bewildered look, I asked, "How did this career opportunity come up anyways, pal?"

"I told you, he's friends with my old man. We were on my parents' boat when Sol, Bernie, and their wives came out for a ride. My mom started making sandwiches while my old man started pouring cocktails. By the time lunch was ready, my old man had just finished his second drink along with Sol and Bernie, and he was preparing a third round. While we were eating, my old man said to Sol, 'My kid here is starting college in a few weeks. Do you have any part-time work? He's a good hustler.' Then Sol says, 'These days it's not easy getting new customers, but if you're a good salesman and are able to get new customers, you can make a nice buck. But you must work hard.'

"Of course, I told Sol I was a hard worker and then asked him if he had room for my friend that I work with at the ballpark, telling him we work on the same souvenir stand at the ballpark and have been splitting the profits all summer. He then told me that when Bernie and he first started, they would call on new customers together all the time. It's actually a pretty good way to get started. Then he gave me his card and told me to come by and bring my friend. It sounded good the way he said it, and it just kind of happened. I must admit that Sol is a hell of a salesman. Anyways, we need to try it for a couple of days, or my old man will go nuts."

Later, after that first day with Sol, we decided to go to the trotters that night at Sportsman's Park. We had gotten a tip from Howie Brown about a sure thing by the name of Colonial Diller with the driver Donald Busse. After we blew ninety-five dollars between us, which was every cent we had on us, Norm suggested I stay over at his house so we could go to work together in the morning. Before going to work, Norm looked in his drawer for his money. Not finding the three hundred dollars he had left in his drawer, he yelled out, "What the fuck, my mom moved my dough." So, Norm called his mom at Community Builders, where she was working as an appointment maker for a home improvement company. "Mom, where did you put my money?"

"In the bank, of course."

"But I need some money."

"Okay, I will give you some money when I get home."

"But I need some now."

"You will have to wait."

"Okay, Ma, talk to you later." Norm said. "I guess we're going to work broke. Let's go—we're going to be late."

We finished our coffee and jumped into Norm's car. When we walked in the door of Happy Shoppers, Sol's secretary told us Sol was next door at the coffee shop. We sat down at Sol's table as the waitress was taking Sol's order. She then turned to Norm and me, asking what we would like.

"Nothing, thank you," I replied.

As Sol was telling us about where we were going today, his food arrived. Sol had ordered a salami and egg sandwich on an onion roll. Norm then said to Sol as both our mouths watered, "Wow, that's a nice sandwich, Sol."

Norm was hoping that Sol might offer to buy us a sandwich. But all Sol said was, "You guys should try one sometime." After Sol finished his sandwich, he asked us to follow him to the Northwest Side around Division and Ashland. It was a nice sunny day when we pulled down Bosworth Avenue just north of Division Street, where Norm parked his Falcon right behind Sol's Caddy. Norm's mom and dad had just last week given Norm his mom's old Ford Falcon to use for going to college and work. Norm's mom, Edie, had just gotten a brand new red and white Pontiac Tempest after his folks came home winners after their recent trip to Vegas on one of Seymour Taradashe's junkets to the Stardust. I later found out that Norm's mom, Edie, had hit a jackpot on a slot machine for one thousand dollars, in addition to Norm's father, Henry, or Hawk as everyone called him, winning a couple of hundred at the craps table.

Sol spent about three hours showing us how to knock on doors and make a cold pitch. The neighborhood was mostly Polish and Puerto Rican, with a few Mexicans and hillbillies thrown in. After over two hours, only two people let us in. One was a Puerto Rican woman, who after spending a good half hour picking out three items and then telling us she had no money, asked us to come back next week when her social security check would arrive.

"Sure, Mrs. Martinez, anything for a new customer. Here is a copy of your order showing one Lady Timex for twenty dollars, and the two beautiful pictures of Jesus for ten dollars each, totaling forty dollars. When we come next week to bring you your watch and your pictures, you will only have to give us twenty dollars, and then three dollars every week till you pay off the balance."

"Gracias, Mr. Sol."

"See you next week, Mrs. Martinez."

After we left, Sol said, "See, fellas, you have made a new customer. All you must do now is come back next week, drop off the merchandise, collect the downstroke, and in a few weeks, you will have made a nice profit. Of course, Happy Shoppers gets a third."

We made one more stop with Sol to one of his old customers, Kim Kowalsky, where he was delivering a large new suitcase. "Hello, Kim. How are you, Alex, and the kids doing? Are you getting ready for your big trip to Poland?"

"Oh, yes, the family's fine, of course. Alex is in Iowa with his polka band, and one of my daughters is living in Downers Grove with her husband and two daughters, three and six. Beautiful girls. My other daughter just left for her third year at the university in Champagne." Then Kim, this 250-pound woman in her housecoat with big, flabby arms and bleached blonde hair, grabbed the suitcase out of Sol's hand

and said in her heavy Polish accent. "Oh, this is a gorgeous suitcase for a trip to Krakow."

"You're going alone, Kim?"

"Of course. My husband is working and my mother is very sick in Poland. I'll leave in two days. Here, I pay you the whole fifteen dollars today for the suitcase. I don't like owing money."

"Thank you, Kim. Oh, I forgot to mention, this suitcase comes with a free cosmetic bag inside."

"Oh, you are vonderful, Mr. Sol."

When we got outside, Sol told us he was going back to the office and suggested we work a few more hours. As soon as Sol left, I yelled, shaking my head at Norm, "Fuck this shit. I can't do this."

"I know, Krock, this shit bums me out too. But what am I going to tell my father?"

"Tell him the fucking truth. Now that you have some wheels, you can deliver pizza."

"Man, that's a boss idea. Let's get out of here and go get something to eat. I'm starving."

"What are we going to do with all these samples and catalogs?" I replied.

"We can drop all this shit off tomorrow. Right now, all I want to do is get some food, except we have no dough. How are we going to eat?" Norm replied.

"We can go to Sarkis. He will feed us and we can pay him tomorrow."

"Good thinking. Right on, Norm. Sarkis always lets us run a tab." By the time we got to Sarkis on the Evanston/Skokie border, it was already two o'clock and would be closing soon.

Chapter 4

The Pan Is Hot!

The Sarkis Cafe was a small breakfast and lunch place with eight stools and three tables. His specialty was a three-egg omelet with onions, green peppers, and Wisconsin brick cheese served with a well-seasoned ground beef patty, which years later would be named the "Disaster" by yours truly, but that story comes much later. He also served sandwiches and a daily special like stuffed green peppers or spaghetti. Sarkis would eventually cut out the daily specials after becoming famous for his omelets and Disasters.

Sarkis Tashjian was a good-hearted Armenian who, along with his wife, Sonny, had come to America from Palestine, where he had worked as a dental assistant and dental lab technician, learning how to make false teeth and bridges while apprenticing to become a dentist and learning how to fill teeth. Soon after coming to America in 1958, Sonny and Sarkis had two young daughters, Elizabeth and Kristina.

Before he left Palestine, Sarkis received his license as a dental assistant, hoping one day he would earn enough money in America to go to college and become a dentist. When he first arrived in this country, he couldn't afford dental school. He tried to get a job, but all he could find were menial labor gigs. So, after quitting his job as an assistant short-order cook in some dive, he decided to take a chance.

Taking the little money he and his wife had saved, he decided to open a dentist's office, buying some used equipment, and hoping to save enough to go to night school. With no license, he found a cheap office right near Chicago Avenue and Damen, treating mostly Ukrainian and Polish immigrants.

Sarkis would charge half the price of a normal dentist. Word got around the neighborhood and he started to eke out a living. Until one day, about a year after he opened his small office as business was starting to pick up, he had a fight with one of his lady patients, Sophie Bolinski, after she accused Sarkis of making a pass at her. She marched out of Sarkis's office after he had finished filling two of her teeth without paying her bill. She then proceeded to go see her brother-in-law, a Chicago policeman who worked out of the Wood Street Station, and asked him to pay a visit to the office of Dr. Sarkis Tashjian.

As Officer Alex Jankowski and his Irish partner, Officer Terry Ahern, walked up the stairs, Alex knew his sister-in-law was up to no good. She was always flirting with her low-cut dresses and heavily made-up face. But he had no choice—she was his wife's sister. He and his partner walked into the small two-room office to find Sarkis alone, eating his lunch.

"Are you Dr. Sarkis Tashjian?"

"Yes, Officer, what can I do for you?"

"Well, one of your patients, Mrs. Bolinski, made a complaint about you being inappropriate with her."

"What do you mean? I fill her teeth."

"She said you made a pass at her."

"No, no, she just wants free filling."

Officer Ahern, looking at the framed foreign language certificate hanging on the wall, asked, "What is this paper and what language is this?"

"It's my dental license from Palestine; this is Arabic," Sarkis replied.

"Where's your American and Chicago licenses, and where is your college diploma?" Ahern asked.

Sarkis looked down at the floor, knowing he was in big trouble. He told the officers he only had a Palestinian license. "I start night school at Illinois Circle Campus next month."

"Sorry, pal, we're going to have to take you down to the station."

Sarkis's office was not far from the Wood Street Station, as well as the Division Street Bathhouse, where on occasion he would go, becoming acquainted with some of the politicians and gangsters who frequented the schvitz. Sarkis was a very funny and entertaining character and made friends very easily. Everybody loved the crazy Armenian at the schvitz.

One of the guys he became friendly with was Harry Krause, a well-known Chicago fixer, head of jury duty for Cook County. Sarkis's bail was set at ten thousand dollars, and he would now have to come up with ten percent, under Illinois law, one thousand dollars in cash, and he didn't have it. After booking Sarkis, they told him he was entitled to a phone call. Not knowing what to do and not wanting to call his wife, Sarkis decided the best person to call would be Harry Krause. As it was already 5 p.m., Sarkis called the bathhouse to see if Harry was there, as he was on most Thursday afternoons.

Izzy, the guy at the front desk who handed out the towels and sheets, answered. "Division Street Baths."

"Hello, Mr. Izzy, this is Sarkis. Is Harry Krause there?"

"Yes, of course—it's Thursday. He and his bunch are in the hot room."

"Please, get Harry for me."

"Sorry, Sarkis, I can't disturb him. He's in the hot room with the other Thursday regulars."

"Please, Mr. Izzy, I'm in big trouble. I've been arrested and I'm in jail at the Wood Street police station."

Izzy could hear Sarkis crying, and knowing that Sarkis was pals with Harry, he told Sarkis, "Hold on." Izzy, who was five-foot-two, always wore a white sailor hat and a bathing suit in case somebody wanted a rub or massage. When Izzy opened the steam room door, he found the Thursday group of Harry Krause, attorney Dean Wolf, the bookie Marv Saks, and a few of the other Thursday guys. A couple of prominent figures who only came on rare occasions and were not part of the Thursday regulars were also there: Judge Abe Lincoln Horovitz and the author Saul Bellow. Izzy called out, "Harry, you have a phone call."

"Tell them I'll call back. I'm about to get a rub."

"It's Sarkis, Harry, and he says he's been arrested."

Harry stepped out of the steam room to pick up the phone extension. He ended his call with Sarkis by telling him to stop crying, that he would be there in a couple of hours. After going back into the steam room, Harry told everyone the story. Everyone shook their heads while also finding humor in this crazy story. After everyone had their platza rub, Harry told the group, "Let's go upstairs and eat; it's on me for all the disturbances." While finishing their skirt steaks, Harry asked Marv Saks, the bookie, "Would you be so kind as to lend me a grand till tomorrow?"

"No problem, Harry."

Then Harry turned to Dean Wolf, who at the time was one of the top criminal lawyers in Chicago. "Dean, will you take a ride over to the Wood Street Station with me?"

"After the rub you gave me, Harry, how could I say no?"

Everybody laughed except the honorable Judge Horovitz. "What's wrong, Judge?" Harry asked.

"Well, for one thing, three felonies that are no joking matter. Harry, this is something I cannot and will not get involved in."

Dean Wolf spoke. "I don't know, with the right legal representation and the right judge, he might have a chance at probation and a small fine."

"Sounds like it's your kind of case, Dean," the judge said, smiling and shaking his head.

Saul Bellow, who until then had been very quiet, said, "I guess this crazy Armenian Sarkis picked the right day to get arrested." He raised his glass. "Here's to America!"

It turned out, Sarkis did get probation, after which he would go on to open the soon-to-be-well-known Evanston establishment, the Sarkis Cafe. And because of his friendly, crazy personality, and his food, he became a famous North Shore personality, especially with the teenage crowd. He also received free publicity from newspaper articles and, from time to time, showed up on special TV segments of the news featuring popular local restaurants.

When Norm and I walked into Sarkis Cafe that day, there was nobody behind the counter. Not even his Mexican helper, Santiago. Then, we heard a woman's voice coming from the basement, moaning, "Oh, Sarkis… Oh, Sarkis…"

Norm and I looked at each other, laughing. A couple of minutes later, the woman's voice stopped, and Norm called out, "Sarkis, are you downstairs?"

"Yes, coming." A few minutes later, Sarkis started walking up the stairs while tucking in his shirt and being followed by a large, six-foot-tall, well-endowed friend of his, Miss Loretta.

"What's up, Sarkis?" I asked.

"Oh, hello, Krockey and Mr. Norman."

"Was just cleaning up. Miss Loretta was helping me. Santiago had to leave early, so Miss Loretta gave me a hand." Some weeks later, Sarkis would come up with a new sandwich called the Loretta, which included ham, melted white cheese, green peppers, tomatoes, onions, and a little mayo all on toasted French bread. "Are you boys hungry? Pan is still hot."

I answered, "We're starving, but we need to pay you tomorrow."

"No problem. I love everyone today," he said as he gave us that big Sarkis smile and then patted Miss Loretta on the ass and gave her a peck on the cheek.

"Please give us both a Sarkis special omelet with a meat patty (Disaster) and hash browns."

After we left Sarkis, we stopped by Gary Shane's. Shane lived in the well-to-do Skokie Devonshire neighborhood. We saw his green Chevelle Malibu SS sitting out front. After ringing the bell and knocking on the kitchen door, Shane finally came to the door in his underwear with no shirt on, looking a little disheveled with his scraggly beard and hair in a mess. When Shane finally opened the kitchen door, his first words were, "What time is it?"

Norm replied, "It's like four o'clock, Shane."

"Fuck, my mom is going to be home from work in like an hour."

Roz Shane worked in the men's department at Marshall Field's in Old Orchard, while Lou Shane had some mysterious job wearing expensive suits and always leaving for work very early in the morning, usually returning after a few drinks over at the Touhy House around midnight.

Then Shane yelled, as he ran up the stairs of this typical Skokie bilevel house, "Bonny, please get up; my mom will be coming home from work soon."

It turned out Shane had snuck his girlfriend, Bonny Kanter, up to his room the previous night after they had both taken a couple of Seconal pills and stayed in bed all day.

"Is your sister Barbara home?" Bonny asked.

"I think she slept at her boyfriend's house last night," Shane answered and then asked, "Why?"

"I need a Tampax."

"Look in her bathroom."

After Bonny stepped into the bathroom, she yelled, "Thank God!"

Then Shane said, while smiling at Norm and me, "I guess she found what she needed."

Bonny was a pretty brunette with long brown hair and a nice figure, and Shane couldn't keep his hands off her.

After Bonny got dressed, she came out of the bathroom while Shane followed her into his bedroom. As Shane got dressed, Bonny straightened up the room and started to make the bed. Then Bonny said, "Oh no, there's a little bloodstain on the sheets. I'm sorry; do you want me to wash them?"

"No, we don't have time. It's okay; it's just a small stain."

Bonny then told Shane, "I can come by tomorrow when your mom is at work and change the sheets and wash them."

She gave Shane a long kiss. "Groovy, but we have to go before Roz gets home," he said.

"Shane, you need to drop me off at Fran's house. I told my mother I slept there, and then Franny could drive me home."

Then Shane asked, "You guys want to take a ride? We can smoke a joint on the way to Fran's."

"Sure," I said.

"You still have some ganja?"

"Yep. I have almost three lids left and it's all tops."

As we were driving Bonny to Fran's, "Hey Jude" came on the radio and Bonny turned her head to Norm and me in the back seat, telling us how much she loved that song.

"I just heard it for the first time last week. I guess it will be on their next album, which should be fabulous."

I replied, "Can't wait."

"I have all of their albums," Bonny told us.

As we were pulling up to Fran's house, "Hey Jude" ended and "Born to Be Wild" came on the radio. Bonny gave Shane a big kiss before getting out of the car and then walked across the street to her friend's house, screaming the words to "Born to Be Wild," shaking her hair around, and then blowing Shane a kiss.

As we pulled away, Norm said, "Man, she is fucking hot. I bet she's a good lay."

Shane replied, "You better believe it. Krockey, you get laid yet?"

"Yes, sir. I met this older girl, Helene, at the Kinetic, and she loves sex, but she's going back for her third year of college at UCLA, Berkeley, right after Labor Day."

Shane replied, "Nice going. You finally got your cherry popped."

Norm then asked, "Hey, Shane, do they need any more drivers at Wesley's?"

"No, but I saw a 'drivers wanted' sign yesterday in Pagliacci's window when I dropped my shirts off at Davis Cleaners."

"Where's that?"

"You know, the joint over on Dempster and Bronx. It's takeout and delivery only. They got a beautiful pizza pie, and you get a free quart of pop with every medium or large pizza. A few weeks ago, I was over at the Royal Cue and the owner's kid, Spencer, gave me a slice to try, and it was right on. And then last week, Bonny and I ordered a pizza from there. It was so good; we ate a whole large mushroom and onion."

Norm then said to Gary, "Shane, do me a favor and take a ride over there. It's like two minutes from here. Let's see if I can get that delivery job." Shane pulled up in front of Pagliacci's, and the 'help wanted' deliveryman sign was still in the window. Norm got out, and then Shane parked around the corner on Bronx Street across from the Royal Cue. As Shane and I waited in the car, we noticed that there seemed to be a big game going on in the pool hall, as a bunch of people were gathered around one of the tables.

"Who's playing?" I asked Shane.

"I can't tell. Too many people blocking the view."

Norm came back, "I got the job. I start Friday at four."

"What about the ballpark? Won't it be cutting it too close?" I asked.

"I'm done for this season. We were only going to work through Labor Day anyhow, and the guy told me he wanted me to work all weekend. I asked him if he needed any more drivers, and he said maybe when winter comes; he starts getting busier when it gets cold out."

I replied, "Cool, come on, let's all go across the street. Looks like there's a big game going on."

As we entered the Royal Cue, Norm pointed out, "Hey, it's a game between Jeff Williams and Jimmy Grimes."

The crowd watching was mostly the older greasers who hung out a lot at All Star Bowl, which included Babe and Nick Caruso, Gene Marines, Chuck Reynolds, Hoppe, Al Pestine, and Ronny Singer. Two of Jeff's good friends, Kenny David and Steve Levin, were also there. Jimmy was a short, skinny, twenty-one-year-old guy who was always looking to bully somebody if he thought they were weaker. He was always picking on Tommy, the mentally handicapped kid, who helped the owner, Ben, and his son, Spencer, around the pool hall with cleaning up, brushing the tables, and, for the big games, racking the balls. As we got there, Tommy was racking the balls, and it was Jimmy's turn. Jimmy was winning and only needed twenty balls to get to the 125 win, while Jeff needed forty-five balls to win. Jimmy then shot a safety shot off the break and wasn't happy, as he left Jeff with a shot. Right then and there, Jimmy slapped Tommy hard in the back of the head. "You fucking retard—the rack was too loose."

Tommy screamed. Then Nick Caruso said, "You hit him again and I will take this fucking pool cue and shove it right up your ass!"

"But, Nick, the fucking retard racked the balls too loose."

"His name is Tommy, and you hit the cue ball too hard. The rack was perfect. It's your shot, Williams."

Jeff replied, "I've got to piss first." Jeff then went into the men's room and took a big hit of hash with his friend Kenny, then walked out of the john smiling. Jeff then proceeded to run three racks to win the game.

"You owe me twenty-five bucks, Jimmy."

"Let's play again."

"Not today; I've got to get home."

"Then fuck you. I'm not paying you, Williams."

Then Nick Caruso grabbed Jimmy by the hair, slamming his head down on table eight.

Jimmy then yelled, "Okay, I'll pay him!"

Tommy started laughing, which got the whole pool hall laughing. Jimmy handed Jeff the money and told him, "This isn't over, you little kike; you owe me a rematch."

"Anytime, Jimmy."

As Jimmy walked out, Norm yelled, "Get the fuck out of here, you fucking antisemite."

Chapter 5

College Deferment and Christmas Tree Weed

On September 9, 1968, Norm and I started Central Y Community College, while many of our friends were going away to other colleges. Some went away not only to escape the draft but also to party, with some fleeing the cold Chicago winters for schools in a warm climate. Many of my friends attended Arizona State, Miami Dade, and a variety of schools that were easy to get into and had reputations for being party schools. The kids from Skokie who wanted to go to college were spread across the country, some by choice, some by affordability, and some by grades.

A few who graduated at the top of their class would end up at Harvard or Yale or one of the other Ivy League schools. While some of the top athletes from Skokie were able to get athletic scholarships to various schools across the country, guys like me and Norm with lousy grades, who needed a college deferment, and had to work, ended up going to a local junior college. On that first day at Central Y Community College, we found ourselves surrounded by the United Nations. What I mean to say is: kids from all over Chicagoland of every nationality, race, creed, and color were our classmates. After orientation, it was time for lunch.

Norm said, "Let's go get a steak. I love Tad's steaks with baked potato and garlic bread for a dollar and forty-nine cents. You can't beat it. Light that joint up, Krock."

I fired up my last joint. Out of the blue, this Black guy, Will, whom I had borrowed a pen from at orientation, tapped me on the shoulder and asked, "How about a hit for me and my friend, Howie?"

"Sure, here you go." Our new friends, Will Johnson and Howie Wong, turned out to be big potheads.

Will then said, "Man, that shit was kick-ass. You got any more, Corky?"

"Not on me, but I might be able to get some for tomorrow. And it's Krockey, not Corky."

Will replied with a big smile, "All right, my man, Krockey. How much for a lid?"

"They're like twenty-five each. How much are you looking for?"

"I don't know, maybe like two lids? One for me and one for my man, Wong."

Wong then said, "I'll take more if you can get it."

I replied, "Let me see what I can do. I can meet you guys at the Little Corporal tomorrow morning before school."

"Where?" Wong asked.

Norm explained, "You know, that coffee shop on Wacker Drive about a half a block from the school." After sharing the joint with our new friends, we decided that instead of Tad's Steaks, we would all go to Wimpy's for a twenty-nine-cent hamburger and a twenty-cent milkshake. After lunch, we all walked back to school.

Norm then said, "C'mon, let's get back upstairs; there's another two hours when we pick out our classes." So the four of us went back up the elevator to the fourth floor, where registration was, and ended up registering for a lot of the same classes while becoming fast friends.

For the first few weeks, Norm, Will, Howie, and I would go to most of our classes, but as the weeks wore on, Norm and I started to cut more and more classes, going to matinees at the great downtown movie houses. We saw some double features for the ages that year. The first matinee double feature was at the Woods Theatre, *The Heart Is a Lonely Hunter,* starring Alan Arkin, and *Guns for San Sebastian,* with two of my favorite actors, Anthony Quinn and Charles Bronson. Although I liked Quinn and Bronson in the movie, I thought *Heart* was a much better movie. Having only seen Arkin once before in *The Russians Are Coming,* I thought Arkin's performance as a deaf mute was very real and well-acted.

That semester, I saw more movies than I had ever seen, these classic old movie houses. I went to the State-Lake Theatre to see *Once Upon a Time in the West* and *Hang 'Em High,* then The Chicago Theatre to see a Steve McQueen double feature, *The Thomas Crown Affair* and *Bullitt,* and The Oriental to see *2001: A Space Odyssey.* We also went to the McVicker's Theater, which had mostly horror movies, seeing both *Night of the Living Dead* and *Rosemary's Baby* there. Pretty scary.

The Clark Theatre stayed open twenty-four hours, showing old movies, and on certain days they showed just Marx Brothers movies. On other days they just showed Bogart movies or other classics. The following year, when we started staying out all night more, we would sometimes end up at the Clark or at The Playboy Theatre, which showed eclectic picks into the wee hours of the morning. It was there I saw films like John Cassavetes's *Faces* or the foreign-made *The Day of the Owl* with Claudia Cardinale. I had always been a big movie fan, and that year set in stone my lifetime appreciation of film.

In cutting classes, we also found ourselves exploring and discovering new restaurants. Some days, Gary Shane would drive downtown to meet us for lunch or to go to the movies. One of our favorites was Bob Elfman's right next to The Chicago Theatre. Elfman's would grill hot dogs and fry potato pancakes right in the window. In those days, you could get a jumbo hot dog with a potato pancake and a drink all for thirty-five cents. We would also discover Little Italy, where we would go for a beef sandwich at Al's on Taylor Street or Mamma Vittori's Italian Beef on Polk and May. We also loved Tufano's Vernon Park Tap for lemon chicken, or my favorite, eggplant parmigiana, all at a reasonable price. Howie Wong introduced us to Chinatown, taking us to his cousin's place, Emperor's Choice Chinese Restaurant, one of the oldest restaurants in Chinatown, which I still go to today.

By Thanksgiving, we were lucky to make it to two or three classes a week. Central Y Community College was not hard, and we needed to stay in school to maintain our draft deferment. But by Thanksgiving, we both wanted to find another school, as Norm and I were getting mostly Ds. Norm had a cousin who was a principal at Robert Morris Business School, also in the Loop. His parents made some kind of arrangement for him to start there in January. With my parents struggling for money and my grades being what they were, I felt I might have to stay at Central Y. I would have to figure it out soon, as registration for next semester would start in January, which was coming up.

The one constant in my life was the Kinetic Playground. Some of the acts I would see and many for the first time that October, November, and the first part of December were:

- October 4–6: John Mayall, Pacific Gas & Electric
- October 11: Jeff Beck Group, Pacific Gas & Electric, Fever Tree
- October 12–13: Rotary Connection, Pacific Gas & Electric, Fever Tree
- October 18–20: Steppenwolf, 18 only, Ten Years After
- October 21–22: Moody Blues, Rotary Connection
- October 25–26: Quicksilver Messenger Service, SRC
- November 1–2: Moby Grape, Eire Apparent, (1st) Rotary Connection
- November 8: Spencer Davis, Rhinoceros

- November 9: Canned Heat, Rhinoceros
- November 15–16: Moody Blues, Rotary Connection, Charles Lloyd
- November 22–23: Blue Cheer, Creedence Clearwater Revival
- November 27–28: Grateful Dead, Procol Harum, Terry Reid
- November 29–30: Canned Heat, Tim Buckley, Terry Reid; Mike Bloomfield sat in with Canned Heat on the 30th
- December 6–7: Deep Purple, Lee Michaels, Buddy Miles Express
- December 13–14: Iron Butterfly, Group Image, Masters of Deceit

This stream of talent was incredible. I became so into the whole music scene and began listening to *Ron Britain's Psychedelic Circus* show on WCFL religiously and reading each edition of *Rolling Stone* from cover to cover. I couldn't get enough of this new wave of rock bands. I also fell deeper into the blues and jazz scene. The Kinetic would soon start booking more blues and jazz, along with some premier rock bands. I had recently put a new eight-track player in my Buick and started buying eight tracks of all these bands while still building my vinyl album collection.

One evening in October '68, Cookie Gordon walked into La Rosa's on Dempster, where I was now delivering pizzas with Norm after he quit Pagliacci's because La Rosa was much busier, allowing us to make more money. "Cookie, what are you doing here?" I asked. "You're supposed to be in Arizona."

"I know, but I brought gifts."

"What are you talking about?"

Cookie whispered in my ear, "Fifty pounds of weed."

"Where is it?" I asked.

"In my trunk."

Just then, Fat Louie yelled out to me that my orders were ready for delivery.

"C'mon, Randy (Cookie's real name), take a ride with me," I said.

"What about my car?"

"Leave it here; nobody's going to bother it," I replied.

On the way to my first delivery, Randy asked me, "Krock, you think I can keep this grass in your parents' basement?"

I answered, "Are you crazy? My parents would kill me!"

"C'mon, Krock, you know the only ones who go down there are your mom and the lady downstairs to do laundry, and the other two apartments use the basement on the other side. You've got that extra shed that you built to keep that shitty old pinball machine your uncle gave you, the one without the flippers. And now that you sold that old pinball machine, all you keep in there are your old baseball cards and those old *Playboy* magazines. Remember when we used to ditch high school and we all played cards down there? Nobody comes down into your basement, especially now that your mom is working. Plus, all the pot is packed up in two suitcases, and the weed's double-wrapped in plastic. I also put some talcum powder in the suitcase for the smell. How about I give you a pound for letting me use your basement?"

"How is it?" I asked.

"Pretty good. It will get you stoned. Not as good as the Jamaican, but you get a nice buzz."

"How much is it?"

"I paid sixty-five dollars a pound. This pilot, who just got back from Vietnam who we met through these chicks at ASU, landed three hundred pounds in the desert outside Phoenix. Me, Daryl Schwartz, and Eddie Barrons are supposed to sell it all. This is a trial run. Daryl and Eddie also did a trial run. All three of us drove straight through in three separate cars."

"That's nuts! You could have gotten busted, especially with your long hair and your hippie garb."

Randy looked at me with a big goofy smile. "Well, I did wear a cowboy hat. A ten-gallon one. But no, you're right, Krock, but we had no choice. Sarge, the pilot, fronted us the weed and said we had to drive the first load ourselves, and after he gets the first payment, we can hire drivers."

"You took quite a chance. Okay, tell you what, you can keep it in my basement shed. But if you can't sell it all in a couple weeks, you're going to have to find somewhere else."

So that night after work and after telling Norm about it, Cookie and I went back to my parents' house, where we decided to leave the weed in the car till morning, as my mom and dad would be working all day. Cookie ended up sleeping on the floor of my bedroom in his sleeping bag. The next morning, he and I walked into the kitchen while my mom was finishing her toast and coffee before going to work. The good thing was my mom didn't really know Randy or his parents, having only met him once a couple of years back when I first met him after he transferred to Niles North from Maine East.

"Good morning, gentlemen," my mom greeted us.

"Morning, Mom. Hope you don't mind; Randy slept over after helping us out on the deliveries at La Rosa's last night. He brought his sleeping bag. You remember Randy?"

"Yes, I think so. Good to see you again, Randy. You boys help yourself to some breakfast."

"Thank you, Mrs. Krockey."

As my mom headed for the door, she turned around and asked me, "Will you be home for dinner?"

"No, Mom, I start work at four. Is it okay if Randy stays a couple more nights? They are remodeling the bathrooms in his parents' house."

"Sure, as long as you both clean up after yourselves. Have a good day, boys."

"You too, Mrs. Krockey."

"You want some coffee, Cookie?"

"No, thanks. Do you have any juice?"

"Yeah, there should be some OJ in the fridge."

"Is it fresh?"

"I don't think so. It's in a carton."

"I only drink fresh."

"What the fuck? That's all we got."

"Do you have any organic tea?"

"Look in that cabinet," I replied, shaking my head.

Since going to college in Arizona, Cookie grew his hair to his shoulders and became a chanting vegetarian. What I didn't know was that he was starting to mess with heroin. We split a pumpernickel bagel and I downed two cups of coffee while Cookie had a cup of Lipton tea before we headed to the basement. Once we were in the shed, Cookie opened the first suitcase, and I looked down to see individually wrapped bricks of grass enveloped in pink or green plastic. Each brick weighed close to a kilo, approximately 2.2 pounds. "Krock, grab one of these keys and we can take it upstairs and weigh up some ounces for samples."

"Randy, I don't have a scale. I only have a lid scooper that measures a lid. Plus, I don't want to smell up my parents' apartment with weed. We can do it down here."

"Krock, you must know someone with a scale. We're going to need one if we're going to move all this pot. Guys buying pounds or keys want the right weight."

I replied, "You know what, Jeff Williams has a triple beam. I'll run upstairs, grab some baggies, and call Norm and ask him to go by Jeff's. Wait here; I'll be right back."

I called Jeff's house first, "Hi, Mrs. Williams, is Jeff there?"

"He just walked out the door for school. Let me see if I can catch him. Oh, Jeff, your friend Krockey is on the phone."

"What's up, Krock? I'm on my way to school."

"I need a favor. I need to borrow your triple beam."

"Okay, but it's in the garage and I have school today. Remember, I'm still in my last year at Niles East."

I then suggested, "How about if Norm comes by and gives you a ride to school, and you give him the triple beam? We really need a scale. We're getting a bunch of pot. Are you interested?"

"Sounds groovy, man. You know me, Krock; I'm always interested in weed. What kind of weed?"

"Mexican from Oaxaca. Pretty good. Not that low-grade Mexican shit with all the seeds," Jeff replied.

"Well, you know, I'm a hash and ganja guy, but I could probably sell a shitload. Have Norm pull around back and meet me in the garage."

"Thanks, man, I'll check you later and lay some of this weed on you for lending us the scale."

I called Norm, and he headed over to Jeff's. After grabbing a box of baggies from my mom's storage cabinet, I ran down the back stairs to the basement. As I walked into the shed, I could see Cookie had rolled a few joints on an old shoebox lid from a box that held my old baseball cards. "Make sure you put the lid back on with the rubber band when you're done rolling and put it back on the top shelf."

"No problem. Let's go outside and smoke a joint in your back-yard," Cookie suggested.

"We better not smoke in the backyard," I said. "We can go down the street to the park. Norm is not going to be here for at least half an hour as he needs to drop Williams off at school. We don't want the neighbors seeing us smoking a joint or smelling anything with all that pot in the basement."

We headed down the alley behind my building to Winnebago Park. It was about eight in the morning when we approached the park, and the only one there was Mike, a mentally and physically handi-capped twelve-year-old shooting baskets whom I was always friendly with. Mike practiced every day, and even with all his limitations, he was a pretty good shot from five or six feet. So much so that we would sometimes let Mike join one of our neighborhood pickup games.

Everybody in the neighborhood loved Mike as he was always cheerful and always offering to help carry a neighbor's grocery bags or help clean up after a neighbor mowed their lawn. My dad would often ask Mike to help him with the lawn, and occasionally as a reward, my dad would take Mike (after checking with his mom) to Mike's favorite place, Cock Robin, for a hamburger and a One in a Million, Cock Robin's name for their milkshake. My dad would sometimes call Mike Mr. One in a Million.

"Hey, Mike. How's it going?"

"Okay, Krockey. You play basketball?"

"Not today, Mike. Here, let me take one shot."

Mike passed me the ball, and I took my eight-footer and missed. Mike laughed and said, "Take one more." He passed me back the ball. Swish. "Nice shot, Krockey."

"See you later, Mike."

Cookie and I walked to the far side of the park behind some bushes and lit up a joint. After we each took a few hits, it started to creep on me, giving me a nice mellow buzz.

"Not bad, Randy. I like it. We can sell this shit."

"I told you, Krock."

On the way back, we saw Norm parking his Falcon right in front of my parents' building. As we reached the front door, Norm was right behind us, carrying what looked like a toolbox but was really the scale case. "Did you call for a plumber, sir?" Norm asked with a smile as we all walked down the stairs to the basement.

"Make sure you lock the front basement door behind you," I told Norm as I went to make sure the back door was double locked.

Norm asked, "How are we going to do this?"

"If we break up one of those bricks, it's going to make a mess."

Randy said, "Krock, hand me that crosscut saw on the wall. I saw these guys at school take a butcher knife and use it to cut sections off before they broke it up to make lids. That saw should work even better."

I replied, "Right on, Cookie, but first let me run upstairs and get some newspaper to lay on the floor."

Cookie said, "You had better bring a couple of brown paper grocery bags and some Scotch tape too if you have them."

(Note: This was right before Ziplocs or people using plastic garbage bags became popular. My family still used brown paper grocery bags for garbage.)

As I spread yesterday's *Sun-Times* on my parents' basement floor, Cookie grabbed the crosscut saw off the pegboard wall and started to cut one of the bricks in half while laying one half on the newspaper to make lids that would weigh one ounce exactly. He put the other half in one of the brown paper grocery bags, then rolled up the bag tightly before placing it in the one suitcase with the other bricks.

Norm said, with a laugh, "Break that weed up with those big hands of yours, Krock."

After breaking up the brick, we weighed out fifteen ounces and rolled about a dozen joints. After Cookie closed the suitcase, I told him to move those paint cans from under the bottom shelf and shove those two suitcases all the way in there, and then put the paint cans in front, blocking the suitcases from sight.

"It still smells a little like weed in here," Norm said.

I went into the clothes closet outside the shed where my mom kept her seasonal clothes and grabbed a few mothballs, spreading them out in the shed. "That should do it. It smells just like my grandma's Persian lamb." While smiling at my friends, I said, "C'mon, let's go upstairs and make some calls."

Once in the kitchen, Norm grabbed the salami hanging from one of the cabinet doors next to the sink, "You guys want a piece?"

"Yeah, cut me off a small piece," I replied.

"How about you, Cookie?"

"Not me, man. I don't eat meat anymore."

Norm replied, "Oh, I forgot you're a flower child now."

Cookie answered, "That shit will kill you guys."

"Yeah, but it tastes so good," Norm answered as he bit into the big chunk of salami he had cut off for himself. He then asked, "Who should we call first, Krock?"

"How about Will from school? He's been buying weed from us every week. He's always telling us how much weed he can sell and asking can we get more."

"You have his number, Krock?"

"Somewhere, but I'll need to look for it. Norm, I think you wrote it down in one of your books when we were all having lunch the other day." Then Norm shouted, "You're right. I wrote it in my Spanish book. I'll be right back. I got it in my car."

When Norm ran up the stairs, Cookie asked, "Who's Will?"

I replied, "Oh, he's this cool Black dude we go to junior college with. We've sold him a bunch of weed before."

Cookie asked, "Do you front him or does he pay up front?"

"No, we front it to him."

"Where's he from?" Cookie asked.

"The South Side," I answered. Norm came back in with his Spanish book and called Will.

"What did he say?" I asked.

Norm replied with a smile, "He said the South Side is dry and he could use all we got. He said he would like to start out with five or ten pounds."

"You guys trust a Black guy from the South Side?" Cookie asked suspiciously.

Norm replied, "Well, listen to Mr. Flower Child. Are you prejudiced?"

"C'mon, guys, I'm not prejudiced. I just don't want to get ripped off."

I said, "You're not going to get ripped off. What do you think, Norm?"

"Nobody's ripping anybody off. I told Will we could meet him halfway. We both agreed to meet in the parking lot at Manny's and then he could follow me a few blocks to one of the streets by those old warehouses where there is hardly anyone around."

I responded, "Good idea, Norm."

Cookie asked, "How much do you want to give him?"

"He said he could move ten pounds in less than a week."

Cookie said, "You sure you want to give him that much?"

"Yeah. If I'm going to drive all the way to Manny's, I'd rather make as few trips as possible."

"Okay, but you and Krockey are responsible."

I agreed. "Cool. Call him back, Norm."

When Norm got off the phone, he told us, "I'm meeting him at one-thirty at Manny's. I told him $135.00 a pound."

Cookie said, "Okay, we can split the profit. I get half, and you and Krockey split the other half."

"Who else can we sell some to, Krock?" Norm asked.

"I'm going to meet Jeff Williams after he gets out of school. He's good for at least two pounds and Shane's good for at least a pound or two."

Norm suggested, "Here, let's make a list."

After making the list and calling everyone, we ended up selling another ten pounds that day to mostly friends or guys we had sold to before, charging a little more for smaller amounts. It turned out Will ended up moving the rest of the pot over the next five or six days and was the quickest to pay us. The following Friday, Norm and I met Will at Manny's for lunch and to get paid for the last of the pot we gave him.

During lunch, Will asked us, "Is there more of this weed coming?"

We told him, "Yes, and we will let you know when the next shipment will be coming in."

Will said, "I haven't seen you two around school too much lately. You don't want to get thrown out and then have to go in the Army or to Vietnam."

Norm replied, "I think we will be okay. We just got our report cards, and I passed everything. Of course, we had to give Mr. Garcia fifty bucks to pass Spanish. Yeah, he passed both me and Krock for half a hundred."

Will and I started laughing as Will asked, "Are you kidding me?" That's crazy. How about you, Krockey?"

"I got mostly Ds like Norm, but I did get an A in business math."

"Yeah, Krock is skilled at math," Norm said.

I said, "The key is always showing up for all the tests. You know, checking in occasionally and staying in touch with other students to make sure you know when the tests are."

"Oh, so that's why you guys call my grandmother's house all the time."

"Yes, Will, and also to see if you could use more weed."

Will asked, "Are you guys registering for next semester?

Norm replied, "No, I'm going to Morris Business School."

"Really, with your grades? How the fuck, did you manage to do that?"

"My cousin's assistant principal is in charge of admissions at Morris, and my dad told me not to ask any questions and that I better not goof off."

"How about you, Krockey?"

"Probably staying at Central Y."

"Well, registration is next week, so you better make up your mind. When do you think the next load of pot is coming in?"

"Our friend said a couple weeks."

Norm changed the conversation, "Krock, do you have any change? We need to call Louie at La Rosa's to see what time he wants us to come in."

"Here's a dime, Norm."

After Norm called, I asked, "What did he say?"

"He said we should be there at four and that Mike Mann is also working."

When we showed up at La Rosa's, Mike Mann was already there, sitting in the back booth. Mike was a year older than Norm and me and had gone to Evanston High. As we approached the booth, he was filling out some kind of form. "What have you got there, Mike?" Norm asked.

"It's an application for this school. I'm going to start in January."

"I have to be accepted and in school by January or I could get drafted."

"What school is it?" I asked.

"It's called the Midwestern Broadcasting School. It's a school that teaches you all about radio and TV announcing. They even help you get your FCC license."

I responded, "Wow, that's cool."

Mike went on to say, "And the brochure says they will help you get a job."

I asked if I could see the brochure. "This looks really cool. Is it hard to get in?"

"Not really. All you need is a high school diploma and 320 dollars."

Norm looked at me and spoke, "Krock, you should go for it. You'd be perfect. You do all those imitations, and nobody knows more about music than you."

I responded, "Yeah, but 320 bucks. My parents are broke. I would have to pay for it myself."

Norm told me, "So, you just made a little over four hundred dollars with the pot, and I know you saved at least a G-note from the ballpark."

"You're right, Norm. This will be way more fun than junior college at Central Y, and maybe Mike and I could become big disk jockeys like Dick Biondi or Ron Britain. What do I need to do, Mike?"

"I'm going down there Monday morning to register. I could pick you up and we could register together."

"What about the application?" I asked.

"You could fill it out when you get there. Just bring a check for $320."

"Can I bring cash? I don't have a checking account."

"I'm sure they will be happy to take your cash. But I must tell you, it is only an eight-week course, and I'm not sure how long the student deferment will last. I figure I can always sign up for more classes."

I looked at Mike, threw my hands up in the air, and replied, "Sounds good to me. I'm in, Michael."

So, the following Monday, Mike picked me up in his Plymouth Valiant and we headed downtown to Wabash Avenue. We parked under Grant Park in the public garage, splitting the two dollars and fifty cents cost for all-day parking. After registering, we looked around the school and saw that they had all this radio and TV equipment, which was very exciting for us both. After everyone had finished registering, the owner of the school welcomed us and told us he would see us all next year.

After we left the school, I noticed a Rose Records store down the street and suggested we go in. I loved going into record stores and talking to the clerks and getting turned on to new sounds. After browsing in this large record store, Mike bought the Beatles' *Magical*

Mystery Tour and I bought an eight-track tape of Janis Joplin's *Cheap Thrills* album.

The next day, Cookie called my house and said that in about a week he was coming in with over a hundred pounds. When Cookie arrived the following week, he called my house. My sister, Sherry, answered. "Al, it's for you. It's Randy Gordon."

"Hi, Krock."

"Where are you?" I asked.

"I'm right outside Madison, Wisconsin."

"What are you doing in Wisconsin?"

"My friend Chris, who drove the load in, has a farm up here, and we are going to unload the truck in his barn."

I then asked, "Truck? What truck?"

Randy replied, "It's a pickup truck loaded with plywood and hollowed out in the middle to hide the weed, with two metal straps tightly wrapped around the wood to keep it in place."

"Pretty cool," I replied.

"Do you have a pen?" Randy asked.

"Here's the directions."

I picked Norm up and we headed for this farm in Wisconsin. When we got there, Cookie was sitting on the porch with his hippie friend Chris, Chris's wife, Mary, and their two kids, six-year-old Arlo and his five-year-old sister, Aspen, along with their dog, Ranger. Chris and Mary were in their late twenties, having met at the University of Wisconsin in Madison before getting married.

Randy told us he had met Chris at a Grateful Dead concert over the summer at The Fillmore in San Francisco. I found out a few weeks later that they really had met at a heroin dealer's house, both stopping there on the way to see the Grateful Dead and becoming fast friends. It turned out that Chris was a truck driver who drove an eighteen-wheeler cross-country a couple of times a month and would stop in Tempe, Arizona, to see Randy and get high. So, when Daryl, Randy, and EB came up with this pickup truck idea, Randy called Chris to see if he wanted to fly out and drive the load back.

Chris said, "Okay, but only if you put on heavy-duty hydraulic shocks, so the pickup truck doesn't look like it is carrying a lot of weight," which was a smart idea.

As we walked up to the porch, Cookie introduced us. "Krock, Norm, this is Chris, Mary, Arlo, and Aspen." After hellos, Mary asked us, "Are you hungry? I have plenty of brown rice with vegetables."

"No thanks; we ate before we came up," Norm replied.

Then Chris, who appeared to be very tired, asked us, "Do you want to get high?" Randy gave him a look, shaking his head no at Chris.

Then Randy said to me and Norm, "C'mon, let's go into the barn and get you guys out of here."

Chris started to walk with us before Randy suggested to him, "Go lie down, as you must be tired after the long trip."

Chris then went back into the house with Mary and the kids following. When we got into the barn, Randy kept scratching.

"What's with the scratching?" Norm asked. Norm and I were still naive about hard drugs and had not yet learned about people using heroin with the nodding and scratching that sometimes went with it.

Randy replied, "I think I got this itch from sleeping in the barn last night. I flew in yesterday and slept in the barn last night to wait for Chris to drive in today with the load."

"How much do you have?"

"Right around 250 pounds. Do you guys think you can move a hundred pounds?"

"I think so," I replied.

Then Norm looked at Randy and told him, "No problem, man."

We loaded up fifty pounds into the trunk and headed back to Skokie. I dropped Norm off, leaving the pot in the car while I slept.

When I got up the next morning, I called Will, telling him the load of pot had come in.

"Krockey, I can use whatever you have."

I replied, "I've got fifty pounds. Do you want to meet us by that spot, a few blocks from Manny's on Polk Street, by that empty warehouse?"

"What time?" Will asked.

"It's now 9 a.m., and I'll meet you there at eleven."

Will ended up selling the fifty pounds in one day and paid us the next day. Norm and I headed back up to Wisconsin after Will had paid us. When we got to the farm, Cookie was there by himself.

"Where's Chris and Mary?" I asked.

Cookie told us, "Chris, Mary, and the kids went up to Iowa to deliver a load of Christmas trees in his eighteen-wheeler."

"How much is left?" Norm asked.

"Sixty pounds. Daryl and EB sold the rest."

We loaded up the car with the remaining sixty pounds that were left and headed back to Chicago.

On Saturday morning, November 16, Will called my house and said he had sold everything.

"When do you want to meet?" I asked.

Will replied, "I'm going to see my friend, Minnie Ripperton, and her band, the Rotary Connection, at the Kinetic Playground tonight. I could meet you guys up on the North Side before the show."

I asked Will, "You know Minnie Ripperton? She is so groovy and a tremendous singer. How do you know her?"

Will replied, "I grew up with her. Her dad and my dad were both Pullman porters and good friends, and we both went to Hyde Park High School."

"Wow, that's so cool. She has such a gorgeous voice, and I love the Rotary Connection," I replied.

Will then told me, "She's been singing since we were little kids and was training to be an opera singer."

Then I suggested, "Why don't Norm and I meet you at the Playground?"

"We planned on going anyway. Plus, I wanted to see the other acts: the Moody Blues, who I have never seen live but always loved the song 'Go Now,' and this incredible sax and flute player, Charles Lloyd, who Bob Koester from the Jazz Record Mart turned me on to. Amazing triple bill. Norm and I will meet you there at eight."

When we arrived that night at the Kinetic Playground, Will was waiting out front with his girlfriend, Kim. Kim was a beautiful, petite, light-skinned Black woman with a big afro who was now in her first year at Northwestern, hoping to follow in her father's footsteps in becoming a doctor. If she knew Will was dealing pot, she would have dropped him like a hot potato. So, we had to be careful around her.

All three bands were very different but exceptional, each in their own distinctive way. Charles Lloyd with the fantastic keyboard player Keith Jarrett, the solid Cecil McBee on bass, and the amazing Jack DeJohnette on drums all blew my socks off. Very groovy with that show, pushing me to expand my interest in jazz. Then, the Rotary Connection came on with Minnie's haunting voice. In this psyche-delic soul band, everyone sang well while complementing each other with a kind of psychedelic harmony. One of the songs that really stood out was an inspired version of the Rolling Stones' "Lady Jane."

Finally, the Moody Blues came on. They had built up a big fol-lowing after coming out with *Days of Future Passed*, combining rock with classical. I had a few friends who were diehard Moody Blues fans and who loved to smoke weed with their headphones on and listen to *Days of Future Passed*. Although I wasn't as big a fan as my friends, I thought they put on an excellent show.

On the way out, Norm and Will slipped into the bathroom where Will gave Norm two paper bags with our cash, which Will had stuffed in both of his cowboy boots. With Norm following Will's lead, stuffing the two bags of money down his Frye boots, they came out, and we all said our goodbyes.

"See you guys in school Monday," Will said as he and Kim headed for Will's car.

By the time we got in my car, it was almost one-thirty in the morning. Norm suggested we drive straight to the farm to give Cookie his money.

"I'm starving, Norm. Why don't we stop at Jack's first and then drive up?"

Norm said, "I'm hungry too."

"But I've got a sneak spot that I went to with a couple of the Hollywood Park guys. You'll love it. It's this cool little twenty-four-hour greasy spoon called Cooper & Cooper. It's right off Lawrence on Kimball."

We walked into Cooper & Cooper, which was a small grill with ten stools and a counter. Sitting there were two three-hundred-pound guys chowing down. One was an older guy, Ritchie Acres, whom Norm had met through Bobby (Buggy) Falstein and I had seen around Hollywood Park. And the other guy was the famous Black soul singer, Baby Huey from Baby Huey and the Babysitters, whom I loved and had seen a few times.

"What's up, Richie?

Richie answered, "How are you doing? I'm sorry, I forgot your name, plus I'm a little stoned."

"I'm Norm; I met you a couple of times when my friend Bobby and his band, the Domineers, opened for Mr. Huey at the Deep End in Park Ridge."

"Oh yeah, you and your friends helped us load the equipment that one night when our roadie didn't show up. Here, let me buy you breakfast."

"That's not necessary," Norm said.

"No, I insist."

Norm said, "Thank you. What's on that cheeseburger you guys are eating?"

"This is a special double cheeseburger with a fried egg on top. And you must try the hand-cut French fries."

Baby Huey said, "These motherfucking fries are out of sight."

Richie introduced us. "This is Ramey (Baby Huey's real name)."

"How's it going?" Ramey said.

"Groovy," I said nervously, as he was a big local star. "I love your music. I saw you a couple times at the Cheetah. Once with the Exceptions and the other time with the band HP Lovecraft. You and the band were smoking both times. And those horns with your voice. Super boss."

"What will it be, fellas?" the counter man asked.

Norm replied, "Give us two of those special double cheeseburgers with the egg on top, an order of fries, and two Pepsis."

While we ate, Ramey and Richie told us a story about the time they were flown to Paris by the Rothschild family to play a coming-out party for their daughter and describing what a wild time they had fooling around with all these rich and wild French chicks who loved to party.

"Sounds like a crazy cool time," I said. "I heard you a couple times on WVON with your version of 'Messin' with the Kid,' which I really liked. When are you guys going to come out with an album?"

Huey answered, "Real soon, my man. Real soon. Look at you, listening to WVON."

"Of course, that's my favorite station. Huey—I mean, Ramey— check out my Buick outside. I've got a WVON sticker on one back window and a WGCI on the other. I'm a big music nut, especially soul."

"Well, shit, my little soul pal, come see us play anytime. Let Richie know and he will get you in for free."

"Thank you. It's been an honor. Do you guys want a joint?"

I handed Ritchie a joint and he responded, "Thank you, man."

Norm and I headed for Wisconsin, arriving at the farm around eight in the morning. When we got there, we looked through the front window and saw Cookie sleeping on the pull-out couch with some gal I didn't recognize. It was about fifty degrees that day, unusually warm for November, with the sun shining. Norm and I decided to wait on the porch until everyone woke up. We both drifted off in big wooden chairs after smoking a joint.

I woke up to the dog, Ranger, licking my hand, and upon opening my eyes there stood Cookie, naked, with a blanket around his shoulders, and with a pretty blonde gal who was also somewhat naked, with just Cookie's button-down long-sleeve shirt on, but open enough where we could see her breasts. Each had a joint in their mouth while holding what appeared to be a cup of coffee, or maybe tea in Cookie's case. "Would you guys like some coffee?" asked this lovely woman.

"Sounds just right. What's your name?" Norm asked.

"I'm Pam, Mary's sister." As she started to go back to the kitchen to get our coffee, she turned around and asked us how we liked it.

Norm answered with a big grin on his face, "Cream and sugar for both of us."

After she went inside, Norm commented, "What nice tits she has."

"Yeah, I know," Cookie said.

While Norm handed Cookie two brown paper bags filled with money, I said, "Here's your cash, Cookie. When's the next load?"

"Not sure, guys."

Arlo and Aspen came out on the porch. We said our good mornings to the kids, who laughed and ran back into the house. Soon, Pam walked out with a big percolator full of coffee, setting it down on the big picnic bench in the front yard. Mary and Chris followed.

Mary asked, "Are you guys hungry? Do you mind eating out here? The house is a mess?"

Cookie smiled. "No problem, but only if you make your famous blueberry and banana pancakes."

Then Mary asked Norm and me, "How about you guys?"

"Sounds delicious," Norm replied as I nodded.

"These pancakes are unbelievable, Mary, and how was your trip delivering the Christmas trees, Chris?"

He replied, "It was super cool. After picking up the trees in Mindoro, which is only about two and a half hours from here, we drove for another hour and a half and delivered the trees to a place in the Dells. We checked into this really nice hotel that the kids love. They have a fun indoor pool with all these slides and an out-of-sight game room. We also really needed the money. Between the money I made from the trees and the money from driving the pot, I was able to pay our mortgage up to date, as we were already two months behind.

"We were going to use the money I gave to the mortgage company to buy more Christmas trees like I did last year, but we were afraid we could lose the house. Last year, I took a whole load of trees to a guy with several lots in Milwaukee and doubled my money. So this year I made the same deal, and now these guys are expecting me to deliver the trees on Thursday or Friday, like I did last year, a few days before Thanksgiving.

"The problem is, last month my cousin had told me he would invest $2,500, which would have paid for the trees. I was going to sell them all for somewhere between five thousand and six thousand and split the profit with him. But my cousin called me last night saying he won't be able to give me the money as his wife is about to have their baby, and it was money his wife's parents had given them to pay for the hospital and baby expenses. His wife, Tina, told him it was too risky. And the guys buying the Christmas trees said they will only pay on delivery and won't front any money as they had been burned before."

I said, "Hey, maybe Norm and I could invest."

Norm spoke up. "Krock, I can't."

"Why not?" I replied.

"I was going to tell you, my dad and I are going into the vending business, and he wants me to use my savings to buy cigarette and candy machines. My dad would get the locations, and I would fill the machines after school. He's putting up $6,000 and I'm going to use the $3,000 that I've been saving since my bar mitzvah. But you should do it, Krock."

I then asked, "What about you, Cookie?"

"Chris already asked me. And I told him all my money is invested in the weed."

I said, shaking my head, "Hey, $2,500 is a lot. I only have the $1,300 we made on this load and a thousand at home. I'm still short two hundred."

Norm said, "I'll lend you the deuce. You can pay me back after the trees are sold."

I asked Chris, "How much can we make?"

"After gas, we should make somewhere between fourteen and fifteen hundred a piece."

"I'm in."

"Cool," replied Chris.

Mary said to me, "That's very cool. Why don't you come up for our big Thanksgiving dinner?"

"Thanks—maybe I will."

I added, "I'll tell you what: Norm and I are going to go back home in half an hour or so. Here's the $1,300 I made on this load and I can meet you halfway tomorrow with the rest."

Chris suggested we meet for lunch at a bowling alley, the Don Carter Lanes in Rockford, tomorrow at noon.

Norm offered to drive. "Give me the keys. I'll get us home." When we got to Norm's house, he handed me two one-hundred-dollar bills along with my car keys. When I got to Rockford the next day, I walked into Don Carter Lanes and spotted Chris sitting in the bar and grill, drinking a Hamm's.

"They have outstanding burgers here, but don't tell Mary. She wants me to be a vegetarian."

The waitress approached me. "Would you like a beer?"

"Sure, I'll take a Hamm's." Then I sang, "From the Land of Sky-Blue Waters," while Chris told the waitress to also bring us two double cheeseburgers with fries. As we ate, I handed Chris an envelope with the money under the table, trying to be discreet. "Chris, you look tired. Are you okay?" I asked.

"I'm fine. I just didn't sleep well. Aspen was up sick last night."

"Is she okay?"

"Just a bad cold. She'll be fine."

I still hadn't realized Chris was doing heroin. He said he was going up to Mindoro on Thursday morning to get the trees and would be delivering them to Milwaukee in the afternoon. When Thursday finally rolled around, I was excited when I woke up around twelve that day. My mom and dad were both at work, so I made myself a bowl of Sugar Pops, sat down at the kitchen table, and began reading the sports section of *Sun-Times* when the phone rang.

"Hi, Krockey, it's Mary, Chris's wife."

"What's wrong, Mary? Why are you crying?"

"Chris has been in an accident, but he's okay. He's in the hospital with a concussion, a broken collarbone, and his face is all cut up. The doctor said it would heal, but he probably is going to have a big scar above his left eye. Thank God it missed his eye."

"Mary, what happened? Do you want me to come up there?"

"No, there's no need."

"What about the trees?"

Mary continued to cry and then shouted, "Fuck, I can't believe this, Krockey—it was just on the Madison *News at Noon*. The truck went over a bridge in Mauston, and Chris was in the cab with the trailer hanging there above the river for close to an hour. The news showed Chris in the cab with the whole rig hanging over the bridge, and the fire department getting there just in time to save him, thank God. A fireman was lowered down on a cable, wrapped some kind of belt around Chris with Chris holding on to him for dear life, then the crew lifted both Chris and the fireman to safety, just moments before the whole cab and trailer with all the Christmas trees fell into the Wisconsin River."

For about a minute, I could not talk.

Mary then asked, "Are you still on the phone?"

I said, "Oh shit, the truck and all the trees are gone. Do you guys have insurance?"

"Yes, but just for the eighteen-wheeler, not the cargo."

All I could say was, "Tell Chris I hope he gets well soon. Goodbye."

After I hung up with Mary, I walked back into my room, grabbing a rubber baseball off the shelf and lying on my bed on my back and just throwing the ball against the wall and catching it for over an hour while listening to the latest BB King album, *Lucille*, which had the tune "No Money, No Luck," which hit home that day. Lying there feeling sorry for myself, I was completely in a daze after losing my life's savings when I heard a knock at the back door. I opened up to find Norm and Gary Shane. "What's up, guys?"

Norm replied, "I heard what happened. I'm sorry, man."

"Who told you?" I asked.

"Mary called Cookie in Arizona and Cookie called me. Cookie told me that Mary was worried they were going to find heroin in Chris's blood when they tested for alcohol. But it turned out they never tested for drugs, just alcohol. Cookie told me he was a stoned junkie."

"Why didn't he tell me this before I invested all my money with him?"

"I think Cookie fucks with it too," Norm replied.

Shane jumped in. "I know he does. Before Cookie drove the empty truck back to Arizona, he stopped by my house, and he was all fucked up and ended up sleeping over after nodding out on our basement couch with the TV on. He told me he just did it occasionally."

"Fuck that shit," Norm said.

"I've got the perfect solution. Did I ever tell you the story about when my dad lost his hot dog store and all his money? And how he was able to come back, making more money than he ever did?" Norm went on in detail to tell us the crazy tale of his father's comeback. I sat there with my mouth open as Norm relayed it.

"I was about four or five, and my sister Judy was like six or seven. My mom at the time was a part-time bookkeeper at Sally's Bar-B-Q. This was back in the '50s when Sally's Bar-B-Q was at their old location north of Devon on Western Avenue, right next to Nortown Olds. Now, whenever she went to work, Sally, the owner, would allow my mom to bring Judy and me. At the time, my dad had a little hot dog store on Lawrence Avenue where he claims he was the first person to serve a hot dog on a poppy seed bun.

"Anyways, one day when my mom was working, my dad walked into the office at Sally's and, as my mother tells the story, he was a little tipsy—or famished—as my mother puts it. You guys know my dad likes his cocktails. It was around three o'clock and the restaurant was empty except for the busboys setting up for dinner. My mom grabs my dad by the hand and takes him to a booth in the dining room, leaving Judy and me in the office with Sally and her husband, Benny. 'What's wrong, Henry?' my mom asked. 'They are not renewing our lease at the store, and now all the money we invested in is gone.'

"Just then, Harry, who was Sally's brother and who managed the kitchen, walked out of the kitchen with a bottle of Chivas Regal and sat down at one of the other tables. A few minutes after he poured himself a drink, he spotted my dad. 'Is that you, Hawk?' 'Harry?' My dad, whose nickname was Hawk, and Harry were old friends from the West Side. Now, Harry comes over and sits down. Says hello to my mom and offers them both a drink. My mom says no and tells my father she must take the kids home and make dinner, telling my father, 'We'll figure something out, Henry. We always do.' Then she tells Harry, 'Don't let him drink too much; he's already had a few.'

"Anyhow, my mom leaves, and Harry and my dad are drinking while my dad's telling him how he lost his lease and all the money he invested. Then Harry asks, 'Have you eaten?' My dad says, 'No.' 'Well, you have got to eat, and I've got the perfect remedy for your situation. My Alabama Kum-Back Sauce on a beautiful slab of ribs with homemade coleslaw and fries.' Then Harry tells him, 'Do you know what the secret of our success is here at Sally's? It's the sauce. The Alabama Kum-Back Sauce is what helped make Sally's Bar-B-Q the success it is today.'

"After that, Minnie, the cook, comes out with my dad's order. Harry then asked Minnie to tell my dad all about the secret powers of the sauce. The way my dad and my mom tell it, Minnie, a three-hundred-pound Black woman with green eyes and a red scarf around her hair, pulled up a chair right next to my dad in the booth. She had this look on her face like she meant business, which grabbed my dad's attention. Minnie started by telling my dad that only two families in the world knew of the sauce's powers: Ms. Sally's family and mine.

"'Harry is doing you a big favor, so, keep it to yourself,' she goes on to tell my dad. 'This sauce is named Alabama Kum-Back Sauce because if you use it right it will help you come back from the setbacks of life. It was originally my grandmother's recipe who was at one time a slave in Alabama.' Minnie goes on to tell him, 'Take your finger and rub some sauce behind both ears.' While my dad, at this point, is feeling no pain from all the booze, he goes ahead and puts the sauce behind both of his ears as Minnie instructed. Then Minnie tells my dad before she goes back to the kitchen, 'All you must do now is wait for the sauce to do its magic.'

"Then Harry says, 'Goodbye,' and he goes back to the kitchen. After my dad finished his meal, followed by two cups of coffee to straighten out, he gets up to go home. Just as he's walking out, he runs into Pip Levin, who came there with his friend Joe, whom my dad didn't know. Pip asks my dad to sit with them while he and his friend Joe eat. So, my dad sits down. Pip and his friend ordered their food, and my dad ordered another coffee.

"While my dad sat there sipping his coffee while these guys ate their ribs, Pip goes on to tell my dad, 'Joe is looking for a salesman for his beer company.' It turns out, Pip's friend Joe Simon was a vice president for Country Club Malt Liquor, and within fifteen minutes of putting that sauce behind his ears, this big shot Joe offers my dad a fantastic job. Of course, my dad tells him 'Yes' and has been selling Country Club Malt Liquor ever since, and the rest is history. So, Krock, that's why we're going to Sally's tonight, to get you that Alabama Kum-Back Sauce to put behind your ears."

We all started laughing. I said, "I do love their ribs, and they put crushed pineapple in their coleslaw to make it sweet. The Big Tuna was the one who told me about the crushed pineapple. The Big Tuna is Sally's cousin, and I think he still works there delivering."

Norm said, "They better be careful or the Tuna will eat all their profits."

Shane added, "Krock, you need to get out of the house and shake this shit off. C'mon, we can go back to my house and smoke some weed before we go to Sally's for that magic Kum-Back Sauce."

We all started laughing again, which is exactly what I needed that day. So, we all went back to Shane's house, as both his parents worked late. His mom, Roz, was working till nine in the men's department of Marshall Field's in Old Orchard, and his dad always came home late.

After smoking a joint on the way over, we settled into the rec room in Shane's basement to veg out before going to Sally's. After turning the channels, we found a rerun of *The Phil Silvers Show* where he played Sergeant Bilko, followed by *The Three Stooges*, which we all still liked. When the Stooges ended, we decided to watch the news. One of the news stories that day was about escaped convicts who robbed a bank in Missouri and then came to Chicago and robbed a couple in the Villa Motel on Lincoln Avenue in Chicago.

Shane said, "Maybe you could rob a bank, Krock."

Norm replied, "Not so funny, Shane. I'm starving. Let's pig out on some baby backs and rub some of that Kum-Back Sauce behind our ears. It's a lot less dangerous than robbing banks."

We jumped into Shane's car and headed for Sally's. Upon arriving at Sally's, we ran into my old downstairs neighbors, Al and Gertie Landerman, along with their two daughters, Cindy and Bonny. After saying our hellos, we sat down and ordered. While waiting for our orders, I was looking around the restaurant and noticed a few people putting touches of sauce behind their ears, including Al, Gertie, Cindy, and Bonny. While pointing this out to Norm and Shane, Howie Brown, whose father's brown Rambler was across the street, had just walked in to pick up an order to go. As he was waiting for his order, he spotted us. "What are you guys up to?"

I replied, "You're not going to believe this, Howie. I just lost my bankroll, and Norm told me this crazy story that this secret way to come back from a setback is to rub Sally's Alabama Kum-Back Sauce behind your ears."

Everybody laughed out loud, with Shane laughing so hard he fell off his chair. Norm then laughed, spitting his water back into his glass.

Howie knew the legend. "Sally, Harry, and Minnie have been telling that story for years. But the crazy part is, people still love coming here for the ribs and the sauce. I guess they figure putting a little sauce behind your ears can't hurt."

"Norm said it worked for his dad, and his mom swore by it. I have to say, it did put me in a better mood."

Skokie, Chicago, and Suburbs

Wrigley Field, back in the day, by Blake Bolinger
(*From Wikimedia Commons*)

Souvenir stand outside Wrigley Field, with
vendors Tuffy and Gary Shane, by R. Gordon

Traffic tie up on South Halsted St. near Maxwell St. Chicago,
by Charles Weaver Cushman (*From Wikimedia Common*)

Sidewalk camp meeting, Maxwell Street by Charles Weaver Cushman
(*From Wikimedia Commons*)

Martin Luther King Jr. assassination aftermath
(*From Adjusters Associated Files*)

Kinetic Playground poster (*From the author's collection*)

Kinetic Playground poster (*From the author's collection*)

Chicago Democratic Convention, 1968, by Fred Mason
(*From Wikimedia Commons*)

Grant Park, during the Democratic National Convention in Chicago,
August 26, 1968, by Warren K. Leffler (*From Wikimedia Commons*)

Pekin House, Chicago (*From the author's collection*)

Take Home A Hot Pie

BARBECUED RIBS OUR SPECIALTY	ALL OUR MEATS BARBECUED ON CHARCOAL

SANDWICHES
(Served with All The Trimmings)

BARBECUED BEEF	.95
CLUB STEAK	1.10
HAMBURGER	.75
RED HOT	.50
BARBECUED RIB	1.50
CHEESEBURGER	.85
BACON, LETTUCE AND TOMATO	.95
LETTUCE AND TOMATO	.40
GRILLED CHEESE ON TOAST	.60
CHEESE ON TOAST	.45

(French Fried Potatoes, Pickle, Cole Slaw and Apple Sauce)

PASTRIES

PIE	.30 - .35
PIE A LA MODE	.40 - .45
WHIPPED CREAM PIE	.40

FOUNTAIN

BANANA SPLITS	.65
SUNDAES	.40
SODAS	.40
MALTED MILK	.45
MILK SHAKE	.40
FUDGE SUNDAE	.55

BEVERAGES

COFFEE	.15	PHOSPHATES	.15
TEA (Hot or Iced)	.20	COCA-COLA	.15
HOT CHOCOLATE	.20	NEDLOG'S ORANGE	.15
MILK, GRADE "A"	.20	GREEN RIVER	.15
CHOCOLATE MILK	.20		
PEPSI COLA	.15	ORANGE DRINK	.15

ENJOY DINNER WITH YOUR FAMILY AT SALLY'S No Service Charge For Children	WE HAVE TRADE THAT GOOD FOOD MADE

DINNERS

BARBECUED RIBS	2.50
CHARCOAL BROILED SIRLOIN STEAK	2.75
FRIED CHICKEN	1.75
FRENCH FRIED SHRIMP	1.75

(Above Orders Served with Salad Bowl or Cole Slaw and French Fries)

JUMBO KOSHER RED HOTS (2)	1.00
GRILLED HAMBURGER STEAK	1.25

(Above Orders Served with Cole Slaw and French Fried Potatoes)

SIDE ORDERS

FRENCH FRIED POTATOES	.30
PICKLES	.30
COLE SLAW	.35
SALADS	.45

(Served with 1000 Island, French or Garlic Dressing)

OUR HOURS

MONDAY, TUESDAY, WEDNESDAY and THURSDAY	12:00 NOON TO 1:00 A.M.
FRIDAY	12 NOON TO 2:00 A.M.
SATURDAY	12 NOON TO 3:00 A.M.
SUNDAY	12 NOON TO 1:00 A.M.

DON'T LEAVE THE PARTY — CALL US
5 CARS AT YOUR SERVICE AT ALL TIMES
PROMPT DELIVERY
Phone AMbassador 2-8800

NOT RESPONSIBLE FOR LOSS OR EXCHANGE OF PERSONAL PROPERTY

Minimum of 50c Per Person

Sally's Bar-B-Q Restaurant menu, Chicago (*From the author's collection*)

Chapter 6

Broken Stride

When I woke up the next day, I knew I needed to get a second job (I was still delivering for La Rosa's). I grabbed our copy of the *Skokie Review* to look through the help wanted ads. I noticed a lot of retail stores were looking for help for the upcoming holiday season, which was just starting with Thanksgiving around the corner. An advertisement for Turn-Style Family Center in Skokie promoting their seasonal work jumped out at me. One of the jobs listed was for a stock clerk in the record department.

Turn-Style was much like the 1968 version of Walmart. It was located across from the Old Orchard Theatre and the Twin Orchard Bowl, down the street from the gigantic Old Orchard Shopping Center. If I couldn't find a job at Turn-Style, I would surely be able to find a holiday job at one of the many stores in Old Orchard. I decided to skip class that day and apply for the job. I showered, dressed, and walked into Turn-Style right at nine when they opened. I asked Florence, the lady at the customer service desk about the position.

She told me, "You'll need to talk to the store manager, Mr. Mages. He should be in any minute. Have a seat over there and fill out this application."

A few minutes later, Mr. Mages walked in and Florence told him I was there for one of the Christmas job openings. "Follow me, young man." As we walked down the hallway past his secretary into a small office, I realized I knew him. When we reached my future boss's office, he sat down behind his desk and motioned for me to take a seat, while I handed him my application.

Before I could say a word, Mr. Mages spoke. "Don't I know you? You're Krockey; you were friends with my son Michael in grammar school."

"Yes, sir. You helped me fix my bike one day in the third grade. How's Mike doing?"

"He's doing well. He goes to Ohio State and hopes to one day be a dentist. How about you, Alan? It says here you attend Central Y Junior College and that you are looking for part-time work."

"Yes, I have a couple more days of school next week, then we're off for Thanksgiving. After that, I don't go back to school until next year."

"It says here on your application that you are applying for the stock clerk position in the record department. Do you know anything about music or records?"

"Yes, sir. Music and records are a big part of my life. I spend hours every week going to different record stores and have a large collection of albums and eight-tracks."

"I understand, Alan, but this job calls for inventory control and display work. Do you have any experience?"

"As you can see, Mr. Mages, on my application, I work as a souvenir vendor at Wrigley Field during the summer. Part of my job as a souvenir vendor is stocking, taking inventory, as well as setting up the displays on the souvenir stand."

"Okay, Alan, I'll tell you what. You seem like a smart, hardworking kid. I'm going to give you the job. Can you start today?"

"Yes, sir."

Mr. Mages explained, "See, our records are stocked by a rack jobber and they happen to be coming in today."

"What's a rack jobber?" I asked.

"You see, this rack jobbing company called Handleman stocks all our records on consignment and helps us with setting up the displays. They come in a couple times a month to count the inventory, replace the records sold, and take back the records that aren't selling. During the Christmas season, they come to the store every week. Your job is to keep them honest by keeping up with the inventory and making sure Turn-Style has an accounting of every record and eight-track tape bought, sold, or returned. You will also be restocking the bins from the overstock and keeping track of what is selling and what is not.

"When you meet Ted from Handelman today, he will show you how to help him keep track of the inventory. Ted's a good guy, and he will better explain their inventory system. Lastly, and extremely important, is helping the customers find the records they're looking for and answering their questions, remembering to always be courteous. How does that sound? Do you think you can handle all that?"

"Yes, sir, Mr. Mages. One more thing, sir. I cannot work after four on Friday or Saturday night, as I have another job delivering pizza for La Rosa's on Dempster Street that starts at 4:30 p.m."

"Okay, you can work today till 4 p.m. Here's a timecard. Write your name on top, and Florence will show you where to punch in. Could you work this Sunday?"

"Yes, sir."

"Okay, meet me here at 8:45 a.m. on Sunday, and we will work out your schedule."

"Thank you so much, Mr. Mages."

Ted Fisher from the Handelman Company showed up at about ten-thirty. Ted was a twenty-six-year-old, five-foot-four-inch, balding Jewish guy from Albany Park dressed in paisley bell-bottoms and a white wide collar shirt. Ted introduced himself and was very friendly and loved talking about music. We hit it off, especially after him telling me how impressed he was about my knowledge of today's music.

After Ted laid a bunch of rolled-up posters on the counter, he handed me the keys to his van and asked. "Al, do me a favor. Please grab a hand truck and go out to the blue Chevy panel truck with the HC logo on the door. In the back, you'll find three boxes of assorted Christmas albums and four big boxes of the new Beatles' *White Album*, along with two boxes of the *White Album* eight-tracks. Also, grab those two boxes marked NR, which have various other artists' new releases."

After Ted showed me how to set up the Christmas and Beatles displays, we went over Handelman's inventory paperwork.

Ted asked me to sign the inventory report. "Here, sign here."

I responded, "Yes, but I haven't counted the records yet."

Ted replied, "That's okay. I did a quick count when you went out to the van."

"But, Ted, what about the returns?"

"Oh, I'll count those when I get back to the warehouse and then add it to the sheet. Just sign it. I will go over everything with you next time. And call me Teddy. Everyone calls me Teddy. Good job, Alan. Next week, I'll take you out to lunch." I knew something was up but decided to keep quiet for now.

I met Mr. Mages that Sunday and he gave me my schedule. On Monday and Tuesday, I had finals at school till noon, finishing up at Central Y. I ended up working every day that week except Thursday, Thanksgiving. On Wednesday, I worked from 9 a.m. till closing at 9 p.m. to get ready for the big day-after-Thanksgiving sale. I had originally planned to go see Terry Reid, Procol Harum, and the Grateful Dead that night at the Kinetic Playground, but since they were also playing Thanksgiving night, I decided to go see the show after dinner with my family.

On Thanksgiving, we had a quiet dinner at home with just my mom, dad, and sister, even though we were invited to my Aunt Edith and Uncle Abe's house. Edith was one of my dad's two older sisters.

But my parents decided to have Thanksgiving dinner at our house because Edith had invited their brother Sol, and his wife, Miriam, whom my dad was not speaking to at the time over some money issues. I spent the day with my parents and my sister. I watched the Thanksgiving parade on TV with Sherry, and I watched football with my dad, while my mom, with Sherry assisting, prepared a delicious holiday meal. Although things were not going well for my folks, and I had just lost all my money, we managed to have a good time with my dad doing his Alan King routine, insisting that Alan King had stolen his jokes from him, even though they had never met. When my dad was on, he could be very funny.

After dinner, Norm called. "Listen, Cuzzi (Bobby) is with his cousins in Highland Park and said he can't pick us up till around ten."

"But we might miss the first two acts," I replied.

Norm told me I should come over to his house because his parents were in Vegas for the weekend and that he had a surprise for me. When got there, he handed me some magic mushrooms. "Try these," he ordered nicely.

"I don't know, Norm. I've never done psychedelics."

"Krock, this isn't like acid. It's just a little bit stronger than weed. You'll like it. I ate mine an hour ago and it's a really nice high. Here's a Dr Pepper to wash it down."

Ten minutes after I ate the shrooms, Cuzzi picked us up. When I got into Cuzzi's GTO, the Chambers Brothers' "Time Has Come Today" was playing on the new eight-track player he had just bought and had installed at Auto Sound on Skokie Boulevard right next to Piazza's. The shrooms had just kicked in when Cuzzi turned up the volume and that really sent me into space, putting a smile on my face for the rest of the night.

I shouted out, "These fucking mushrooms are out of sight."

Norm, sitting in the shotgun seat, turned around with a big smile while raising his eyebrows and just said, "Groovy."

We walked into the Playground and saw that Procol Harum had just finished their set, and the stage crew was setting up for the Grateful Dead. Right before the Dead came on, the shrooms came on even stronger. All my senses seemed to be heightened; the light show was incredible that night and seemed to be moving to the beat of the psychedelic sounds coming from the music. I was truly "psychedelicized," as the Chambers Brothers put it in their song "Time Has Come Today," which I had heard earlier in Cuzzi's car.

The Dead were a remarkable jam band. I never really appreciated their albums as much as I enjoyed hearing them live. I danced all night with this sexy, fat girl who traveled with the Dead, and Cuzzi and Norm danced with her friends.

After the show, the girls invited us to a party with them. As high as I was, I almost forgot I had to be at work in the morning until Norm reminded me. Norm and Cuzzi really wanted to go to the party and had just eaten more mushrooms. I really wanted to go too, but I knew better, that I could lose my job If I showed up late or fucked up.

Earlier that night, I ran into Freddie Vedder, Chuck Perkins, and Don Grayless. Fred lived around the corner from my parents' place, so I asked them for a ride, which they were happy to do. I had gone to high school with all three of these guys. Fred and I also went through grammar school together. These guys were all part of a crowd everyone called the surfers. In high school, they dressed like surfers and even tried surfing on Lake Michigan. After jumping in Chuck's Volkswagen bus, I lit up a joint. It turned out that all three were real Dead Heads and were planning to go see them again on Sunday in Detroit.

Waking up a little groggy, I downed two cups of coffee, took a shower, and headed for work. I arrived at Turn-Style the next morning at 8:00 a.m., an hour before opening. Because of the Black Friday sale, there was a long line waiting to get in and take advantage of the deals. It was a cold, windy, and gray day for these anxious shoppers to stand in line, freezing.

After punching in, I grabbed my Turn-Style orange vest with my new Alan pin-on name tag and walked into the employee lounge for a meeting called by Mr. Mages. To my surprise, Teddy Fischer was there with a cute girl whose Handelman name tag said "Rosie." I noticed he had brought bagels. I also noticed a man from Mattel who brought donuts, and a woman from Revlon who was handing out sample bottles of perfume to the employees, and I grabbed a few for my mom and sister. The meeting was basically a pep talk for the busy day we were about to have. After the meeting, with everyone leaving except Teddy, Rosie, and me, Ted came over and suggested we sit at one of the tables in the corner. Ted then handed me a raisin bagel from New York Bagel and Bialy and asked, "Would you like some cream cheese? There's plain and chive."

"Chive sounds good, Ted."

"Please call me Teddy."

"Okay, Teddy."

Then Teddy said as he reached into his briefcase, pulling out a bunch of inventory forms, "Now, we can go over how I like the inventory done. I brought Rosie, my assistant, to help. She's going to start counting while we talk."

"But, Teddy, aren't I supposed to check the count?"

"That's what I want to talk with you about. You see, Alan, I have my own method." He showed me the paperwork already filled out. "You see, all you need to do is let me know what records and tapes are selling and which ones are not. Rosie and I do all the counting, and all you need to do is sign the sale and return sheet. For this, you get fifty dollars in cash."

I gave Teddy a questioning look and spoke, "But Mr. Mages—"

"Don't worry about Mr. Mages; you won't have any trouble from him. Nobody's going to know. Better in our pocket than the shoplifters'. Everybody in the record business does it. All the record companies allow a ten percent breakage allowance for broken or missing inventory." Just then, Rosie walked in. "Isn't that right, Rosie?"

"Whatever you say, Teddy."

I thought about my options: I could quit; tell Mr. Mages, who might be in on it; or I could take the fifty and keep my job, which is what I decided to do. I could see there was something going on between Teddy and Rosie, even though Teddy was engaged to be married to another woman in a few months.

After a few weeks working at both Turn-Style and La Rosa's, things were starting to look up as I went to work on Friday, December 20, the last weekend before Christmas. I had been able to save up around three hundred dollars after that day's paycheck, Teddy's fifty dollars, and my tips from La Rosa's. When Teddy came in that day, we slipped into the washroom, and he handed me an envelope. "Open it later, I put a little extra in."

After we walked out, we ran into Mr. Mages, who asked Teddy to come into his office. After Teddy came out of Mr. Mages's office, he walked over to the record section, shaking his head.

"What's wrong, Teddy?"

"You know, Krockey, I thought for Christmas I would give Mr. Mages a few promo records. So today I gave him Glen Campbell's newest record, Dean Martin's *Greatest Hits*, and *The Funny Girl* soundtrack, because he had told me his wife likes showtunes. He then tells me he can't accept presents from vendors. I told him these are promotional records for radio stations, record store owners, store managers, and buyers. I then told him to at least take *The Funny Girl* LP as that was for his wife. He reluctantly took it. I knew he was a straight arrow, which is why I'm glad I made the deal with you instead of him. Did I tell you I'm going to Hawaii tomorrow with Rosie and that I broke off the engagement with Marcy?"

"No, but have a good time. I will see you when you get back."

Just then, Gary Shane walked into the store with Howie Brown. Howie greeted me. "Hey, Krockey, how's it going? Do you have the Temptations' *Greatest Hits*?"

"Yes, we do, Howard. Right over there in the bin that says Temptations. Hi, Gary, how about you? Are you looking for any new albums?" Shane and I both chuckled.

"Maybe, let me look around." Shane and Howie were browsing the record bins when Shane asked, "Are you working at La Rosa's tonight?"

"Yeah, I start at 4:30 p.m. and I work till midnight."

Howie said, "Too bad. I've got a sure thing at Balmoral running tonight. Mothers Bonda, who is a favorite at two-to-one with Frank O'Mara driving."

Shane then suggested, "Krock, you should see if you can get off tonight. You can use a night off. You've been working night and day for almost a month. This is a sure thing, right from the trainer."

"You're right, I've been working my ass off since Thanksgiving, and this sounds like something I can't pass up. I have not been to the Trotters in ages, and I would love to double my money. The last time Howie had a tip, you guys cleaned up, and I didn't go because I had to work. Do you have a dime?"

Shane gave me a dime, and I called Mike Mann from the pay-phone in the employee lunchroom to see if he wanted to work for me that night. He agreed. I told him to tell Louie I would be in tomorrow at 4:30. Howie picked me up that night in his '67 red Rambler Rebel convertible. Shane was sitting up in front, reading the racing form, which he had picked up earlier at the Main Street News Stand in Evanston, along with a copy of *Rolling Stone*, which I had asked him to get for me.

We arrived at Balmoral around 8 p.m., just in time for the first harness race. I had brought my whole bankroll, $320, with me. Our horse was running in the sixth race. I started off good, winning the first race with a horse named Dominator paying $11.80 for my $2 wager. But by the time we had reached the sixth race, I had lost $40. With my $280 left, I decided to put $100 to win on Mother's Bonda, but when I got up to the window, I had this urge to bet more, and I plunked down $200.

When I went back to where Shane and Howie were sitting, Shane asked, "How much did you bet?"

"I bet two hundred."

Shane replied, "You bet a deuce? I thought you were only going to wager a hundred bucks."

"I don't know, something came over me. I'm feeling lucky. How about you, Shane?"

"I bet my whole bankroll, $110."

"Howie, how about you?" I asked.

"I'll tell you after the race. C'mon, let's go outside by the finish line."

I responded, "It's freezing outside, like twenty degrees freezing."

Shane and I followed Howie outside to stand at the finish line. There was a group of five or six guys all standing around the finish line, sipping coffee while one guy was drinking whisky from a bottle he had pulled out from his coat and was passing it around to his friends. Howie knew all these track rats and, apparently, they all had the same tip on Mother's Bonda. Right before the race started, the odds had dropped to 4-to-5. This meant I would only get back $360 for my $200 wager. No sooner had the race started, and like a bad dream, Mother's Bonda broke stride. The whole entourage of us standing at the finish line began screaming obscenities, except for Howie.

"How much did you bet, Howie, on Mother's Bonda? I lost $500 on the horse."

I asked, "I thought your info was solid. Aren't you pissed?"

"The trainer's tips have been solid, but breaking stride is part of harness racing. I couldn't be too pissed. At the last minute I put $50 on the winner, Orphan Audrey. Orphan Audrey paid $19.40." For his $50 bet, Howie received $485.

Shane borrowed $200 from Howie. Then, Shane and I decided to pool our money and bet whatever Howie was betting for the remainder of the night, hoping to get our money back. We lost every race.

When the three of us left Balmoral that night, the only money Shane and I had left was the $25 Shane still had in his pocket. We jumped into Howie's car and headed for Jack's Restaurant. I was broke once more and really pissed at myself when we sat down. Howie and Shane were still talking about what horses we should have and could have bet. In the meantime, I had brought the new *Rolling Stone* magazine into Jack's and was thumbing through it when I noticed an article mentioning the Miami Pop Festival.

I said, "Hey, Shane, look at this big concert in Miami at Gulfstream Park. They're calling it the Miami Pop Festival, and what a lineup. Look at this." I read off:

- Chuck Berry
- The Amboy Dukes
- Blues Image
- The Box Tops
- Paul Butterfield Blues Band
- Canned Heat
- Wayne Cochran
- Cosmic Drum (aka Train of Thought)
- James Cotton Blues Band
- Country Joe and the Fish
- José Feliciano
- Fish Ray
- Flatt and Scruggs
- Fleetwood Mac

- Marvin Gaye
- The Grass Roots
- Grateful Dead
- Richie Havens
- Ian & Sylvia
- Iron Butterfly
- Junior Junkanoos
- Jr. Walker & The Allstars
- The Charles Lloyd Quartet
- Hugh Masekela
- Joni Mitchell
- Pacific Gas & Electric
- Procol Harum
- Terry Reid
- Buffy Sainte-Marie
- Steppenwolf
- The Sweet Inspirations
- Sweetwater
- Joe Tex
- Three Dog Night
- The Turtles

Shane said, "Marvin Gaye, are you kidding? We should go, but my dad will only let me use my Malibu for work or until I start going to school."

I replied, "We could take my Buick, but we don't have any money for gas or food, or a place to stay, plus my heater isn't working, and my back plastic window on my convertible has a hole in it."

Shane replied, "I still have my mom's Standard gas credit card, and we could take blankets."

I countered, "Let's think about it; I've got to go to work in the morning."

Howie said, "You guys are crazy. You can't go to Miami with no money."

On the way home, Shane suggested I stop by his house tomorrow when I got off from working at Turn-Style, before going to my other job delivering at La Rosa's. The next morning when I walked into the stockroom, I remembered I needed to unpack and put away the eight-track order that Teddy had dropped off yesterday. The eight-track order consisted of forty-eight assorted artists and forty-eight of the Beatles' *White Album*. After I opened the *White Album* box, I had forgotten that there were only twenty-four of the Beatles *White Album*, as it took two eight-tracks for the whole album and they were packaged as two tapes. I sorted the eight-tracks and put them in the eight-track display. I had an extra box of twelve eight-track double *White* Albums, which I went to put in the back overstock area, when I noticed the back door had been left open by one of the guys taking a cigarette break.

I looked outside and nobody was there. Since my car was only twenty feet from the door, I decided to do something I had never done before and could get me in real trouble. I walked to my car with the box of *White Album* eight-tracks and threw them in the trunk of my Buick. The store was super busy, and I was nervous all day that someone had seen me take them. Back then, stores did not have security cameras.

I left the store at four and stopped at Shane's before going to my job at La Rosa's. I grabbed the tapes out of the car to show Shane and to leave them at his house while I delivered pizzas that night, just in case I got stopped. Shane's kitchen door was unlocked, so I walked in and yelled, "Shane!"

Chapter 7

Life Is a Highway
of Roundabouts

"I'm up here, Krock."

When I walked into Shane's room, he had a suitcase lying on his bed with clothes, toiletries, his camera, and an electric razor already packed, even though he had a three-day-old beard with his hair in a ball. Shane was a couple inches taller than me, about five-foot-nine, with his belly hanging over his belt and a receding hairline. He looked older than me, even though I was nine months older than him.

"What's all this?" I asked.

"I just hung up with Barry Paddor in Oklahoma. He said if we pick him up in Oklahoma, he will pay for a room in Miami and let us stay in the room with him. If there is only one bed, we can sleep on the floor. I've got these extra blankets to keep us from freezing in your car with no heater. Do you have any sleeping bags, Krock?"

"No, my family aren't campers. What about gas and food?" I asked.

"I've got my mom's credit card for gas, and Barry said he'd pay for food on the ride down to Miami."

"I don't know, Shane. Let me get to work and think about it."

"Okay, Krock. I'll ride with you on your deliveries tonight, and we can talk about it. What's that box in your hand?"

"I stole twelve Beatles double *White Album* eight-tracks."

Shane responded. "Good. If we go, we can sell them when we get to Oklahoma."

After taking one tape out to play in my car that night, I laid the rest of the tapes next to Shane's suitcase. "Let's go—I'm going to be late." When we got into my car, it was freezing out. So, Shane went back inside to get the old blankets he had taken out of his mom's storage closet. Upon arriving at La Rosa's, I told Shane to wait in the car.

Shane responded, "I'll be next door at the Q-Inn. Come get me when your orders are ready."

When I walked in, Norm and Mike Mann were already there, and so was Louie's nephew, Pete.

Louie said, "Because you didn't come last night, I wasn't sure you would come in tonight, so I called my nephew, Peter. You can take one of his nights during the week."

"Didn't Mike tell you I'd be in tonight?"

"No, he no tells me, and I no hear from you today, so I call Peter."

Mike said, "I did tell you, Louie, when I walked in yesterday."

"I don't remember. You should have called me, Krockey. Anyway, you take the night off, Krockey."

"Okay, Louie."

While Norm and Mike were waiting for their delivery orders, we all sat down in the back booth, and I told them all about me losing my dough at the track and that I was thinking of going to this pop festival in Miami tomorrow with Shane. Norm tried to talk me out of it and said I should stay here and work. I was about to ask Norm for a loan but remembered I still owed him two hundred from the Christmas tree fiasco, and decided I better not.

Then, Mike told me that a few of his friends—Jeff Render, Kenny Goss, and Chuckie Goldwynn—were all going and he wished he could go to hear all that groovy music.

"Hey, Mike," I said. "Aren't you a big Beatles fan?"

"The biggest," he said.

"Do you have an eight-track player in your car?"

"Sure do. Why?"

"I've got a copy of the new Beatles double *White Album*. If you'd like, I can sell you my copy for two bucks. They are on sale at Turn-Style for seven dollars and twenty-nine cents."

"You got a deal," Mike said as he handed me two dollars, and I handed him the *White Album* eight-tracks. I told Norm that if we decided to go to Oklahoma in the morning, I would call him. I grabbed Shane from the Q-Inn and told him I wasn't working tonight.

I said, "Let's hit the road."

"Good, we can leave in the morning. You can sleep in the extra bed in my room, and we can stop at your house in the morning to pick up your clothes."

"No, I don't want my parents to know I left until I'm in Florida. Let's run by my house now. My parents went to the movies and my sister is sleeping at her friend's house."

After packing a small duffle bag and grabbing the last of my pot, we proceeded to go through my mother's kitchen cabinets looking for snacks for the road trip. We found two packs of Twinkies, a can of Pik-Nik brand shoestring potatoes, and a package of Hershey's small bittersweet chocolates my mom used for baking.

While Shane was going through the fridge, he said, "Hey, your mom has some deli in the fridge. I'm hungry. Is it okay if I make a sandwich?"

"Forget it. I want to get out of here before my parents come home. I don't know what time they went to the movies. Let's go to Zweig's and get the soup and half a sandwich for eighty cents. We can each get our own order with the two bucks I got from Mike for the Beatles tapes I sold him."

While driving to Zweig's, Shane pointed and said, "Pull into that Standard station on the corner so we can fill the car up, check the oil, and get some roadmaps for the trip."

"Good idea, we can plan our trip while we eat." While we sat in a booth, eating our food, Shane began studying the maps. I asked Shane, "How long do you think it's going to take to get to Oklahoma?"

"Looking at these maps, we go right through St. Louis, which should take us about five hours, and then another eight or maybe nine hours to get to Norman, Oklahoma. Maybe it's a little longer with gas and bathroom stops."

Then I asked, "How long from Oklahoma to Miami?"

Shane answered, "Give me a minute—I need this other map. Oh, shit, it's like twenty-two hours from Oklahoma to Miami."

"Are you kidding? That's about the same time it takes to drive from Chicago to Miami."

Shane lifted the bowl to his mouth and downed the rest of his soup. "This mushroom barley soup is out of sight."

"I know, Shane, the soup is terrific, but do you really want to drive fourteen or fifteen hours out of our way just to pick up Paddor? That's crazy."

Shane replied, "It's not just to pick up Barry. Remember, we are broke. He's going to pay for a hotel room in Miami and let us crash there. Plus, he is going to pay for our meals on the drive down, and we might be able to borrow a couple of dollars from him as well. We might even be able to get some trim from one of those nice University of Oklahoma college girls when we stop to pick him up."

"Maybe, I don't know. We've got no money. We've got very little pot, and we're going to freeze our asses off in my car. Like I said, it's nuts."

"C'mon, Krock, we are already freezing our asses off right here in beautiful Skokie. Your job at Turn-Style ends after Christmas. Doesn't warm weather sound nice? And this Miami Pop Festival sounds out of sight. We can't miss that. Have you heard that there's a new documentary film about the Monterey Pop Festival coming out soon? This Miami Pop Festival looks like it's going to be just as big of a happening as Monterey, with many of the same bands."

"Okay, I guess. When do you want to leave, Shane?"

"Let's try to leave early in the morning before my parents get up. We can shower tonight and leave at maybe four or five in the morning." Shane set his alarm for 3:30 a.m. When we got up that Sunday morning, December 22, 1968, it was twenty-six degrees out. We jumped in my car with our winter coats, knit stocking caps, and gloves, and headed for Norman, Oklahoma. Shane also brought along a pair of yellow ski glasses, which he had perched on top of his red knit stocking cap. The only money we had between us was $1.78 that Shane had all in change. As soon as we got in the car, we opened one of the packages of Twinkies we had taken from my house.

After each of us we downed a Twinkie, Shane said, "Let's stop at New York Bagel and Bialys on Touhy. We can get a dozen bagels with my change and take the cream cheese my mom has in the fridge, which should fill us up and last us the whole trip to Oklahoma." We walked into the New York Bagel and Bialys on Touhy at 4 a.m. that cold morning. You could smell the deliciousness of those freshly made bagels and bialys. In line ahead of us were two young couples, a few years older than us, dressed like they had been out all night. This was a popular place to stop on the way back to Skokie or Lincolnwood for people who were out partying all night. When it was our turn, the lady behind the counter asked us, "What will it be?"

Shane replied, "Give us a dozen. Two pumpernickel bagels, two onion bagels, two sesame bagels, four raisin bagels, two poppy seed bagels, and two garlic bialys."

The counter lady told us, "You get a free one with every dozen."

I replied, "Give us a mishmash bagel. Is the coffee still free?"

"Yes, help yourself." She added it up and said, "That will be a dollar and thirty-four cents."

When we walked outside, I opened my trunk up to grab my eight-track collection, only to realize I only had three tapes with me.

I told Shane, "I fucking forgot to bring the rest of my music. I only brought three tapes, plus the Beatles tapes I stole."

Shane asked, "What tapes do you have?"

"The Four Tops' *Greatest Hits*, Joplin's *Cheap Thrills*, and *Sinatra at The Sands*, plus I can also open the *White Album* tapes, which I would like to hear."

Shane stuck the Four Tops in the player and we were off to Oklahoma. We were about an hour out of St. Louis when we stopped to get gas and pee. When Shane came out of the restroom, he said, "Looks like a good hamburger place next door."

"You just ate four bagels with cream cheese. Aren't you full? I only ate two bagels, and I'm full."

"Not really. Smell those onions, Krock?"

"Yes, but we only have forty-four cents."

Shane said, "We have just enough for two burgers, and anyways, I need to warm up."

We both sat down at the counter and ordered a couple of burgers from this cute teenage girl, whom we found out later was only fifteen. She and Shane started talking, and before long, Shane had talked her into giving us some free French fries and a couple of Cokes. When we got in the car, Shane offered to drive. As Sinatra's "Luck Be a Lady Tonight" played, I nodded off for three or four hours until Shane nudged me.

"Where are we?"

"In a gas station right outside Springfield, Missouri."

"Shane, why are you wearing those goofy yellow ski goggles?"

"I like to wear them when I am tripping. The colors come on trippy through these yellow goggles. You better drive. I just took some acid I found in this winter coat before we left. I think I'd like to hear that Beatles album now."

"Give me the fucking keys, Shane. I unwrapped the two Beatles tapes and stuck one in my player and headed for Norman, Oklahoma, with "Back in the USSR" coming out of my car speakers. While we drove toward Norman, Shane hardly spoke, but would occasionally turn his head toward me with those yellow ski goggles on and this crazy smile and just say, "Far out, man." A few hours later, I saw a sign. "Oklahoma Turnpike Ahead."

When we reached the turnpike, I drove up to the toll booth and a lady handed me a card and asked, "Where are you boys headed?"

"Norman, Oklahoma," I answered.

She told us, "Take the tollway all the way to the end, which is where you will pay."

Ten minutes before we arrived at the end of the tollway, Shane started to talk, "Man, what a magnificent trip. You should try LSD."

"Well, maybe one day, but for now, what am I going to tell them when we must pay the toll?"

Shane replied, "Tell them you don't have any money. What can they do?"

"I don't know, arrest us, maybe?" I suggested he take off the goggles.

He just looked at me and said one word, "Negative," while making a negative sign using two fingers.

The sun was just about to go down when we pulled up to the one open toll booth. I could also see that to the side of the tollway, about ten feet from the booth, was an Oklahoma state trooper car. I still had one joint on me, which I stuffed in my sock.

I looked at Shane, who was still wearing the ski goggles. "Here we go," I said, right before I handed the lady in the booth the toll card I had received when we first entered the tollway.

"That will be one dollar and twenty-five cents."

I looked up at her and spoke. "We don't have any money."

She replied, "You both have no money? How are you paying for gas?"

Shane leaned over and told the lady, "My parents gave me a gas credit card. Will you take that?"

The toll lady replied, "No, I'm sorry, sir," as she turned a bright red light on. A minute after the light came on, this six-foot-four state trooper straight out of the movies came walking over after the toll lady told him we didn't have the money for the toll.

He leaned into my window and said with his Oklahoma accent, "Why don't you pull your Buick over to the side in front of my trooper car?" After we pulled over, the trooper told us to step out of the car and asked for my license and registration. After fumbling through the glove box for my registration, I handed him my license.

Then the officer asked, "Where are you guys headed?"

"U of O in Norman," I answered.

"How are you guys traveling with no money?"

Then Shane spoke, while he rested his goggles on top of his ski cap, coming up with a colossal bullshit story about how he'd lost his wallet. That it must have fallen out when he was taking a crap in St. Louis, and that he hadn't realized it till we had gotten to Springfield, Missouri. He went on to embellish, "Fortunately, just before I went to take a crap, I gave Alan the credit card to pay for the gas, which Alan stuck in his pocket."

The trooper asked, "What's your name, son?"

"Gary Shane, sir."

"That's quite a story, Gary. I tell you what, fellas, I have two boys around your age, and it being Christmastime, I'm feeling a bit charitable. I might be able to lend you the money for the toll. That is, if you have something of value that I can hold till you mail me back the money? How about that nice eight-track player in the car?"

Shane looked at the trooper right in the eyes and said, "Negative," while making that same negative sign, moving both his index fingers back and forth.

I thought this state trooper was sure to get mad and arrest us after that.

But to my surprise, it turned out he was a really nice guy, telling us his name was Officer Terry, and proceeding to ask us, "Do you have anything else of value?"

Shane asked me to open the trunk. He then started rummaging through his suitcase and a few minutes later turned around holding up a Kodak Instamatic camera in his left hand and a Shick electric razor in his right. "Well, boys, I already have a Kodak just like yours, Gary, but I always wanted to try one of those electric razors. Let me see that, Gary." Gary handed him the box with the electric razor in it. After the trooper took the razor out of the box and looked it over, he asked, "Do you mind if I try it?"

Gary said, "Sure, of course."

Trooper Terry then walked over to the toll booth with us following. He asked the woman in the booth, "Cousin Rita, would you mind terribly if I came into the booth to plug this electric razor in, to see if it works and give myself a shave? I'm thinking about lending these boys the money for the toll." When Trooper Terry went into the booth, he plugged the razor in and then asked his cousin, "Rita, could I borrow that little makeup mirror of yours?"

"I'll hold it for you, Cousin Terry."

Shane and I could not believe our eyes and good fortune as we watched Officer Terry give himself a shave as we both shook our heads and chuckled. After shaving, he rubbed his hands over his face while smiling as Cousin Rita nodded her approval. Before coming out of the booth, he wrote down his name and address. He then walked over to my car, where Shane and I were standing. "This here Schick gave me the smoothest shave. I don't know why I never tried one before. Here's my address and ten bucks; this way, you have some eating money for the road. I also gave my cousin Rita the money for the toll. Gary, if you ever want your razor back, just send me a check and I will mail you back the razor."

Gary replied, "No, sir, you keep it."

"Well, thank you, Gary. I know these Schicks go for twenty bucks or more."

Shane and I both said, "Thank you, Trooper Terry, and Merry Christmas." Then we both yelled over to Cousin Rita, "Merry Christmas."

It was about 9 p.m. when we reached the University of Oklahoma campus. Shane told me, "Pull into that gas station and we can call Barry for directions to his dorm. Here's his number. Give him a call while I go take a whiz. Also, see if he wants to go eat. I'm starving."

"Me too," I replied.

When Shane came out of the men's room, I told him, "I spoke to Barry; he said we were only a few minutes away, and that he and his friend and roommate, Murph, would be waiting outside their dorm." When we pulled up, I could barely recognize Barry, who was about my size. He had grown his hair much longer and had grown a thick black mustache. His friend Murph was well over six feet, with a full, dark brown beard and a brown ponytail.

After Barry and his friend Murph crawled into the back seat, Shane asked, "Are you guys hungry?"

"No, we already ate; this is my friend Murph."

After introductions were made, Barry went on to say, "If you're hungry, I know a cool spot with good food and cold beer. The Denco Cafe is where we usually go late at night after partying. Go down this street and I'll tell you where to turn. You guys want a hit of some righteous Afghani hash?"

"Sure," I said.

Barry replied, "Here, Shane, you hold the pipe for Krock, and then you take a hit. Here's my lighter." While at a stop sign with nobody around, Shane held up the hash pipe to my mouth, and I took a big hit, causing me to cough while I blew out the smoke. I immediately felt a buzz.

After Shane took his hit, he said, "How far is the restaurant? I'm starving."

Barry told me, "Krock, turn left at the light and it's about a half a block."

As we walked to our table, Murph shouted out, "Four bottles of Coors, please."

"What's good here?" I asked.

Murph answered, "Only one thing to eat here and that's the Denco Darlin."

Shane asked, "What the hell is a Denco Darlin? Some kind of fancy hamburger?"

Barry said, "No, the Denco Darlin is noodles, chili, and some kind of cheese concoction upon which two eggs sunny-side-up usually are placed to look at you, as the saying goes. You eat it with either catsup, hot sauce, or this green salad dressing. I like to mix all the garnishes together. It comes with a side order of chips, and they bring you the hot sauce in baby bottles. It's out of sight, especially after a few beers."

Gary Shane replied while shaking his head, "I don't know. Sounds kind of weird."

"Trust me, if you don't like it, I'll eat it." Shane ended up eating two orders, and we both had to admit it was out of sight.

After finishing our Denco Darlins, we all hung around the Denco while downing another four or five beers each and using up the whole ten dollars Officer Terry had given us. It was already 1 a.m. when I pronounced that I was exhausted, and Shane nodded his head in agreement.

Murph said, "Barry, you can drop me off at Frenchy's house and I can sleep there, then one of these guys can have my bed and the other can sleep on the sofa."

Frenchy, whose real name was Lisette, was Murph's girlfriend, a beautiful, petite, dark-skinned Cajun girl with green eyes from Lafayette, Louisiana. Earlier while we were shooting the shit and downing cold Coors, Murph had shown us a picture of her. He told us how they had met in the emergency room at the local hospital where she worked as a nurse, when Murph broke his arm after falling off his Harley and totaling it.

After dropping off Murph, we headed for the dorm. When we arrived back at the dorm, Shane and I flipped to see who got the bed and who got the pull-out sofa bed. I won the flip, and two minutes later, after taking my shoes and pants off, I flopped down on the bed and passed out. I woke up around 2 p.m. to "Rocky Raccoon." I had given Barry a copy of the eight-track *White Album* the previous evening, and now Barry and Shane were smoking hash and listening to the whole double album, which they both seemed to love.

"Good morning, guys," I said as I walked into the living room.

"Well, look who's up. You want a hit of hash?" Barry asked.

"No, not till I have some coffee."

"Sorry, Krock, no coffee, but there's Pepsi in the fridge."

"That will do. Do you mind if I take a shower?"

"Sure, there's a clean towel in the hallway closet, but you better wait a little, as Shane just showered and there might not be a whole lot of hot water."

After showering, I asked Barry, "Do you know any people who might want to buy any of these *White Album* tapes?"

"Right now, most of the kids are gone for Christmas break. But I bet the guy at the record store by Campus Corner would buy them all for the right price."

So the three of us strolled over to this record store called Friends and ended up selling the last eight *White Albums* for two bucks each to the hippie clerk behind the counter. The hippie clerk, whose name was Jocko, told us that the wholesale price was much more and that he planned on buying a couple for himself to give out as Christmas presents. Then he called his boss to get permission to pay us out of the till. After paying me, I looked through the store's eight-track selection for the new Stones release, *Beggars Banquet*, and not finding it I asked, "Jocko, do you have the new Rolling Stones on eight-track tape?"

"Let me check. There might be more in the back." Jocko came out with the new tape, "Here you go."

"How much?" I asked.

"I'll charge you the same you charged us, two bucks. Merry Christmas."

With the fourteen bucks in my pocket and my new Stones tape, I was ready to hit the road. I asked Shane and Barry when they wanted to leave. Barry answered, "Not till later tonight. Murph just called to tell us that Frenchy is inviting all of us to her place before we hit the road for her famous shrimp and andouille sausage jambalaya. Murph asked me if we wouldn't mind picking up a couple of six-packs of Coors and then asked us if we would be okay dropping Frenchy, Lisette, off in New Orleans on our way to Miami, as Murph was catching a flight back to New York in the morning to spend Christmas with his family."

Shane asked, "Isn't that way out of our way? The map I looked at says that we are supposed to be going through Arkansas, Tennessee, Mississippi, Alabama, and Georgia, and then into Florida."

Barry said, "It's a much cooler ride through Texas into Louisiana, and it takes the same time to get to Miami."

Shane pulled out the map and, after studying it, stated that it was true. "You're right, it takes about the same time, and New Orleans has got to be groovy." As we all agreed.

Later that day, as we were getting ready to go over to Frenchy's, Shane asked Barry, "What time are we going to leave for Frenchy's?"

Barry yelled back, "Around 6:30. Make sure you guys don't call her Frenchy to her face. Only Murph calls her Frenchy. You guys need to call her Lisette."

"Okay, cool," I responded. Just before we left for Lisette's, I asked Barry if it would be cool to call my parents from his phone, and that I would pay him back.

"Go ahead, Krock, but don't stay on the phone too long."

I dialed my number, and my mother picked up the phone. "Where are you? I haven't heard from you in a couple days and was beginning to worry."

I obviously didn't want to tell her I was on my way to Miami for Christmas break to go to a rock festival. So, I came up with a story. "Sorry, Mom, I meant to call you yesterday, but I forgot. We are on our way to work at the Orange Bowl football game in Miami. I'm with Gary Shane and Barry Paddor. We just stopped in Oklahoma to pick up Barry at his college."

My mom replied in a suspicious way. "Isn't Oklahoma a little out of the way to drive to Miami?"

"Yes, but Barry put up the money to buy all the souvenirs we are going to sell. I think we can clean up."

"Miami, what about this new broadcasting school? You know you start school on January 6th."

"The game is on New Year's Day, and we are driving back the next day."

Then my dad got on the phone and asked, "Why are you driving all the way to Miami to work? You could have worked here, in Chicago."

"Yeah, Pops, I know; I thought I could take a little break before school started and make some good money at the same time, especially after the Christmas tree fiasco."

My dad responded, "I understand. As long as you can make a buck and get back for school in time, I guess it's okay. How's the car?"

"It's running just fine."

"Well, be careful and don't forget to check the oil and tires. Remember, safety—"

I answered, "…first… See you, Pops. Say goodbye to Mom."

"Call us from Miami and maybe go visit your Aunt Lill and Uncle Jack. I'm sure they would let you stay there."

Barry yelled, "Get off the phone!"

"Got to run, Pops, bye."

We headed over to Lisette's house, which she shared with two other nurses. Murph answered the door, greeting us with a joint in his mouth. I put the beers in his hand. "Here, Murph, these are still cold."

We followed Murph to the kitchen. He introduced us. "Guys, this is Lisette. Lisette, this is Krockey and Gary.'"

"Good to meet you guys. Dinner will be ready soon."

Gary replied, "Thank you—smells out of this world."

"You guys want one of these beers?" Murph asked. "We also have wine and Lisette's favorite, Dr Pepper."

Barry said, "A Coors sounds good."

Shane and I opted for a Coors as well. When we walked into the living room we were introduced to Lisette's roommates—Tula, an attractive, curvy, full-blooded Choctaw woman with brown hair down to her ass who had grown up only a few miles from the Oklahoma campus, and Margie, a tall, beautiful blonde with blue eyes who hailed from Santa Fe, New Mexico. Next to Margie was her boyfriend, John, a six-foot-five guard for the Oklahoma Sooners football team. Marge and John, like Murph and Lisette, had also met at the hospital. John had dislocated his shoulder in October against Iowa State and was hoping to play in the upcoming Bluebonnet Bowl on New Year's Eve against SMU.

Lisette came into the living room and announced dinner was ready, asking Tula and Margie to help her serve the large bowls of Jambalaya dished out of a giant pot on the stove. As we settled in to eat, Murph suggested we add some Louisiana Hot Sauce.

Lisette said, "I prefer a little green Tabasco but not too much," and passed the hot cornbread she just made.

As we sat there eating this exceptional meal and drinking cold beer, we talked about everything from football to music to cooking. While we were finishing and I was wiping my plate clean, soaking up the gravy with the outstanding cornbread, Murph stood up to make a toast to Lisette. "Thank you for this wonderful meal, Cheri. Your food and, more importantly, your love, are the secret ingredients to happiness. I love you, babe." Murph kissed Lisette.

Lisette said, "I have coffee and homemade chocolate cake in the kitchen. Girls, would you mind serving coffee and cake? Tom (Murph's first name) and I need to talk privately in my bedroom before not seeing each other for a couple weeks."

Tula and Margie both smiled and happily agreed. By the time we finished our coffee and cake, with all of us cleaning up, it was 11 p.m. As I was drying the last dish, Murph and Frenchy walked out of the bedroom.

Murph asked, "Any more chocolate cake?"

Margie answered, "Yes, help yourself, Murph. We need to get ready for work. Tula and I are working the night shift at the hospital tonight."

You could see Shane was disappointed as he was hitting on Tula all night, and she seemed to like him too.

Around a quarter to twelve, we all said our goodbyes. John was giving Margie and Tula a ride to the hospital. Murph kissed Lisette goodbye, and he was on his way, walking back to his dorm room. Before I jumped into the driver's seat, I went into the trunk and grabbed my wool peacoat and the two blankets I had. "Here,

Lisette, please take this blanket. My car gets cold with just that piece of thin plastic for the rear window. Also, my heater doesn't work."

"I'm warm in my fur-lined suede coat," she responded as she ran her hand over the fluffy white lining.

Shane said, "You better take the blanket; it can get pretty cold in the old Buick."

As soon as we hit the road, Barry pulled out his hash pipe, and we all took a hit except Lisette, who reminded us we had a long ride. Shane and Lisette were in the back seat, and after driving for a while, Shane asked Lisette if she wouldn't mind sharing the blanket.

"Sure," Lisette said.

Then Shane asked, "Does Tula have a boyfriend?"

"No, she had been seeing this older doctor last summer, but he broke her heart when he told her he was married. So she stopped seeing him, and she hasn't really been seeing anybody since then. You should come back and visit. I think she liked you, Gary."

Barry, who was wrapped up in the other blanket, asked, "Where is that new Stones tape, Krock?"

"It's in the glove box."

Barry then turned off the country station on the radio and stuck *Beggars Banquet* in my eight-track player. Upon hearing "Sympathy for the Devil," Barry said, "I love this record."

We all agreed. As we were approaching Dallas, I said, "I've got to pee, plus we need gas."

We pulled into a truck stop and got gas while we all used the washroom. Barry and Lisette went in to buy some snacks while Shane was filling the car up using his parents' credit card and I cleaned the windows with the truck stop squeegee. Barry and Lisette bought a big bag of Cheetos and four Moon Pies. Shane said he would drive as I took shotgun seat. On the road, we all took another hit of hash, and this time Lisette joined in.

After eating enough Cheetos to turn my hands orange, I took a bite of my Moon Pie and started to fall asleep when Marvin Gaye's "I Heard It Through the Grapevine" came on the radio; it had just come out. I dozed off while the Glen Campbell song "Wichita Lineman" played next. I was awakened a few hours later when I heard the car door open. Lisette and Shane had switched places, and Lisette was now driving. Shane and Barry were passed out in the back seat. We were just outside Alexandria, Louisiana. I put *Cheap Thrills* in the eight-track player.

"I love Janis Joplin," Lisette told me.

"Me too. How do you like being a nurse?"

"I love it." She went on to tell me that her mother was also a nurse and that her grandfather had been a doctor back in Lafayette. He would often take her and her sister to his office when they were kids, where they both saw how much people adored him. Her sister was also a nurse and now lived in New Orleans, where Lisette was stopping before she showed us around.

Lisette's sister, Sarah, wasn't at home when we arrived. She had left a note that she had gone up to her grandmother's house with her husband, Angus, and their eight-year-old daughter, Seraphine, and five-year-old son, Roscoe, to help her Maw-Maw, Corrine, prepare all the food for tonight's festivities.

The plan was for us to clean up at her sister place, then have a little tour of New Orleans. After that, we planned to meet up with her family at their property along the Louisiana Great River Road. The property had been in Lisette's family since the Civil War. This was her family's tradition, to every year watch and participate in the traditional Cajun Christmas Eve bonfires on the levees along the Mississippi River.

We all showered and changed our clothes. Shane said he was hungry.

Lisette told him, "Don't worry, we are going to have plenty of food later tonight. We can get a snack when we get to the French

Quarter. Let's go. We can fool around in New Orleans for a few hours and then head up to my family's spot along the levee for the festivities."

After jumping in Lisette's sister's 1956 Chevy station wagon, we headed for the city. Lisette first took us for a ride through the Garden District, pointing out Lafayette Cemetery #1 before deciding to park the car.

She then suggested, "Let's do a little walking around the Garden District, and then we can take the St. Charles Avenue Streetcar over to the French Quarter." After soaking in the Garden District, we hopped on the streetcar to the French Quarter. During our trip on the historic streetcar, Lisette pointed out Auburn Park, Tulane and Loyola Universities, the central business districts, beautiful mansions, restaurants, hotels, parks, and museums. I was taken in by the different architectural fabric and sounds of the Crescent City, The Big Easy.

As soon as we got off the streetcar, Shane said, "I'm hungry."

Barry added, "Me too."

Lisette thought of something. "Have you guys ever tasted beignets?"

We all shook our heads no.

"Well, you are in for a treat. Follow me." As we approached Cafe Du Monde, the sweet aroma of freshly fried beignets filled our nostrils. We sat down in the cafe's open-air space and ordered a dozen of these beauties along with the chicory coffee Lisette suggested. We could hear a street performer playing a pretty good version of "The Christmas Song" on his sax, which made the perfect soundtrack for enjoying the warm doughy treats.

After finishing, we walked across the street to Jackson Square with Lisette pointing out the St. Louis Cathedral. She said, "You should see the inside. It's so beautiful. We don't have time now, but if you guys like, some of my family and I will be going to Midnight Mass after the bonfires and you're welcome to join us. I know you guys are Jewish, but everyone is welcome. It's a beautiful mass that you might enjoy." We walked around Jackson Park and all through the French Quarter with Lisette as our guide. She showed us the French Market, Bourbon Street, and all the little shops, restaurants, and jazz clubs.

We were in front of the Preservation Hall a few hours later when Lisette said, "Let's get back on the streetcar and grab the car." We all got back into Sarah's station wagon and headed to the levees.

As we approached the earthen levees, the sun was just going down, and the Christmas Eve bonfires were just beginning. Within minutes, twenty- to thirty-foot-high flaming log pyramids began to rise. While the bonfires were, of course, the star of the show, I found myself watching and admiring Lisette's Maw Maw, Corrine, dishing out her famous gumbo to her twenty-five or so family members of all ages who were enjoying the festivities. The children were playing games while the grown-ups enjoyed their gumbo and beer. As Shane, Barry, and I sat eating our gumbo, I asked Maw Maw Corrine, "Why are the bonfires celebrated here?"

Maw Maw, a heavy-set, dark-complected Cajun woman with gray-haired braids, told us with a big, warm smile while a half dozen children sat at her feet, "The fires illuminate the way for Papa Noel, Santa Claus, flying his sleigh and eight reindeer to find the homes of good girls and boys. Isn't that right, Seraphine?"

"Yes, Maw Maw." Seraphine was Maw Maw's great-granddaughter. Although most of the bonfires were pyramid-shaped, I noticed one in the shape of a cabin and one in the shape of an alligator. Throughout the night, other families and friends stopped by, while some of Lisette's family would stroll down the levee to do the same. Soon, a fireworks display was going off, and I decided to take a walk down the levee, where I could hear and see a joyful group of people playing energetic zydeco music and dancing up a storm. Lisette would tell me later that these folks were black Creoles. All in all, it was an amazing, memorable evening.

Lisette asked us if we wanted to go to Midnight Mass. We told her thank you, but we were tired and wanted to get an early start in the morning. "Okay, here's the keys to the Chevy and a key to Sarah's house. I'm going to sleep at my parents' house; and Sarah, Angus, and the kids are staying at Maw Maw's place down the road from my folks." She then gave each of us a big hug with kisses on both cheeks. Angus asked us to help him put the wash tub that held the drinks in the back of the Chevy Wagon, which still had a couple of six-packs of Falstaff Beer and a few bottles of Nehi orange and grape soda.

"Help me pour out the water from the melted ice?" he asked.

Then Angus said, "Wait here." He went and got one of the big pots of leftover gumbo, placing it in the back of the wagon and telling us, "Maw Maw wanted you to have some food in the morning before you leave. Also, there's some cornbread in the breadbox on the kitchen counter at the house. Help yourself to whatever you like."

We thanked Angus and waved goodbye to Maw Maw, Lisette, and the whole family, all of us yelling thank you and Merry Christmas. As we got in the car and drove away, this wonderful family continued to wave goodbye.

Shane said, "Wow, what cool people. I'm ready to move here."

Barry seconded that. "I hear you, brother. Super nice folks."

I nodded and smiled in agreement as we headed to the house. We woke up early that Christmas morning, around seven, after which we warmed up the gumbo and ate every last bite, while mopping it up with the cornbread and washing it down with some Orange and Grape Nehi.

Shane then asked, "Krock, how much dough do you have left?"

I told him, "Eight dollars and eighty-eight cents. How about you, Barry?"

"Around fifty bucks and my Diners Club card, which we can use to pay for the hotel when we get to Miami."

Shane said, "Look at this. I found a two-dollar bill that I forgot I had folded into my wallet the last time we went to the track."

After washing the dishes and putting our bags in the car, I noticed Shane going through the cabinets in the kitchen. Just then, the phone rang, and Shane yelled to me and Barry, who were now outside. "Should I get it?" Barry answered.

"Yes, Lisette said she would be calling around this time."

Once Shane hung up with Lisette, he told us she said to put the keys in the porcelain owl on the porch, and to have a safe trip. Shane said he found some peanut butter and jelly in the cabinets and that there was bread in the breadbox. I asked Lisette if it was okay to make some peanut butter and jelly sandwiches for the road, and she said that it would be okay—not to worry. We finally hit the road around 9 a.m. after pulling into a Standard gas station, telling the attendant to fill it up and check the oil. The attendant yelled out to us when we came out of the washroom, "You boys are down over a quart of oil according to this here dipstick. You want me to top it off?"

"Go ahead," Shane said, handing him his folks' credit card.

Barry was the first one to take the wheel. I was sitting up front while Shane was stretched out in the back seat. Barry handed me his pipe and his large stash of hash. "Krock, fill up a bowl for me." After putting some hash in the pipe, I held it up to Barry's mouth as he took a big hit with me holding the lighter over the bowl. Then I filled up another bowl for Shane, handing him the pipe and the lighter. After he took a big hit, it was my turn. The hash really hit the spot. I stuck the Four Tops *Greatest Hits* tape in the eight-track and "Baby I Need Your Loving" filled the air as we all sang along.

"Wow, man, look how empty the roads are," Barry said.

"Of course, it's Christmas—everyone's home," I replied.

Shane said, "Please, turn the music down a little. I'm going to crash. I didn't sleep too good last night."

"Cool," I replied.

Oklahoma, New Orleans, and Miami

Oklahoma Turnpike (*From the author's collection*)

Denco Café, Norman, OK (*From the author's collection*)

Café Du Monde, New Orleans, 1955, by David Lofink
(*From Wikimedia Commons*)

Christmas Eve bonfires, Mississippi River levee, Louisiana
(*From Wikimedia Commons*)

New Deauville Hotel, Miami Beach (*From Wikimedia Commons*)

Wolfie Cohen's Rascal House postcard, late 1960s
(*From Wikimedia Commons*)

Wolfie's Coffee Shop, Miami Beach, postcard
(*From the author's collection*)

Pumpernik's Restaurant & Coffeeshop, Miami Beach,
postcard, by Curt Teich & Co., Chicago

Miami Pop Festival, Gulfstream Park, poster
(*From the author's collection*)

Miami Pop Festival, Gulfstream Park, poster
(*From the author's collection*)

Chapter 8

The Sunshine State

After stopping in Pensacola and then Tallahassee for refreshments, gas, and to use the facilities while enjoying the PB&J sandwiches along the way, I took the wheel in Tallahassee and drove to Orlando, where Shane took over driving us into Miami. We were making record time as the roads were empty most of the way, with all of us going 80 mph in my big Buick. It was around 10:30 p.m. when we neared Miami and Shane asked, "Where should we go first?"

Barry answered, "I'm hungry. Let's check into the hotel first, and then we can go right down the street and eat at Pumpernik's."

Shane replied, "You mean the Brazil Hotel where we stayed last spring?"

Barry said, "That's right. It's only twelve dollars a night with a student ID. Just go straight down Collins; it's right down the street from the Deauville and Pumpernik's."

Shane remembered, "And there is Texas Burger right across the street. Mouth-watering charbroiled burgers. I love that place."

When we arrived at the Brazil Hotel, we had to park a few blocks away, and when we walked past Pumpernik's and Texas Burger, they were both closed for Christmas. As we walked up the steps of the Brazil Hotel, Mooch Sands, Chuckie Goldwynn, and Al Katz were walking out. We stopped for a few minutes to talk.

Shane asked after we all said our hellos, "Do you guys know where we can get some food? Everything seems to be closed for Christmas."

Al Katz, whose nickname was Kutz in high school, answered, "We're on our way to Wolfie's Deli right now. It's open 24/7. Why don't you meet us there?"

Then Chuckie Goldwynn handed us a joint and said, "Here, smoke this and work up an appetite."

We thanked him and told them we would see them there later.

Mooch Sands offered, "I've got more weed if you want to buy some."

Shane answered, "No, we're good right now. See you at Wolfie's."

Barry walked over to the desk where this old man named Oscar was smoking and chewing on a big cigar. Barry asked, "Sir, could I get a room for tonight with three beds?"

"Call me Oscar. We only have rooms with two beds, but we can get you a roll-in for two bucks more, or if you book more than one night, it's free."

Barry answered while showing Oscar his student ID, "Give us two nights."

"That will be thirty dollars."

Barry replied, "I paid twelve dollars a night last spring."

Oscar smiled, telling Barry, "We raised the price in October."

Barry handed him his Diners Club card.

Oscar then said, "It's going to take about a half hour to get you the roll-in bed and have it made up. How many keys do you need?"

"Three," Barry said.

Oscar handed Barry three keys. He walked over, giving us each room key. "Here you go, Mr. Shane, Mr. Krockey. You guys owe me ten bucks each for the two nights, but after that, you're on your own. You can mail me the money when you get back to Chicago. This Friday, I'm going to stay at my cousin's place in Fort Lauderdale till I fly back next week, but you're good for tonight and tomorrow night.

We put the bags in the room, then jumped in the Buick. Shane said he would drive and suggested putting the top down. "It's beautiful outside. I love these Miami nights."

Barry and I agreed. We headed down Collins in my Buick convertible, smoking the joint Chuckie had given us and going past the big hotels like the Eden Rock and the Fontainebleau and seeing all the giant yachts on the intercoastal. I wondered if I would ever be able to stay in a hotel like the Fontainebleau or own one of those big yachts someday. I reached into my pocket and felt the eight dollars and eighty-eight cents and thought maybe someday. We walked into Wolfie's around 1 a.m. and sat in the booth across from Chuckie, Mooch, and Kutz.

Chuckie asked, "Did you guys enjoy that pot? We bought it down here. They call it Panama Red."

Barry said, "I never heard of it, but it tasted sweet and sure got us stoned."

Then I pointed out, "Isn't that the comedian who is always on Hollywood Squares?"

Al Katz answered, "Yes, sir, that's Jan Murray, and you know who's with him? That's Jackie Mason. He's that Jewish comedian that used to be on *The Ed Sullivan Show* when we were kids. My dad loved him but told me that Jackie Mason once gave Ed Sullivan the finger and was banned from the Sullivan show for life. That's why you hardly ever see him on TV anymore."

I replied, "You're fucking right. I saw an advertisement on the cover of the entertainment magazine in the lobby of the Brazil that he was appearing at the Eden Roc."

"Do you guys need a minute, or do you know what you want?" the waitress asked.

Barry answered, "I'll have a pastrami sandwich on rye. What does that come with?"

"Coleslaw and either fries or a potato pancake."

"Fries and a chocolate phosphate."

I said, "I'll have the same."

Shane ordered a brisket sandwich on an onion roll with fries and a Coke. When our food came, Mooch, Kutz, and Chuckie got up to leave.

I asked Mooch, "Hey, Eric, do you think you could loan me twenty dollars?"

"Can't do it, Krock."

"How about a sawbuck?"

"Hey, man, I barely have enough for myself. You know I'd lend it to you if I could. What about you, Gary?"

"I'm broke too, Eric."

"I know you have money, Barry."

"Listen, Eric, I've already lent them money for our room."

Then Eric, or Mooch as we called him, got up to leave with Kutz and Chuckie. "Pass the mustard, Krock."

"Here you go, Barry." As we sat there eating our sandwiches, Jackie Mason and Jan Murray were walking out right by our table when one of the waitresses went up to them.

The waitress asked, "Would you two mind giving me an autograph?"

"Our pleasure, Shirley. Didn't I just give you an autographed picture a few weeks ago?" Jackie Mason answered. "Yes, but my cousin from Jersey is in town and asked me to get your autograph, as I told her you were one of my regulars. Thank you so much, Jackie, and you as well, Mr. Murray. I see you're playing at the Eden Roc, Jackie. Where are you playing, Mr. Murray?" Jan Murray answered as he handed Shirley his autograph.

"Oh, I just appeared on *The Jackie Gleason Show* and decided to stay for a few days and play some golf."

"God bless you both."

When we finished eating, Barry asked for the check.

Shirley handed Barry the check and said, "I hope you boys enjoyed your sandwiches. That will be five dollars and seventy cents; you pay at the register."

Shane was about to hand Barry his two-dollar bill when Barry said, "Dinner is on me. Krockey, leave the waitress a dollar tip, and I will pick up the check."

"Thanks, Barry," I replied.

We arrived back at the Brazil Hotel a little after 3 a.m. Oscar, the desk man, was fast asleep on one of the couches in the lobby. On the other couch, directly across from Oscar, sat Al Katz, next to what appeared to be a very tall, blonde, semi-attractive hooker. She was dressed in a red miniskirt with white fringe go-go boots and a black top with blue sequins.

Kutz called out, "What's going on, fellas? I want you guys to meet Darlene, the 1961 Miss Knoxville, Tennessee."

"Hello, Darlene."

In unison, Barry, Shane, and I all said, "Hi."

"Hello, boys," Darlene said in her southern accent. "Are you boys looking for a little fun like my friend Alan?"

Kutz said, "Darlene is more than fun; she enjoys her work. This will be my second night with Miss Knoxville."

Shane asked, "How much?"

Darlene stood up, came over to Shane, and whispered in his ear as she rubbed against him, "Ten dollars, cutie."

Shane answered out loud, "I'm a little short right now, but maybe tomorrow. How do I find you?"

"Big Al knows. I live right down the street at the apartment building right next to the Sherry Frontenac Hotel."

Turning to me: "How about you, little guy?"

"I'd love to, but I'm a little short myself."

Darlene replied, "Well, you let Big Al know. I should be around all week. Let's go, big guy," as she grabbed Kutz by the hand and headed for the elevators.

When we got to our room, we were asleep in minutes. We woke up around noon, and after we showered and cleaned up, Shane suggested, "How about we go across the street for a beautiful Texas Burger, and after that we can go to the beach and look for girls?"

Barry replied as he took a puff of hash, "Sounds groovy; let's put our bathing suits on."

Barry and Shane put their bathing suits on, but the closest thing I had to a bathing suit was some ragged blue jean cut-off shorts.

After we all had our burgers, fries, and Cokes, we stepped outside and ran into Chuckie Goldwynn. I asked, "Chuckie, do you know where the best beach is? The one where all the girls are?"

Chuckie replied, "Fuck the beach—you guys need to check out the pool at the Deauville Hotel. It's swarming with chicks from all over the country."

Barry asked, "Chuckie, don't they check to see if you're a guest? I know when I was younger and my parents would stay at the Fontainebleau, they would always ask me for my room number."

Chuckie replied, "Here's the deal. There is a Cuban guy named Bembe who gives out the towels and escorts you to a lounge chair. All you guys need to do is give him a buck each and you're in. Although Krockey, you're supposed to wear a bathing suit. Maybe he'll give you a pass."

So, we all followed Chuckie into the Deauville and up to the pool area to the towel bar. The place was packed with families and college students, including some super-hot chicks. Chuckie, looking like he owned the place, handed Bembe a dollar, and we all did the same. Bembe started to lead us to our lounge chairs when he looked at me and said, "Hey, man, don't you have a bathing suit?"

"No, I forgot to pack one," I replied.

"Well, you are going to have to leave and find a bathing suit."

Chuckie spoke up. "Can't we work something out?"

Bembe replied, "It's going to cost you another buck," as he motioned for me to follow him.

"Okay," I said as I followed Bembe to the men's locker room. Bembe opened one locker, and there were a bunch of bathing suits as well as sunglasses and containers of suntan lotion that people had left behind.

"These were all left behind by guests. Give me another buck and pick one out." So, I handed him the dollar, and he said, "Here, amigo, put the lock back on after you pick out your suit; make sure it fits. I've got to get back to the towel bar."

"Cool. Thanks, man."

After rummaging through the pile of bathing suits, I picked out a really cool Miami Dolphins aqua and orange bathing suit that seemed to be my size. After washing them off in the bathroom sink with soap and water, I put them on and they fit perfectly. Before I closed the locker, I started to rummage through the sunglasses and found a nice pair of Ray-Ban sunglasses, which I stuck in my blue jean shorts pocket while grabbing a half container of Coppertone and sticking it in the other pocket.

Carrying the shorts while concealing what I had just taken, I walked out of the locker room and ran smack dab into Bembe. "Hey, man, I never saw that bathing suit, or I would have taken it for myself. That is super boss. You should give me another dollar."

"My money is in my shoes underneath the lounge chair."

Bembe said with a smile, "Amigo, I was just messing with you. Just bring me a joint when you come tomorrow."

"Okay, thanks." As I walked toward my friends, I realized that Bembe was wearing the same type of Ray-Ban sunglasses I had just stolen. I decided not to wear the Ray-Bans till I left the pool in case Bembe recognized them.

When I arrived back with my friends, Shane said, "Wow, cool bathing suit."

"Thanks. I also found this Coppertone suntan lotion, which helps you get a better tan."

Back then, you used suntan lotion instead of sunscreen, which kind of had the opposite effect, helping you tan easier instead of protecting your skin. Who knew? After I rubbed the Coppertone all over my face and body, I passed it to Shane, telling him to share it with Barry and Chuckie when he was done using it. As I looked around, I saw some familiar Skokie faces from people in our age group, as well as a few parents' I recognized.

"Hey, Krock," Barry called. "Isn't that Andy Cohen, Donna Lachman, and Cindy Lavin over on the other side near the lifeguard stand?"

"I'm going to walk over," Shane said. "I always thought Andy Cohen was sexy."

"I'll go with you," Chuckie shouted and then said, "That Cindy Lavin is a knockout. But I think she is still going with Bob Stiller. Let's check it out."

So, Shane and Chuckie walked over and sat with the girls. As soon as they sat down, Bob Stiller came walking over with drinks for the girls. Bob Stiller was probably the only guy tougher than Chuckie from Skokie, and they were friends. I could see from afar that Chuckie looked disappointed until one of the girls hanging around the pool came over and started talking to him. I also noticed that Shane and Andy were getting up to take a walk. A few minutes later, Bembe asked, "Are your friends coming back?"

"No, I don't think so," I answered.

Bembe then said, "Here, girls, take these two lounge chairs," as he laid beach towels on the two chaise lounges next to us.

"Hi, I'm Suzie, and this is my cousin, Lois."

"Hi, I'm Barry, and this is Al."

I asked Suzie, who was sitting next to me, "Where are you from?"

She answered, "We are both from Philadelphia—well, the suburbs of Philly. How about you guys?"

"We're from Chicago," Barry answered as he moved to the empty seat next to Lois. "Where do you girls go to college?"

Lois answered, "Oh, I'm in my senior year in high school, but my cousin Suzie here is a freshman at NYU."

"Wow, how cool, New York City, wow," I replied.

"The only bummer is we came down here with our parents, and they did get us our own room," Lois said with a smile.

Suzie chimed in, "Our moms are sisters, and ever since our grandparents moved here ten years ago, we've come here on vacation once or twice a year. We even got to see the Beatles when *The Ed Sullivan Show* did their broadcast from right here at the Deauville in 1964."

Suzie and I had been talking for almost a half hour when the music that was playing through the pool's loudspeakers stopped for an announcement. "Hello, folks, I know some of you may recognize me, but for those who don't, let me introduce myself. I'm Morry Guntty, the comedian, and today's social director, who will be opening for the fabulous 5th Dimension right here in the Deauville's beautiful Casanova Room."

Then, Morty announced, "It's time for the Deauville Beach Hotel's Twist Contest. Ladies and gentlemen, please make your way over to the dancing area for our twist contest. The winning couple will receive two tickets for tonight's 5th Dimension show. C'mon, grab your partner and get your tushies out here."

Out of nowhere, Suzie's mom, Sylvia, came by, accompanied by an awkward-looking guy with glasses. "Suzie, I brought Mrs. Weinberg's son Stephen over for you to dance with. Stephen, this is my daughter Suzie; she's a terrific dancer."

"Hi, Stephen, I'm sorry, but my mom's mistaken. I'm not a very good dancer."

"Now, Suzie, you're a terrific dancer. You remember, Stephen's parents are Bubbe's neighbors, and Stephen is an accounting student at the University of Florida. Now dance with him, because we must leave soon to get ready for tonight."

"Where are we going tonight?"

"Your father's favorite, Joe's Stone Crab. Stephen and his parents are also coming with Grandma and Grandpa. Your bubbe went out of her way to invite them for you two to meet."

Stephen started turning red while looking up in embarrassment. Barry, Lois, and I were trying not to laugh. Suzie said, "Okay, okay, I'll dance," as she gave me an embarrassed look. "I'll be right back." Stephen looked terrified as he and Suzie headed for contest. As soon as they hit the dance floor, "Let's Twist Again" by Chubby Checker started playing through the pool's speakers. Stephen started doing his version of the twist, looking like the future Big Bird, while Suzie was doing her own hippie free-style dance. They were soon eliminated. Suzie and Stephen walked over to Suzie's parents' cabana to talk to her mom, who I could see, along with her father and Lois's parents, were getting ready to leave. After a few words, the two came back over by us.

Lois noticed, "Stephen, you're bleeding."

Stephen, looking down at his flip-flops, saw that he had cut his big toe.

Suzie said, "Stephen, you better go take care of that."

"Okay, Suzie, see you tonight."

After he had walked away, Suzie said, "You guys, I'm so embarrassed."

We all started laughing, including Suzie.

"Hey, girls, you want a hit of hash?" Barry asked.

Suzie responded, "I'd love some, but where can we go?"

Lois said, "Look, our parents are about to leave the cabana. We can smoke there when they're gone."

So, Suzie and Lois walked over to the cabana and said goodbye to their parents, telling them they would meet them in the lobby at five to go to Joe's Stone Crab. When Barry and I entered the cabana, Suzie pulled the flap across the front, and we all took a hit. Lois commented, "That's some heavy hash. Do you guys have more? We have some good grass along with some acid in our room, but this hashish is out of sight." Barry broke off a little piece of his hash and handed it to Lois.

Suzie brought up the Miami Pop Festival. "Are you guys going to Gulfstream Park this weekend?"

As I was about to reply, a man who appeared to be Suzie's father pulled back the flap and walked into the cabana. "Suzie, why is the flap closed to the cabana, and what's that smell?"

"This is my father, Stanley Simon," Suzie said, trying to introduce us.

"I think you boys should leave now, and Suzie and Lois, you need to go up to your room. Suzie, I came down here because your mother wants you to see the new dress she bought for you to wear tonight."

"Bye, girls," Barry said.

"See you later," I said, giving a little finger wave.

As we walked out, I could hear Suzie call after us. "It was nice meeting you. Hope to see you at the pool tomorrow."

"Hey, where's Shane?" I asked.

Barry replied, "I don't know. He took off with Andy Cohen and never came back. Let's go back to the room and mellow out."

"Cool, but first I want to stop by my car for a minute. I think I left my hairbrush there, and there should still be some snacks in the trunk."

Sure enough, after grabbing my hairbrush from the back seat, we opened the trunk and found the container of Pik-Nik shoestring potatoes and the package of bittersweet baking chocolates we had taken from my house. I also found three joints, which I'd forgotten I had hidden in the wheel well just before we left Oklahoma. When we got back to the room, we smoked one of the joints, kicking back on the two single beds.

Then Barry said, "I'm thirsty and my throat is really dry from all the hash. I think I'll go get us some beer."

He came back with two six-packs of Jax. "Hey, Barry, why did you get two six-packs?" I asked.

"They were on sale, two six packs for three dollars while one was two dollars. For an extra buck, we got six more beers. Cheers, Krock," Barry toasted as he handed me one of the beers and put the rest in the room's not-very-cold small refrigerator. After that, we polished off the shoestrings and the chocolates, washing them down with a couple beers each.

We watched the news with Walter Cronkite, which showed a whole platoon of soldiers celebrating Christmas in Vietnam. I thought to myself how lucky I was to be here and not fighting a war I did not understand. It was 7 p.m. when Cronkite signed off as he did every night, saying, "And that's the way it is, December 26th, 1968." After the news, we turned on an old *Honeymooners* rerun that we had both seen before. Within minutes, I was fast asleep and didn't wake up till I heard Dean Martin sing his theme song, "Everybody Loves Somebody Sometime." It was now about 10 p.m.

I asked Barry, "Are you sleeping?"

Barry replied, "No, I woke up about an hour ago, took a shower, and got dressed." He then pulled back the drapes and told me to come see what was going on outside, as I could hear old Dino announce his guests for his show that night, which included Zero Mostel, Buddy Ebsen, Shecky Greene, Lena Horne, and a TV actress named Barbara Heller. Looking out the window, which faced Collins Avenue, we could see that the street was packed with college kids and traffic was bumper to bumper. "Hey, Krock, why don't you clean up and get dressed, and we can go hit the streets. There's a ton of pretty chicks on the street, and I'm starting to get a little hungry."

"Go ahead, Barry, I'll catch up with you later. I need to take a shower, and you're ready to go."

"Okay, Krock, see you later."

After Barry left, I took a couple more hits off a joint and grabbed another Jax for my dry mouth. When the *Dean Martin Show* was over, I jumped in the shower. After getting out of the shower, combing my hair, and brushing my teeth, I threw on my blue jean shorts and my only clean t-shirt and lay back down on the bed. The eleven o'clock news was almost over as I finished that third beer and was about to finish getting dressed, then *The Joey Bishop Show* came on. I couldn't believe that Red Foxx was his guest that night. This was a few years before *Sanford and Son*. I loved Redd Foxx, having learned about him from listening to his records.

You see, my dad, in addition to being a scrap peddler, would also take jobs offered to him because he had a big truck. One day, a guy asked him to pull down an old frame garage in an alley in Chicago's Lawndale neighborhood. My dad had learned that he was able to take these small wood frame garages down by wrapping big chains around the garage and attaching them to the back of his truck and then moving slowly forward in the alley where the garage faced. Before he pulled any garage down, he would naturally clean out the inside.

Well, one day he came home with a treasured box of records after the owners had told my dad to dispose of everything left inside the garage. The box contained records by Sarah Vaughan, Nat King Cole, and Etta James, among about a dozen others, including two Redd Foxx albums. When my dad came home with this box of records, he left them outside on our back porch. Later that night, my dad told me to go clean up the records and put them in my closet, since at the time, the only record player in the house was in my room. I was about fourteen at the time, and the next day after school, with my friend Gary Garfield, we started going through them.

I didn't know anything about the Redd Foxx records, but Gary, having worked at his uncle's record store in the South Loop that catered to a Black clientele, knew all about these very funny party records, which contained brazen talk of sex and color using four-letter words. Gary told me that the reason I'd never heard of Redd Foxx before was because the only places these party records were sold were in the record stores where Black folks shopped. For the next few months, my friends and I wore these records out, and we all became big Redd Foxx fans.

Anyhow, I grabbed another beer and settled back to watch Redd do his thing that night on the *Joey Bishop Show*. Although it was nothing like those party records we had listened to, he was still very funny. Redd cracked me up that night. After finishing another beer and smoking more weed, I had fallen back to sleep only to be woken a few hours later by a lot of noise outside.

When I looked out the window, it appeared that one of the couches from the Brazil Hotel lobby, along with Oscar, was now in the middle of Collins Avenue with horns blowing and traffic backed up, even though it was almost four in the morning. Upon seeing this, I rushed down the stairs barefoot onto Collins Avenue, only to see Oscar still sleeping on the couch, even with all these cars blowing their horns, while trying to avoid hitting the couch and Oscar. Now, with all that noise and commotion, and these college pranksters laughing their asses off, many of whom I knew, I ran into the middle of Collins Avenue and shook Oscar until he finally woke up. After he came to, he looked up at me and said, "Where the hell am I?"

I put his arm over my shoulder and walked him to the curb. I told him, "You were sleeping on your couch in the middle of Collins Avenue. Who did this?"

As he looked over at the guilty ones, who had stopped laughing, Oscar whispered in my ear, "Tell those motherfuckers to put the couch back where it belongs. I need to put some water on my face and make some coffee."

So, I started screaming at Mooch Sands, Al Katz, and a bunch of other Skokie guys I could tell were in on it. Then I yelled at these guys that they had better move that couch back in the lobby or Oscar says he's going to throw them all out. After the guys moved the couch back into the lobby, Oscar put his hearing aids back in and then walked into the lobby and told them, "No more shenanigans, fellas, or you can all leave. And if you don't think I'm serious just try me." He pointed a gun at the ceiling that he had just pulled out of the safe under the front desk.

Oscar turned to me after putting the gun away and asked, "What's your name, kid?"

"Al," I said.

"Didn't I hear them call you by another name, like Rocky?"

"No, they called me Krockey. That's my last name."

"Well, Mr. Krockey, I want to thank you for saving my tuchus. I'm Oscar Rosen."

I replied, "Rosen, that's a Jewish name. I thought you were Cuban."

"I am. I'm a Cuban Jew, originally from what they now call Belarus, but when I was first growing up there, it was still mostly Lithuanian and Polish, and then in '39 it became occupied by the Soviets."

"Wow, that's really interesting. How did you end up in Miami?"

"Listen, Krockey, are you hungry? Come, follow me."

So, I followed Oscar to a small apartment next to the hotel lobby. "I'm going to make us both a little Cuban breakfast and then we can sit and talk. Do you like Cuban coffee?"

"I don't know. I've never tried it."

"I'm going to make you the best Cubano coffee with steamed milk. What we call café con leche."

"Thank you, Oscar; you don't have to go to all that trouble."

"Don't be silly—I make it for myself anyway. So now I make double." He nodded and smiled at me, saying, "Bueno!" Oscar had this strange accent, always going back and forth using English and Spanish and throwing in Yiddish. Come to think of it, he sounded just the way you would expect an Eastern European Cuban Jew to sound. Then, as we ate our breakfast, which was amazing, we started to talk.

I asked, "Do you live here?"

"No, sir, I have a beautiful apartment at the Coral Sea Towers, where I live with my wife, Leah, and my sixteen-year-old daughter, Laura. My oldest daughter, Francine, goes to school in Gainesville, where she is studying medicine at the University of Florida Medical School."

"That's great. You must be very proud."

"Yes, of course, but it's because of the influence of my wife and my wife's father, who is a doctor, that she followed that path. Very smart people and a very warm, nice family. I'm blessed. You see, after the war, I left my country, arriving in Cuba in 1945 with only a few dollars in my pocket. My older brother Alex had been in Cuba since 1940, going there right after the Germans invaded Poland in 1939 and trying for years to bring me to Cuba. But I couldn't get out till the war ended. So, I joined the Jewish resistance in Belarus called the Bielski partisans. We fought against Nazis using guerrilla warfare much like the way the Vietcong are fighting our troops. These war years were the hardest years of my life. I lost many friends and family. May they rest in peace.

"You see, my brother Alex had a childhood friend from Grodno who was a big Jewish businessman named Meyer Lansky. In the 1940s, Meyer, along with his brother Jake, was running all the gambling operations in Cuba for the mob and Batista. So, when my brother Alex arrived in Cuba, Meyer and his brother Jake taught my brother the gambling business and eventually made him a pit boss in the casino at the Nacional Hotel. It was in 1945 when my brother arranged for me to come to Cuba.

"When I arrived, Alex was able to get me a job at the Nacional Hotel as a desk clerk, and then eventually I would move up to assistant manager. Then in the '50s, Meyer and Jake opened the Habana Riviera, and so both Alex and I moved over to this brand-new beautiful hotel casino, with Alex as a pit boss in the casino and me as the assistant manager of the hotel, as well as the high rollers' concierge. But, of course, having come from Grodno, the same town as the Lanskys, we became close friends with the two Lansky brothers, playing Partnership Gin Rummy every week with them. Whenever we were together, we only spoke Yiddish.

"Fortunately, Meyer, Jake, Alex, and I all made it to Miami, and the four of us still play gin once a week. In fact, I met my Leah through Jake. It was only a few months after I had arrived in Cuba. I was working one day at my job as one of the front desk clerks at the Nacional Hotel when a little kid dropped a bottle of Coca-Cola right in front of the desk. I walked over to see what had happened and to see if the kid was okay. Anyhow, for some reason instead of waiting for the porter to come and clean up the mess, I started to clean up. That's when I cut the shit out of my index finger. Look here, you can still see the scar.

"Anyhow, Jake, whom I had barely known at the time, happened to be in the hotel lobby and rushed over to help me, giving me his handkerchief to wrap around my finger and then walking me around the corner to Dr. Schwartz's office. As soon as we walked into Dr. Schwartz's office, Leah, a nurse, who also happened to be Dr. Schwartz's daughter, saw that I was bleeding and took me into one of the examination rooms, which is where we first met. After her father stitched me up, I asked Leah to dinner, and six months later we were married.

"Earlier, you asked me how I arrived in Miami. Well, Castro took over Cuba on New Year's Eve, 1959. Meyer and Jake lost the hotels and casinos and all that went with it, and we all ended up here in Miami Beach, leaving our homes and investments in Cuba. I tell the guests here that I'm the hotel's manager, but I'm really one of the owners of the Brazil Hotel. When we arrived here in Miami, and with whatever money my brother Alex and I were able to get out of Cuba, we decided to invest in hotels with Leah's uncle Seymour Schwartz, the doc's brother. A few months ago, Seymour caught the Brazil Hotel's old manager and the desk clerks stealing. Of course, we had to let them go. So now, we are both coming in a few days a week until we get a full staff we can trust, while my brother Alex runs our other hotel called The Senator.

"So, what's your story, Krockey?" As I told Oscar a short version of my life story, he would nod and make an occasional short comment like yes, no, uh-huh, really, that's too bad, or that's impressive. But Oscar waited until the very end of my tale to give me longer comments, resulting in some good advice from this seasoned and wise sixty-two-year-old man.

He went on to say, "So, Krockey, you're quite a go-getter. Working at the ballpark selling souvenirs, a little door-to-door sales, selling pants out the trunk of your car, it's all quite admirable. It was too bad about those Christmas trees. You took a calculated risk using your case money. But you're young and I'm sure, with all that hustle, you will be back on your feet in no time. If I were you, I would try and take something you enjoy and turn it into a business. Maybe a little store."

"Wow, Oscar, that's exactly what Arnie Fisher, the one who sold me the bell-bottom pants, told me."

"Well then, maybe you should listen. I see you guys are checking out today. Where are you going to go?"

"I'm not sure; my friend Barry paid for the first two nights, and now he is leaving. He made plans to stay at his cousin's place in Fort Lauderdale, and my friend Shane and I don't have enough to stay even for one more night."

"How are you going to get home?" Oscar asked me while shaking his head.

"That's a good question," I replied.

"I tell you what I'm going to do, Alan. You and your one friend can stay here tonight, on me. Although tonight, Seymour, my partner, is coming in, and I'll be gone till Monday. So, if you decide you want to stay longer, you will have to pay, which is why I'm going to lend you a hundred dollars; this way, you will have money to stay a few more nights, and plenty left for food and gas to get you home."

"Oscar, I don't know how to thank you."

He replied, "Well, first, when you get back and start this new radio school, make sure to do your best. And then once you get back on your feet, you can mail the money back to me. Here is my home address and telephone."

"I can't thank you enough. Why are you doing this? We just met, and you hardly know me."

Then Oscar said, "I know you better than you think, and besides, you saved my ass and now I'm helping to save yours. Remember, no racetrack or gambling."

"Okay, Oscar, and thanks again."

I smiled at him and he said, "Goodbye, boychick. Stay in touch."

As I walked through the lobby, I hadn't realized how long Oscar and I had talked until I noticed the clock behind the front desk showed it was almost noon. I decided to take a walk over to the Deauville to see if I could find Suzie. She had mentioned going to the Miami Pop Festival, which I did not want to miss.

When I got to the Deauville, I gave Bembe a dollar and he told me, "Follow me—all your friends are over here. Hey, those are the same Ray-Bans I have. Nice glasses, aren't they?"

"The coolest," I replied, laughing to myself. Then I asked, "Isn't that one of the guys and one of the girls from the 5th Dimension sitting on the edge of the pool with their feet in the water?"

"Yes, amigo, that's Marilyn McCoo and Billy Davis Jr. I think they are married. Anyway, they tip us good and asked us to help them try and keep a low profile so that too many people don't bother them. Which is a little hard, since they are the only Black people staying at the hotel."

As we approached where a bunch of my friends were lying on the Deauville's chaise lounges, I spotted Shane sitting next to Andy Cohen while both were sipping on one of those tropical drinks with an umbrella sticking out. I asked Shane, "Where did you sleep last night?"

"Andy and I went to see my friend Lee Liss over at Miami Dade Junior College. We ended up sleeping in his dorm room, where there was a spare bed. Krock, I think I'm going to ask my parents if I can go to school down here and register at Miami Dade for next semester. I love Miami."

Andy said, "I love it here too. I graduate from Niles East next June, and I for sure want to go to college in Miami and get away from those freezing Chicago winters. Plus, this way me and Sugar can be together."

Then, I saw Suzie's cousin Lois sitting in her parents' cabana, and sitting right next to her was my friend Barry. I walked over to the other side of the pool where the cabanas were and asked, "Barry, what are you doing here? I thought you were staying with your cousins in Fort Lauderdale."

"I am, Krock. This is my cousin Jeff. I spoke with Lois on the phone this morning, and she suggested we come meet her at the Deauville pool. I'm glad I did." Then, Barry and Lois clinked their glasses with the little umbrellas together as they smiled.

I asked Lois, "Where's Suzie?"

"She and both our parents are still with our grandparents."

"When is she coming back?"

"Probably tomorrow. Our bubbe is making a big Shabbat dinner tonight for our family, and Suzie said she is going to sleep there tonight."

"Isn't she going to the festival?"

"I know she's definitely going the second day, Sunday, and probably Monday, but not sure about tomorrow, Saturday."

I grabbed the chaise lounge next to Shane, where Bembe had laid one of those fluffy Deauville beach towels. I asked him, "What are those drinks with the little umbrellas that everyone is drinking?"

Andy answered, "They're called piña coladas. They make them with rum, coconut milk, and pineapple juice, and they're delish. You want one? I have my parents' credit card."

"That's okay, Andy, thank you. I was able to put my hands on a few bucks and get one more night in the room."

Shane asked, "Where did you get the money?"

"Oscar, the Brazil Hotel's manager, lent me a couple bucks. I will tell you about it later."

Shane replied, "Okay, let's drink up." He motioned for Peggy, the waitress, to come over. "Peggy, we need a few more drinks. We would like three of these piña coladas with plenty of rum, and my friend Krockey is buying."

I asked Peggy, "How much for these drinks?"

"All the drinks today are seventy-five cents."

"Well then, bring us three."

Andy said, "I'll buy the next round." I was not used to drinking hard liquor, and after two strong piña coladas, I ended up falling asleep by the pool until Bembe woke me up around four. As I looked around, I asked him, "Where is everybody?"

"Your friends left about an hour ago. That guy Shane said to meet him at the hotel."

When I walked into the room, Andy had just gotten out of the shower and was wrapped in two towels, one around her body and one around her hair. I could see Shane was under the covers and fast asleep, snoring like a moose. Andy said, "Let him sleep. He drank about five piña coladas. Tell him I'm taking a cab back to The Castaways and remind Gary that you guys should come by about ten to pick up Donna and me."

"Where are we going?"

"Oh, that's right, you were sleeping. When we were lying out at the pool, Cindy Lavin came by to tell us that she was going to put Gary Shane, you, Donna, and me on the guest list of this discotheque called The Barn on the 79th Street Causeway. It turns out her father, Mel Lavin, who lives over in West Palm Beach, came down to Miami to see Cindy and her brother, Michael. He told Cindy that his good friend owns this place called The Barn, and he wanted to take her and her friends to see this white soul singer, Wayne Cochran, and his band."

I said, "Really, a white soul singer? How good could he be?"

Andy answered, "Cindy said he was unbelievable."

"Andy, how are we supposed to get into a bar that serves drinks? I don't have any fake IDs."

"Don't worry," Cindy said, "there is a special under-twenty-one area for us to sit in. And her father has made all the arrangements. We are meeting her and Bob there at ten-thirty."

After Andy left, I walked down to the lobby to get more towels so I could take a shower. When I got to the desk, Oscar was gone, and a very fat, Jewish-looking older man with glasses was sitting behind the desk, whom I assumed was Oscar's partner, Seymour. I asked if I could get more towels. He asked me for my room number. After I told him, he looked up and spoke. "Oh, you're that kid Krockey that Oscar told me about. I'm Oscar's partner, Sy Schwartz. Oscar told me you're a good kid. He also mentioned you might be staying a few more days and to not reserve the room for the weekend until I talk with you, just in case you want to stay a few more days."

"Can I let you know tomorrow, Mr. Schwartz?"

"Sure, as long as it's before ten, as checkout is at eleven and we're expecting to sell out this weekend with all the kids here for Christmas break, and please call me Sy or Seymour."

"Thank you, Sy." When I got back to the room, Shane was still sleeping, and I decided to take a shower, after which I also decided to take a little nap. I was awoken by the phone in the room ringing. I was about to get up and answer, but heard Shane say "Hello" to Andy. After he got off the phone, he nudged me, "Wake up." I sat up. "We need to get ready for tonight."

"Okay, go take a shower, Gary. I already took mine. Whose pot is this on the dresser?"

"Oh, Andy must have left it here."

"I'm going to roll a few joints for tonight." I started to roll a few joints after lighting the half joint that lay in the ashtray.

Soon we were both getting dressed when Shane said, "C'mon, Krock, let's go over to Texas Burger and eat before we go pick up the girls. Do you have any money left?"

"Yep, I still have a few bucks. I can buy dinner." I didn't want to tell Shane that I still had ninety-six dollars and fifty cents, as he would have asked me to borrow some. Plus, Andy had slipped and mentioned she had lent Shane fifty dollars, which he had not bothered to tell me. So, I told him I had six bucks and a little change. When I was getting dressed, I put ninety in my left pocket while I put six-fifty in my right.

After we both finished our double Texas Burgers, fries, and an Orange Julius, we headed to The Castaways Hotel to pick up the girls. Shane really liked Andy, and I was always friendly with Donna, but not in a girlfriend kind of way, as she was going steady with Jim Gunderson, who was away somewhere out west in college.

Donna and I had become friends a couple of years earlier when she asked me if I would follow her father from his store. She suspected he was cheating on her mother and even offered to pay me a dollar an hour to do so. Sure enough, the first time I watched him, he was working at his fur store on Dempster, while I sat next door in the parking lot of this strip center, clocking his store. Then, after he left his fur store on Dempster, I followed him to the Touhy House Bar

& Restaurant. Once inside, I saw him walk over to the bar, ordering a drink for himself and the redheaded woman next to him. I soon realized it happened to be the same lady I'd seen working in the fur store earlier that day.

When I told Donna, she couldn't believe it was Doris, her mother's good friend who worked at her parents' store. After I told her, she started crying, saying, "Oh my God, that's my mother's best friend." She wanted to give me five dollars for the hours I spent watching her father at his store and then following him, but I refused to take it as she was crying and very upset. Ever since then, we had been pals.

When we arrived at The Castaways, the girls were waiting outside. On our way over to The Barn, Shane asked Andy if she'd brought the bottle of rum they had stolen earlier from the pool bar. Andy responded, "It's in my purse, babe."

Shane replied, "Cool. Keep it hidden in your purse until we're inside the club."

I parked my Buick about two blocks away because The Barn's parking lot was full. As we walked up to the nightclub, we saw Cindy standing outside with her boyfriend, Bob, and her brother, Mike "Dizzy" Lavin, and Mike's girlfriend, Annette. I said, "Hey, Mike, I haven't seen you since the Doors concert when I was selling binoculars and sold you some pot."

Mike replied, "Unbelievable. That was the night I was dancing on top of those big speakers when they fell, and I sprained my ankle. Unbelievable."

"You're a wild man, Dizzy."

Then Donna asked, "Cindy, where is your father?"

"He just left. We all went out to dinner and then we came here. When we got here, his girlfriend wasn't feeling good, so after he set us up with his friend Junior here, he went back to West Palm Beach. Guys, this is Junior; he works here and has us all set up in the under-twenty-one section." Once we were seated in the underage section, we ordered some Cokes and waited for the show to start. I noticed that Mike and Annette had snuck off into the over-twenty-one area.

Shane announced, "Pass your Cokes to me one by one, and Andy will add some of this Myers's Rum." Soon after Wayne Cochran and the CC Ryders hit the stage, I would find out what a first-rate singer he was and what a tight band the CC Ryders were. I was truly impressed. He sang Otis Redding songs, Wilson Pickett, and even sang and danced like James Brown. He and his band reminded me of Baby Huey and the Babysitters, both with intensely soulful voices and a smoking horn section. The energy of the show from this crazy-looking guy with his outlandish outfit and platinum blond hairstyle just blew the crowd away.

As the show went on, Shane and I wound up finishing the Myers's Rum as Bob and Cindy weren't drinking, and Donna and Andy only had one drink with the rum added. By the time the show had ended, I was buzzed and sweating my ass off as it was so crowded and hot in the club, especially since Donna and I did a lot of dancing. When we finally got outside, Shane told me he was going back to The Castaways with Andy and that Cindy's boyfriend, Bob, was giving them all a lift since they were all staying at The Castaways.

Just then, I saw Dizzy Lavin lay some rubber as he pulled out of the nightclub's parking lot in his GTO. I said goodbye to everyone, thanking Cindy for getting us in. Getting in my car, I was still a little tipsy. I drove away in my Buick, jumping on the 79th Street Causeway. Driving back to the hotel, I had trouble staying awake, even with the top down and the tropical Miami breeze. Suddenly, I heard a loud noise as my head hit the steering wheel. Realizing I must have dozed off, I looked up and saw that my car was in the middle divider of the causeway with my front bumper wrapped around a palm tree.

I tried to back up but my car wouldn't move. Upon inspection, I could see the front axle was broken. I saw the cops were about to pull up, so I got back in the car, picking up the roach in the ashtray and swallowing it, dry mouth and all. Soon, the squad car came to a halt and two policemen walked over to the car. One was a tall, young, white cop who wore a neatly pressed policeman's uniform and hat. The other was an older Hispanic-looking, heavy-set cop, with a sergeant patch on his uniform but wearing no hat, showing his bald head. Then the older cop asked me to get out of the car and went on to ask, "What the hell happened here?"

I then lied, "Well, Officer, you see this other car cut me off and I had to swerve and that's how my car ended up going over the embankment in the middle of the causeway and hitting that tree."

"Let me see your license and registration," which I gave him. I noticed the name badge on his shirt said Arturo Garcia. After looking at my license and registration, he handed them over to his young partner and told him, "Tommy, go run his plates and his license and wait for me in the squad."

"Okay, Sarge."

"Listen, Alan, I see you're from Illinois, and your sweaty shirt smells of liquor. Right now, I'm sure if I gave you a sobriety test, you would fail. And, in addition to arresting you for a DUI, I could throw you in jail for destroying public property and reckless driving."

I was about to say something when Officer Garcia told me, "Do not say a word and go sit in your car till I return."

As I sat down on the passenger side of my Buick, Officer Garcia walked over to his squad car, where he talked with his partner through the squad car window. While I sat there waiting, all I could think of was going to jail and having to call my parents. Then, after about fifteen minutes, Officer Garcia walked back to my car and got in on the driver's side, pulling the front seat back as far as it would go.

"Well, Alan, looks like your plates are clean and you have no warrants. Alan, you seem like a nice kid, and I really don't want to arrest you and have to do all that paperwork. I'm sure you can see your car is so badly damaged it can't be driven and will cost more to fix than it's worth. But, I do love these old Buicks. The problem is what to write in the report. Also, if you are arrested, you will be responsible for paying the cost of having the city tow your car away. The city will then charge you at least a hundred dollars for the tow in addition to the fine, which will be at least $500. In addition, a DUI could possibly land you in the slammer and possibly have your license suspended. But, if I decide not to arrest you, the city won't charge you for the tow if you surrender the title. Do you have any money on you?"

I then reached into my left pocket and pulled out the ninety dollars I had and showed it to Officer Garcia, while telling him, "It's all I have."

"Do you have the title for the car?"

"Yes, right here in the glove box."

"Well, Alan, today might be your lucky day as my shift ends in an hour and I really don't want to spend a couple of extra hours doing paperwork. So here is what I suggest: Unless you prefer I give you a sobriety test and put you under arrest, you can lay that ninety dollars right here on the seat, which I will donate to my favorite charity," he said with a wink. So, I put the money on the seat and then Officer Garcia handed me my license back, shaking my hand and squeezing it hard while telling me, "You are now a free man. Do not say anything about this to anyone." Officer Garcia then asked, "Where are you staying?"

I told him, "The Brazil Hotel over on Collins Avenue."

"Since it's not too far, I will give you a ride there while my partner waits for the tow truck." He then walked over to the squad car and told his partner, "I'm letting the kid go."

Then his partner asked him, "Why are you letting him go?"

"Tommy, I believe the kid's story, and since he has no record, and the plates checked out, I am going to let him go." Officer Tommy Flynn looked up at Officer Garcia with a puzzled look. Garcia then went on to say, "You know, Tommy, the kid just lost his car, which he told me was given to him by his father and was his prized possession. And sometimes you need to give a kid a break, especially since no one was hurt."

Officer Tommy Flynn responded, "I guess you're right, Sarge."

"I'm glad you understand. I'll be right back. I'm going to take the squad and run the kid over to the Brazil Hotel on Collins. Here's the title of the car. You wait here for the tow truck. It shouldn't take more than fifteen minutes each way. Do you want some coffee and donuts?"

"That would be great, Sarge. Do you need some money, Sarge?"

"No, I got it this time."

"Thanks, Sarge."

I realized right then that Officer Garcia would be keeping all the dough for himself, and I thought to myself how lucky I was that this old-school cop was on the take and I was not going to jail. When we were a few blocks from the hotel, I asked him, "Would you mind pulling over here? I don't want my friends or the hotel manager to ask any questions about why I'm being dropped off by the police."

"That's smart, Alan. Remember, don't tell anyone." After pulling onto a secluded side street to let me out, he shook and squeezed my hand again, but this time smiling and wishing me well.

As I walked back to the hotel, it started to hit me that I was completely broke once more, and that my car, my beautiful Buick that my father was so proud to have given me, was now headed for the junkyard. When I got back to the room, I could see the sun coming up as I closed the drapes and took my shoes off. I lay down on the bed, looked up at the ceiling, and wondered, "What now?" I had only been sleeping for a short time when the phone rang.

"Hi, Alan, it's Sy Schwartz. What did you decide? Are you staying or checking out?"

"Checking out, sir. I think I might be heading back to Chicago later today."

"That's too bad. Please be out by eleven."

"Will do. Thank you." After I hung up with Sy, I realized I had left my eight-track player and my tapes in the car as well, which made me even more depressed. After showering and getting dressed, I packed my few pieces of clothing in my duffel bag and headed for the lobby.

When I got to the front desk and handed Sy the key, he asked me, "What's wrong? You looked troubled."

"Nothing, I just have a lot on my mind with going home and starting school and everything."

"I understand. When are you leaving?"

"Probably later tonight. I was wondering if you had a washing machine I could use."

"Well, Alan, we only have the ones for the sheets and towels, and the guests are not allowed to use them. But I guess I can make an exception this time."

Sy called out to one of the housekeepers, "Maria, please take this young man's clothes and wash them." She walked back into the laundry room and came out holding a pillowcase she was about to wash. "Please put your clothes in here." She grabbed the pillowcase and my duffel bag and said, "You come back later."

"Thank you, Maria."

Sy said while he reached out to shake my hand, "Alan, you have a safe trip. I won't be seeing you again as I'm about to leave for the day. Hector here is training to be the new manager. If you need anything else, just ask Hector." Then he said something to Hector in Spanish.

"Thank you, Mr. Schwartz. You and Oscar are really nice people."

"You're welcome."

As soon as I hit the sidewalk, reality set in. I started thinking, *Where would I go? What do I tell my parents? Do I ask them to send me money? Do I call my Aunt Lill and Uncle Jack? How am I going to get back to Chicago?* With all this running through my head, I decided that I needed to take a walk and clear my head. I started walking. After about a mile, I saw a payphone and decided to call my Aunt

Lill and Uncle Jack. They had retired to Miami a few years back from Cleveland, where my Uncle Jack had driven a laundry truck and at the same time ran a small bookie operation. My Aunt Lill had worked in the children's clothes department at The May Company in Cleveland. They had married in their forties and had no children.

In my summers between the ages of six and twelve, my parents would ship me off to stay with them for a couple of weeks. And then, when my sister became six or seven, they sent both of us off to Cleveland, where my aunt and uncle would spoil us by taking us to this amusement park called Euclid Beach. My uncle also loved taking me to see his beloved Cleveland Indians, while my aunt loved schlepping my sister and me to see children's plays like *Peter Pan* with Mary Martin or *Davy Crockett* with Fess Parker. I have to say, they were fun times. All in all, my sister and I were loved by Lill and Jack, and we both loved them too.

The only thing was, I had only seen them twice since my bar mitzvah and rarely called them. Now, I would be calling and asking them to help me. I found a phone booth, and after dialing Information to get their phone number and street address, I wrote it down on a book of matches I'd had in my pocket. I stuck a dime in the payphone and dialed their number nervously. When they didn't answer, I felt a little relieved and walked across the street to a gas station to ask for directions to their place. The man at the gas station, after giving me directions, told me it would take me over an hour to walk there and suggested I take the bus. I started walking in the direction of their house, taking side streets. After a few blocks, I saw an old lady struggling to carry a big tray of food from her car into what appeared to be a synagogue. I ran up to her, asking if she needed help.

"Oy," she said, "that would be terrific. Are you Jewish?"

"Yes, I am."

"Wonderful. You can help me set up the food for the Kiddush following the Shabbat services. Do you live in the neighborhood?"

"No, I'm from Chicago." And just like that, I was back in a temple. "Come, you can enjoy the service after we set up. Temple Shalom is a Reform synagogue and we have a beautiful choir. There's a bar mitzvah today."

"I'm not sure how long I can stay."

"Stay as long as you like. If you decide to stay for the service and you help me serve, I will give you a ride wherever you want to go. I'm Fanny Goldberg. Good to meet you."

"I'm Alan Krockey."

"Okay, let's get everything set up quickly so we can both enjoy the service."

I started to hesitate, but then thought, *Why not? What else do I have to do? Maybe this is a sign.* After setting everything up, Mrs. Goldberg handed me a yarmulke and took me into the temple, sitting down next to what appeared to be her husband.

The service was about to start when her husband turned to her. "Why didn't you come and get me to help?"

"Alan helped me set up. This is my husband, Herb Goldberg."

"Thank you for helping my wife. Are you and your family members? I don't think I've seen you here before."

"No, I'm from Chicago." Just then, the service started. I had never been in a temple where they had a choir, let alone a band featuring a guitar player, a piano player, and a percussionist.

I'd been reared in a traditional synagogue. I found myself enjoying the service and praying with the music. I thought, *In almost six years since my bar mitzvah, I have not been to a synagogue more than five or six times, and then mostly on the High Holidays with my father.* Now, the bar mitzvah boy was starting his Haftarah. As Jeffrey Finkelman chanted, I thought that this sounded very familiar. Could this be the same Haftarah I said for my bar mitzvah in 1963? No, it couldn't be. But then I thought, *Maybe it is since my birthday was coming up in a little over a week, and who knows with the way the Jewish calendar works?*

As Jeffrey continued, I realized it was the same Haftarah, having listened to a recording of this Haftarah every day for a month and memorizing it to prepare for my bar mitzvah. Was I meant to be here? Maybe this was a sign. After they had put the Torah away, Jeffery gave his bar mitzvah speech and thanked everyone for coming. After that, the rabbi gave his sermon, talking about overcoming obstacles in life, about getting back on your feet after falling, that sometimes failing or having something bad happen can be a path or a lesson and a means to get where you are going. He went on about gratitude and being grateful—and how all of us, no matter what we are going through, have reasons to be grateful.

The rabbi closed his sermon, saying, "Remember, most things are out of our hands. All we can do is trust in God and do what's in front of us. Have a good Shabbat." After this moving sermon, the cantor came on and sang a beautiful version of Hatikvah, which is the Israeli national anthem. The worry I had felt earlier had gone away, and I now felt more relaxed. Thinking about starting school and finding a new job gave me new hope. Following the service, I helped Mrs. Goldberg serve the after-service Kiddish, which consisted of honey cake, cookies, wine, and grape juice for the kids, along with coffee. After we cleaned up, Mrs. Goldberg asked, "Where can we drop you off?"

I answered with a question. "Is there a payphone here?"

"Follow me," she answered and took me into the synagogue's office. "Here, you can use the office phone."

I tried calling my aunt and uncle again, but there was still no answer. I would find out when I got back to Chicago that they had gone back to Cleveland to attend my Uncle Jack's old boss's funeral.

After hanging up, I asked the Goldbergs, "Would you mind dropping me off at the Brazil Hotel? It's on Collins down the street from Pumpernik's."

Then Mrs. Goldberg asked me, "Would you like to come to our house and join us for dinner?"

I thanked them and told them I had already made plans, even though I didn't have a clue where or what I was going to do next. When we arrived at the hotel, Mr. Goldberg handed me his business card that said Goldie's Dry Cleaning, then told me, "During the week, we are always there if you ever need something."

Mrs. Goldberg gave me a kiss on the cheek and said in Yiddish, "Zei Gezunt."

I replied, "I wish you both good health as well." I waved goodbye and walked into the Brazil Hotel to get my clothes.

At the front desk, Hector handed me my duffel bag and said, "Good luck."

Before I left, I turned around and asked Hector if he had a pad of paper and a pen or pencil I could have. "Yes, sir." He handed me a little white pad that had the Brazil Logo on top, along with a Brazil Hotel pen.

"Thanks, Hector. Take care." As I walked out, the anxiety I had felt before I stumbled into Mrs. Goldberg and Temple Shalom's Shabbat service started to slowly creep back into my psyche. As I walked down Collins Avenue, I remembered that there was a nice sitting area in the lower level of the Deauville Hotel next to the restaurant where maybe I could gather my thoughts and write down a to-do list. When I reached the lower level of the Deauville, I saw that no one was sitting on the couch next to the restaurant. After glancing at the menu in front of the entrance, I started to get hungry, looking at all the selections and the people eating as I glanced inside. I started to think maybe I should have taken the Goldbergs up on their dinner invitation. Or maybe I should have taken some of the cookies or honey cake I served at the temple. At least I would have had some food in my belly while I tried to figure things out.

Sitting on the couch outside the restaurant, my anxieties and worries started to increase. I started to write some thoughts down, but my mind was racing. Should I call my parents? Should I try and borrow forty or fifty bucks from my friends so I could fly home? Or try and get a ride back from people I knew who had driven down here? But where would I stay? I saw a few payphones down the hall and started to walk over to try and reach my aunt and uncle again. As I started to get up from the couch and walk over to the phones, I spotted Suzie and her parents walking out of the restaurant. I called out to Suzie to say hi and she replied with a hi back.

Her father said, shaking his head, "Isn't that one of the boys from the cabana? Let's go, Suzie, we are going for ice cream."

As she started to walk away with her parents, she turned her head around to face me without her parents seeing and mouthed silently to me without speaking, "Wait here—I'll be right back." As I sat there waiting for her to return, my anxiety increased along with my hunger. It was now getting close to an hour since Suzie said she would be right back. I thought about leaving, but I didn't know where to go. Just then, Suzie came skipping down the hallway looking beautiful with her long brown hair and a flowing, long hippie-type dress. "Hi, Al."

"I almost left," I told Suzie.

"I'm sorry; my father insisted on taking a little walk after we had our ice cream and then walking me back to my room. Which, thank God, is on a different floor than my parents. Then, once I went into my room, I decided to change. Thank you for waiting. So, what should we do? It's too late to go to the Miami Pop Festival, but we can go together tomorrow."

"That sounds nice, but I must tell you something." I told Suzie all about what had happened to me since I saw her last and how I wasn't sure what I would do next.

After I finished telling her all my woes and how hungry I was, Suzie gently placed her hand on my cheek, and with her big brown eyes looked at me. "Don't worry, you can stay in my room, Al." She gave me a quick little kiss. "C'mon, I'll buy you some dinner. I can charge it to my room. My father never looks at the bill, although sometimes my mother does." Suzie laughed.

We walked into the Deauville restaurant, and the maître d sat us in a nice corner booth away from the other people dining, as we looked like a couple of hippies. Looking at the menu, I commented on how expensive everything was.

"Get whatever you like, Al."

"Suzie, I promise to pay you back when I get home and back on my feet."

"It's not a big deal. My father said the steaks here are some of the best. Of course, I wouldn't know because I don't eat meat."

The waitress walked up and asked, "Would you two like to start with a drink?"

Suzie replied, "Yes, I'll have an iced tea, but I think my friend here is ready to order some food, as I already ate."

Smiling, the waitress replied, "Yes, I waited on you and your parents earlier. What would you like to eat, young man?"

I told the waitress, while pointing to the menu, "I will have this New York strip steak with a baked potato."

"How would you like it cooked?"

"Medium rare."

"Would you like butter, sour cream, and chives on your potato or on the side?"

"Oh, you can put it right on top."

"It also comes with our dinner salad."

"No salad for me."

Suzie said, "I will take his salad."

"What do you want to drink, sir?"

"A Coke would be great."

While we were eating, we talked about the festival and all the incredible music we would be seeing. Suzie told me how she loved going to college in New York, and we discovered that a lot of the bands she had seen at the Fillmore East I had seen at the Kinetic Playground.

Suzie also pointed out, "Hey, there's the guy from *Bonanza*."

"You're right, that's Loren Greene, and that must be his daughter who he is sharing that giant strawberry cheesecake with."

The waitress walked back to our table. "Will there be anything else? Dessert maybe?"

Suzie replied, "Could you please bring us one of those strawberry cheesecakes to go?"

"Oh, those are so good—we get them from Pumpernik's across the street. Anything else?"

"No, just the check." Suzie told the waitress she would be charging it to her room.

When the check came, along with our cheesecake to go, Suzie signed and gave the waitress a big tip. Then the waitress said, "You tip much better than your father," while smiling with a little laugh and thanking Suzie.

I thanked Suzie as we walked out and suggested we take a walk on the beach. Suzie smiled at me and grabbed my hand. "It is so beautiful outside. Let's drop your duffel bag off in my room first, and I can roll a joint for our walk."

When we got to her room, she turned to me, giving me a long kiss, after which she sat on the edge of her bed and rolled a joint, and when she stood up, we kissed again and she grabbed my hand. "Let's go take that walk on the beach."

We walked down the beach smoking and talking. Time flew by and we kissed. I hadn't realized we had been walking for almost two hours until I noticed a large clock on top of one of the hotels. We headed back to her room. Once there, Suzie lit a candle along with some incense and turned the radio on. "Crimson and Clover" came on as I turned the bedroom lights off and headed for the bathroom. After peeing, washing my face, and brushing my teeth with my finger, I walked out of the bathroom to find Suzie undressed and under the covers.

That night, although I had had sex a couple times before, I had never really been this intimate with a woman or made love the way we did that night. Suzie was obviously more experienced, but she somehow made me feel like I was the one teaching her. As an inexperienced eighteen-year-old about to turn nineteen, I started to think that maybe this was love. I woke up that Sunday morning with a smile on my face to the sounds of "Soulful Strut" playing on the radio and we made love again. Soon after, there was a knock on the door. Suzie asked, "Who's there?"

"Room service." Suzie motioned for me to go into the bathroom, which I did. Grabbing her robe, she walked to the door. "You can just wheel it inside the door and I can take it from there."

"You don't want me to set it up, ma'am?"

"No, thanks. Here, let me sign." The waiter rolled the cart just inside the door and then backed his way into the hallway. Suzie handed him the signed check.

"Here you go. I put a nice tip on for you. Happy New Year."

"Same to you, miss, and thank you."

I thought to myself how life can change on a dime, as I stared out the hotel window at the beautiful blue sky with its pink and white clouds and the sun reflecting off the ocean. Then I remembered a line from the rabbi's sermon from yesterday, which fit this moment: "Gratitude can transform common days into thanksgivings." Suzie and I proceeded to devour the wonderful French toast and eggs while finishing off a pot of coffee.

After we showered and dressed, Suzie suggested we walk out separately so as not to run into her parents together. She picked up the phone and called her parents' room. "Oh, hi, Mom. I just wanted to let you know I'm going to that concert with Lois that I told you about. No, I don't want to go to Jai Lai tonight. I should be back by ten or eleven. Bye, Mom." Suzie walked over to me and asked, "What are you smiling about?"

"Just you," as I pulled her toward me for a kiss.

"Al, let's meet in front of the Brazil Hotel. I'm sure one of your friends or one of the college kids staying there is going to the festival."

"Okay, you walk out first and I will meet you there."

Suzie grabbed one of the small blankets from the closet and left. I waited a few minutes. Then, to make sure I didn't run into her parents, I took the back stairs, going out the back entrance of the Deauville and walking along the beach to the Brazil pool and entering through the Brazil's back entrance. When I walked into the lobby, giving Hector a nod, I could see Suzie standing on the front porch veranda, talking with Al Katz and his friend Darlene, the former Miss Knoxville. I thought to myself, I hope Suzie does not find out Darlene is a hooker. Apparently, Al Katz had seen Suzie and me talking at the Deauville, so Katz had asked Suzie if she knew where I was. Suzie told him I was meeting her in a few minutes.

When I walked outside to the veranda, I found out that Al and Darlene were also looking for a ride to the Miami Pop Festival at Gulfstream Park Racetrack. Just then, I noticed Dizzy Lavin's GTO parked on Collins Avenue halfway between the Brazil and the Deauville. His girlfriend, Annette, was sitting in the car with the top down. I decided to walk over and ask Annette where Dizzy was. As I approached the car, I could hear Dion with his new release, "Abraham, Martin and John," coming out of Dizzy's car radio, "Hi, Annette, how are you?"

"I'm doing good."

"Where's Mike?"

"Oh, he's just finishing up his shift as a car jockey at the Deauville."

"How long has Mike worked there?"

"Well, when Michael came down here to attend Miami Dade, he started working as a car valet, first at the Caroline, and after a few weeks, he moved over to the Deauville at the end of October, because the tips are much better. He should be here soon. We're supposed to go to the pop festival at Gulfstream."

Then I heard, "Hey, Krockey."

"Dizzy, how you doing, man?"

Mike, responded, "I'm cool. We're going to see all these great bands at Gulfstream Park."

"Wow, Mike, so am I and my new girlfriend. She's standing on the front porch of the Brazil talking to Al Katz and his girlfriend. We're all looking for a ride to the fest."

"Unbelievable! Hop in—you can go with us." So, we all piled into Dizzy's silver convertible GTO and headed for the racetrack called Gulfstream Park, site of the Miami Pop Festival. As we were driving, Al Katz lit up a joint and passed it to Dizzy. "Here you go, Mike, this is some killer Panama Red."

Mike responded, "Unbelievable! This is the same pot I have."

Katz said, "Yeah, I bought a pound from Bembe, the towel guy at the Deauville. You must know him. You both work there."

"Unbelievable! I sold Bembe a whole bale of this grass."

Mike "Dizzy" Lavin started almost all his sentences with "Unbelievable." As we were driving, the song "Going Up the Country" by Canned Heat came on. As the tune played, I said, "Wow, I can't believe they're on Top Forty radio. I sold Canned Heat some reefer the first time they played at the Electric Theatre."

Katz said, "I saw them there too. They were out of sight."

"Michael and I also saw them there, last summer in Chicago," said Annette.

When we arrived at the Miami Pop Festival, we joined a big line of cars trying to get into the parking lot. We sat in line for about ten minutes when suddenly, Dizzy said, "Ah, fuck it." He decided to back his car into the other lane, which was the exit lane going in the wrong direction. Since there weren't too many cars leaving, Dizzy, driving backwards, was able to avoid the few cars that were exiting and ended up in the valet area after scaring the shit out of us. It turned out Dizzy knew the valet guys at Gulfstream and was able to valet his car with no problem. After we got out of the car, we parted ways. All four of the others headed for the racetrack bleachers where Steppenwolf and the Grateful Dead would be playing.

Suzie said, "Let's head to the other stage where everyone sits on the grass."

"Are you sure? I wouldn't mind seeing the Grateful Dead."

"We can go there later. I'm sure they're closing the show. When I spoke to Lois this morning, she said that the grass area is way cooler than the bleachers."

As Suzie grabbed my hand, I said to the others, "See you guys later." When we got to the other stage area with everyone sitting on the grass, Suzie laid the blanket down that she had taken from the Deauville. As soon as we sat down, we started kissing, and Suzie said, "Close your eyes and open your mouth," which I did. Upon which, Suzie threw a tab of acid into my mouth.

"What is this?"

"The grooviest LSD I have ever taken since I started tripping last year. They call it Orange Sunshine."

"I don't know, Suzie. I have never taken acid before, although most of my friends have."

"Trust me, Alan, it's trippy but mellow."

So, I swallowed the tab after some of it dissolved in my mouth. Then Suzie pointed to a blonde folk singer walking out on the stage with only a guitar. She said, "I know her. I met her in the Village just a few months ago when she was playing at this club, Café Au Go Go.

Her name is Joni something." We then heard, "Please welcome, Joni Mitchell."

Suzie turned to me, "That's right, Joni Mitchell. I really like her music. She writes beautiful songs."

"I never heard of her." As we lay back on the blanket with Suzie putting her head on my chest, I said, "I'm not feeling the acid yet."

"Don't worry, you will. Just lie back and look at the beautiful pink and white clouds," as she handed me a joint. And almost on cue, Joni started singing "Clouds (Both Sides Now)" while Suzie and I both looked up at the sky, enjoying the remarkable cloud formations. Along with Miami's tropical air and the scent of Suzie's hair on my face, I felt a new freedom of life's grace. Joni closed her set that night with Dino Valenti's song "Get Together," as she invited Graham Nash from the Hollies, along with Richie Havens, on stage to sing with her.

When Joni finished her set, I turned to Suzie, saying, "Wow, is that the acid?"

She responded, "No," pointing to the beautiful sky with a gentle smile. "That's the spirits working along with a beautiful soundtrack." Just then, Suzie saw Joni Mitchell coming our way. Suzie got up to say, "Hi, Joni, do you remember me? We met in the village."

Joni said, "Oh, hi. Suzie, right? How are you?"

"I'm good. That song 'Both Sides Now,' especially before the Miami sunset with the pink sky and all the clouds, was perfect."

Joni said, "Well, sometimes things come together and there is no explanation. It's kind of how I came to write this song."

Suzie said, "Oh, I thought Judy Collins wrote 'Both Sides Now.' I heard her sing it on the radio just this morning."

"No, I wrote it, but a lot of people think Judy wrote the song, because her new record is covering my song."

"What a lovely song you wrote, Joni. Please tell me, how do you write something so beautiful?"

"Well, thank you. Let me tell you how I came to write 'Both Sides Now,' which is quite a story in itself. You see, I was on this airplane reading Saul Bellow's book *Henderson the Rain King*, where, coincidentally, the protagonist is on a plane looking out the window. At that point, I looked out the plane window at all the clouds, and that gave me the inspiration to write 'Clouds' or 'From Both Sides Now.'"

"Far out," Suzie responded.

Then Joni said, "Sometimes the spirits align." I looked up from the blanket at these two beautiful women as the acid was starting to kick in.

Gazing up into Joni's lake-blue eyes, I told her, "Wow, you were wonderful."

"Thank you. Good seeing you again, Suzie."

Graham Nash walked up, grabbed Joni's hand, and walked away with her. Suzie sat down next to me, as Procol Harum stepped on stage with the sun about to go down, while Suzie and I were now tripping our brains out. The peak of my acid trip that night was when Procol Harum played "Whiter Shade of Pale." To this day, whenever I hear that song, I start to trip a little.

As we lay there on that warm Miami night looking at the stars and listening to the music, I was in heaven, especially when Suzie touched me or we would kiss, as all my senses had been elevated to a place I had never felt or experienced before. This was all new to me. I didn't want this trip to end. When Procol Harum ended their set, Suzie asked, "Please go get us some drinks and hurry back. Marvin Gaye is next. I know you said he's one of the reasons you wanted to come today."

So off I went. Standing in line to get the drinks, I ran into Shane's friend Lee Liss. "Hi, Lee. Is Shane here with you?"

Lee just smiled at me, lifting his shoulders and shaking his head, and responded, "Not sure," and he walked away with a strange trippy look in his eyes.

When it was my turn, the lady at the drink booth asked, "What will it be? Lemonade or Pepsi?"

I responded, "I will have two of those far-out looking pink lemonades. Wow, check it out!"

"Okay, young man, that will be one dollar."

"Wow," I said, handing the lady the dollar Suzie had given me. When I got back to our blanket, Suzie was talking to the couple sitting next to us, along with their little baby. "Isn't she cute?"

"Wow, yes, she is." I must have said "wow" a hundred times that night.

I handed Suzie her pink lemonade and she said to me, "Thank you, sweetie."

"It's pink, just like the clouds and that baby's tush," I said, as I pointed to our neighbors changing their baby's diaper. We both laughed. As they were setting up the stage for Marvin Gaye, the crowd became larger to the point where there were no more places to sit. Many of the new arrivals were Black and came just to see Marvin Gaye, which made sense as Marvin had the number one pop and R&B hit at the time. I was still tripping my ass off when I saw the stage crew wheel out two giant kettle drums, and when the spotlight shined on those drums, I saw loads of psychedelic images flying around in my head.

When I told Suzie about the images, she just said, "You're tripping, man. Enjoy the good vibes."

The stage lights lowered and two guys started hitting the kettle drums, playing the bassline from "I Heard it Through the Grapevine." It was incredible, I never heard that arrangement before or after that night. Then, Marvin hit the stage and the crowd went wild. It was a spectacular set that included two songs made popular by The Drifters, "Some Kind of Wonderful" and "There Goes My Baby," two of my favorites. I would find out later that these songs were on

Marvin's new album, *In the Groove*, which also included "Heard It Through the Grapevine." When Marvin started to sing "How Sweet It Is," Suzie and I got up and danced. After Marvin finished his set, Suzie said, "Let's go over to the other stage and see if we can find your friends."

As we reached the other stage, the Grateful Dead was just starting their set. A few people were starting to come down from the bleachers so they could dance. A few jumped over the racetrack's fence so they could dance in front of the stage on the racetrack's turf. Suzie and I were about to climb over the fence when a giant hippie guy pushed one of the gates open, and Suzie and I, and much of the crowd, came down in front of the stage to dance. We danced joyfully, losing our shoes and spinning in a world of colors from the light show projected on a screen behind the Dead. When the music was over, we headed for the exit.

As we walked, I turned to Suzie and said, "Wow, I forgot my shoes," and noticed that she was carrying hers in her hand.

"No hassle—you can get a new pair in the morning." Just then, I saw a sign that said valet parking.

"Hey, look, Suzie," I said as I pointed at the sign, "maybe Dizzy is still there." As we neared the valet area, we saw Dizzy's GTO with Annette behind the wheel and Dizzy standing next to the car talking to one of his car jockey friends who worked at Gulfstream. I yelled, "Hey, Diz!"

"Unbelievable, what a night." Dizzy told us about the fantastcal acid he took, offering us some and babbling on and on. As high as I was, Dizzy looked light-years beyond.

Annette said, "Where's Al Katz and his girlfriend?"

"I have no idea."

"I thought he was with you guys," I responded.

Annette said, "We should go."

Dizzy said, "I'll drive."

"No way," Annette responded. "You're high on LSD and I'm not. I'll drive."

On the road, Annette suggested we stop at The Rascal House in Sunny Isles for breakfast. By now, the acid was starting to wear off. Suzie turned to me for approval, saying, "We should eat something. We haven't eaten anything since breakfast. I could go for some pancakes."

I just nodded. I was so spacey and not thinking about food until we walked into the crowded Rascal House and were hit with its delicious smells. The aromas of all the different foods began to fill my nostrils with a bouquet of deli smells, which reminded me of my childhood and the first time I walked into the Ashkenaz Deli in Chicago with my parents when I was five. As I was coming down, it seemed like all my senses had been heightened, as I could hear every conversation in the restaurant.

Each plate of food on everyone's table looked like a Picasso painting to me. And when the food came, everything tasted like never before. Suzie ate her banana pancakes with maple syrup. I threw down three orders of blintzes. One cheese, one blueberry, and one strawberry. Dizzy was eating French toast made from challah, which he soaked with syrup along with a side of scrambled eggs, while Annette had lox on a toasted bagel with cream cheese and tomato. We all ordered giant fresh orange juices, which tasted amazing. When we got back in the car, it was almost four in the morning and Suzie suggested we go watch the sunrise. By this time, Mike was cool to drive, and he told us, "I know the perfect place, Bal Harbor Beach."

As we sat on this beautiful beach waiting for the sun to come up, a hippie couple walked by us with their dog. The beautiful yellow lab wandered over to us and Annette and Suzie both petted the dog.

Annette said, "What a beautiful dog. What's her name?"

"Daisy," the couple said in unison, smiling as they both walked away with Daisy running ahead.

We all sat there quietly as the sun slowly started to rise above the horizon. Suzie stroked my cheek, and I could feel the soft Miami breeze. As we sat serenely on the beach, out of the blue my serenity was interrupted by a seagull landing his shit right on top of my head, while at the same time I thought I had heard the seagull laughing. I told Suzie that I thought I heard the seagull laugh.

She smiled and told me, "That's why they call them laughing gulls. It's true—my grandpa taught me that when I was eight."

Everyone laughed, including me, and I wiped the bird shit out of my hair as best as possible. Soon after, I stood up and suggested, "Let's go home." When we got back to the room, I jumped into the shower to wash the bird shit out of my hair. A few minutes later, Suzie joined me. After we washed each other off, we made love in the shower and again in the bed and fell asleep. We woke up to the sound of someone knocking on the door, even though we had put the Do Not Disturb sign on.

Suzie yelled out, "Who's there?" while putting a finger to her mouth to give me the shush sign.

"It's your mom. Are you okay? We've been trying to call you all day. Your phone must be off the hook."

"I went for a walk on the beach early this morning and while I was walking. I got my period, so, I came back to the room to rest and took the phone off the hook." I looked at Suzie smiling, almost laughing, and shaking my head.

"Well, we're on our way to Bubbe's for dinner. You know they like to eat early. Why don't you join us? You know we are leaving in two days."

"I'm not feeling well, Mom. I'm still in bed with these cramps, which is why I didn't come to the door when you knocked."

Susie's mom replied, "Poor thing."

"Please tell Grandma I will spend all day tomorrow with her."

"Do you need me to get you something for your cramps?"

"No, I just took something. Okay, Ma, I'm going back to bed."

"Goodbye, darling." Suzie put her fingers back up on her lips, signaling me not to talk. After about five minutes of silence, Suzie walked over to me, gave me a kiss, and whispered in my ear. "Let's get dressed quietly. I want to make sure she is gone. I think she suspects something." Suzie turned the TV on, and we didn't talk until the room's phone rang ten minutes later. Suzie answered the phone and turned to me and mouthed "Lois." When she hung up, she told me, "Lois, Barry, and his cousin Lenny are picking us up in a half hour to go to the festival."

I said, "Then I need to get some shoes."

"Oh, that's right. I saw some flip-flops at the drugstore down the street. I think they even had some cheap sneakers there."

"I better get the flip-flops as I have a wide foot and don't think those cheap sneakers will fit. I usually wear Converse because they come in wide sizes."

Suzie ran down to get the flip-flops and returned with not only the flip-flops but with coffee and Danishes for both of us. As soon as we got downstairs, Barry's cousin Lenny pulled up in his little Volkswagen convertible. Lenny was a few years older than us and stood about six-foot-six with a red ponytail down to his ass. He had played college basketball at Florida State till a broken knee ended his b-ball career. Lenny's petite, five-foot-two girlfriend, Maria, a beautiful Cuban girl with long brown hair, was sitting in the front bucket seat. It was a tight fit in the back seat of Lenny's VW, with Lois on Barry's lap and Suzie on mine. As we were driving, Suzie yelled out, "Stop, pull over."

"What's wrong?" I asked Suzie.

"Nothing, sweetie, look." Suzie was pointing to the window of the Jefferson Super Department Store and a sign that said "Converse All Stars $6.99."

"Suzie, that's too much. You've paid for everything since we met. I'm cool with these flip-flops."

"Well, Alan, what are you going to do when you get back to Chicago? Walk into your parents' house with flip-flops covered in snow?"

"I guess you're right. But I insist on paying you back everything."

So, we both walked into the store and bought the Converse All Stars plus a couple pairs of white crew socks. I told Suzie, "I think I'll wear these flip-flops for the festival and put the pair of Converse and the socks in the front trunk of Lenny's VW."

We arrived at Gulfstream on the opposite side of where we came in the day before, where we found it easier to park. We entered Gulfstream Park on that sunny Monday, but it still felt like the weekend. Walking in from this side of the venue, we found ourselves much closer to the grass area stage than the bleachers stage. Suzie suggested, "Let's sit over there," while pointing. "We sat here yesterday, and we were able to see and hear everything perfectly."

As Suzie and Lois were laying out the blankets they had both brought, Lenny said that he and Maria were going over to the bleachers where he knew some of his friends were sitting. Lenny said, as he and Maria were walking away, "Meet you at my car when all the music's over."

After we sat down, Lois asked Suzie, "Did you bring the sunshine?"

"Yes, but we took one tab each yesterday and I only have two left. Why don't you and Barry split one and Al and I will split one?"

Lois answered, "Cool, that's all we wanted anyway. Barry and I split a tab yesterday and it was groovy. You and Krockey must have gotten super high yesterday taking a whole tab each."

Suzie and I both smiled and nodded. She then said, "Open your mouth, Al," and proceeded to put half a tab of acid on my tongue. A cool band I was unfamiliar with named Sweetwater came on stage. About halfway through Sweetwater's set, the acid kicked in, and the music intensified as Sweetwater sang and played "Motherless Child," blowing all of us away. Come to think of it, all the acts we saw that day sounded terrific. The acid wasn't as intense as that first trip, but it still amplified my senses.

We kept going back and forth between both stages, listening to fantastic artists. That day the acts that stood out to us were a fairly unknown Three Dog Night, Canned Heat, the Sweet Inspirations, Joe Tex, the Charles Lloyd Quartet, and Iron Butterfly doing their hit "In-A-Gadda-Da-Vida," with that ten-minute drum solo that the crowd went crazy for.

At the close of the festival, José Feliciano was on one stage while the Turtles were on the other. I was a big José Feliciano fan, so we parked ourselves in front of the stage. When José finished to a standing ovation, closing his set with his version of the Doors' "Light My Fire," we could still hear the Turtles finishing their set on the other stage. As the four of us headed to the car, I ran into Jeff Render and Kenny Goss standing by Jeff's yellow Oldsmobile 442. Kenny asked, "What's up, Krockey?"

"Incredible show. How are you guys doing? Are you guys going back home soon?"

Kenny answered, "Yeah, we're leaving tomorrow."

"Do you have room for one more passenger?" I asked.

Jeff said, "Well, right now, it's just Kenny, Chuckie Goldwynn, and me. I think we can give you a ride back to Skokie if you can pay for your share of the gas and food. We are driving straight through, and only stopping for gas, food, and to pee."

"That would be great."

"Okay, meet us in front of the Deauville Hotel at 10 a.m. tomorrow."

Jeff turned to Suzie and asked if she needed a ride as well. Suzie replied, "No, I'm going back to school in New York."

Just then, Barry and Lois, who had walked ahead to Lenny's car, called out, "Hurry up—Lenny wants to leave! Maria must get home."

"See you guys tomorrow. I really appreciate you giving me a ride back to Skokie."

When Suzie and I arrived back in her room, she suggested we take a bath and told me to open the bottle of champagne that had been sitting in the room's small refrigerator. The Deauville had a big bathtub, and Suzie had made a bubble bath. We ended up staying up till five in the morning, soaking in the bath, drinking champagne, smoking reefer, and then moving to the bed, talking and making love. Suzie woke me about 8:30 a.m. and told me she had to leave right then to go meet her parents in the Deauville coffee shop before going to see her grandparents. She sat beside me on the bed and we kissed goodbye. "Call me when you get back to Chicago, and you better come and see me in New York. I put forty dollars on the dresser for your car ride back, along with my phone number and address of my dorm. Love you—got to go."

And just like that she was out the door. At that moment, I thought I loved her. How could I not think that with all she had done for me and the marvelous sex? I was still young and inexperienced. After cleaning up, I got dressed in a pair of jeans, a t-shirt, and my new white Converse All Stars. While packing my few things I thought to myself, *Oh shit, I left my peacoat in the Buick.* Well, at least I had a hooded sweatshirt, which I could throw on when I got cold on the drive home. I left the Deauville at about 8:30 a.m. to go to Pumpernik's for something to eat before meeting the guys for my ride home.

I walked into the restaurant and was about to sit at the counter when I heard, "Hey, Krockey."

There were the same guys I would be driving home with: Kenny Goss, Jeff Render, and Chuckie Goldwynn. I really didn't know Kenny too well, even though we were the same age and had a couple of classes together at Niles East; we had hung out with different crowds back then. Kenny was part of a collegiate crowd who all went away for college and came from more affluent families. Also, I hardly knew Jeff

Render as he had graduated from Evanston and was a year older and was part of the same crowd as Kenny. Chuckie was also a year older and had graduated from Evanston. But Chuckie and I became friends a few years back, when we both would hang out at the Q-Inn. I asked Jeff, "What did you spend on gas coming down to Miami?"

"I'm not sure, maybe forty or fifty altogether. That 442 of mine does not get good mileage."

We finished eating and headed for Chicago—well, Skokie, where we all lived. Chuckie and I were in the back seat with Jeff Render driving his 442, while Kenny sat in the other bucket seat. When we were an hour out of Miami, I fell asleep and didn't wake up till we hit Ocala, Florida, when Chuckie shook me and asked if I wanted a cheeseburger. I looked out the window and saw we were at some little hamburger place. I got out of the car and joined the line for food behind my friends.

After we chowed down on double cheeseburgers and gassed up, Jeff said he would pay for the gas the whole way, and then we could figure out what each owed once we were back in Skokie. Chuckie took the wheel, while Jeff sat in the shotgun seat. Jeff then turned the radio off and put the eight-track tape *Wheels of Fire* in the car's built-in eight-track machine and blasted his JBL speakers while we all shared a joint. It was really the first time I had heard the whole *Wheels of Fire* double album. It sounded amazing coming out of those JBL speakers, which were top of the line back then. After *Wheels of Fire*, Jeff put in *Greatest Hits* by the Young Rascals, whom I had always loved and had recently seen back in late September when I was working and selling binoculars at the Coliseum in Chicago. The ride between Ocala and Atlanta flew by as we listened to albums and talked about music, girls, and football.

When we got to Atlanta, Jeff asked Ken, "Do you want to drive?"

"No, let Krockey drive to Nashville, and I will drive from Nashville till we get back home."

So that's what we did. I had never driven a car as fast as Jeff's Oldsmobile 442. He also mentioned that he and Kenny bought like ten tapes from Stereo City on Dempster before they left for Florida. After stopping in Nashville for something to eat at a place called Brown's Diner, we headed home. Kenny took over driving the last stretch. Somewhere around Louisville, Chuckie pulled out our last joint, holding it up and saying Happy New Year and passing it around as we ushered in 1969.

When we were back in Skokie, Jeff told Kenny, "Drive over to the gas station and automatic carwash on Skokie Boulevard near Searle. The car is filthy, and this carwash gives you a complete carwash, inside and out, for fifty cents with every fill-up of ten gallons or more."

After filling up the car, Jeff did the math and told us we each owed him fourteen dollars for the gas and the snacks he had bought for the trip. I was the first one to be dropped off as I only lived a few blocks away from the gas station/car wash. It was around noon on this New Year's Day, 1969, when we pulled up to my parents' apartment building at 8239 Knox in Skokie. I handed Jeff the fourteen bucks and grabbed my duffel bag. "Thanks for the ride. I'll see you guys."

Stepping out of the car, my face was slapped by the wind on this cold, twenty-degree day. Then, upon entering my parents' building, standing in the hallway before running up the stairs to their apartment, it hit me all at once as I realized 1969 was here.

I started to reflect on this past crazy year. All the ups and downs and my wild traveling adventures—and meeting Suzie was a journey I could have never imagined. Would the new year hold more new opportunities and adventures? The world was changing. With me starting this new broadcasting school, my hustler's quest for adventurous ways to make a buck, all the new bands that I had never seen that would be coming to the Kinetic Playground and different festivals, along with my wanderlust, my gut was telling me that 1969 would be a year like no other.

COMING SOON!

Coming in 2026

Straight Outta Skokie: Krockey Road Ahead: 1969 takes you on a wild ride through one unforgettable year in the life of Al Krockey. From chasing dreams at broadcasting school and running a scrappy two-man radio show, to hustling souvenirs at Wrigley Field and rolling the dice in Las Vegas, every chapter pulses with the restless energy of a young man carving out his place in a changing world. It's a year of big highs—on stage at Woodstock, a sun-soaked adventure in Jamaica, and the spark of an idea that would become The Record Shack—and heavy lows, from the Cubs' collapse to brushes with the law and the looming draft lottery. With music, rebellion, and possibility at every turn, 1969 becomes the year Al learns that coming of age means stepping boldly into the unknown.

Coming in 2027

Straight Outta Skokie: The Record Shack Years: 1970–1974 dives headfirst into the gritty, electric world of a young dreamer who turns a wild idea into a legendary record store. From battling distributors, hustling bootlegs, and dodging gangsters and busts, to running concerts and crossing paths with Chicago's counterculture underground, The Record Shack becomes more than just a store—it's a front-row seat to an era exploding with music, rebellion, and risk. Between stolen records, celebrity visits, and nights tangled in love, heartbreak, and haze, Al Krockey learns that running a store means juggling business, chaos, and survival. As competition grows and the pressure mounts, the ultimate question looms: Is it time to sell the dream—or double down on it?

About the Author

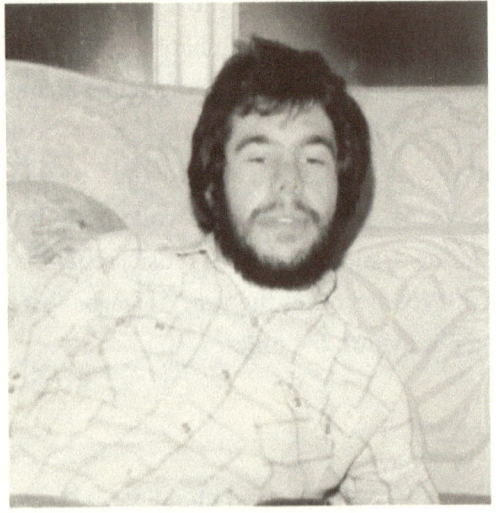

Just beginning

Al Krockey was born in 1950, and only a few months later his parents settled in Skokie, Illinois. Raised in a working-class Jewish family that often struggled to make ends meet, Krockey learned the value of hard work early on. By the time he was twenty, he had already opened a record store, The Record Shack. His passion for music led him through a whirlwind career in the 1970s—running a store, starting a record label, and even producing music—before leaving the business in the early 1980s.

He went on to build a successful career in insurance consulting, ultimately becoming vice president of a national firm. At 68, he reached the final table of a World Poker Tour Main Event, and at 75, he embarked on a new journey as an author.

Today, Krockey reflects on a life shaped by grit, reinvention, and a love for the hustle—whether in business, music, or cards.

Still becoming